Sustainability in Global Value Chains

Measures, Ethics and Best Practices for Responsible Businesses

Edited by
Michael Henke
Holger Kohl

KoganPage

First published in Great Britain and the United States in 2021 by Kogan Page Limited

2nd Floor, 45 Gee Street
London
EC1V 3RS
United Kingdom

122 W 27th St, 10th Floor
New York, NY 10001
USA

4737/23 Ansari Road
Daryaganj
New Delhi 110002
India

www.koganpage.com

Kogan Page books are printed on paper from sustainable forests.

ISBNs

Hardback	978 1 78966 264 1
Paperback	978 1 78966 262 7
eBook	978 1 78966 263 4

British Library Cataloguing-in-Publication Data

A CIP record for this book is available from the British Library.

Library of Congress Cataloging-in-Publication Data
Names: Henke, Michael, 1971- author. | Kohl, Holger, author.
Title: Sustainability in global value chains : measures, ethics and best practices for responsible businesses / edited by Michael Henke, Holger Kohl.
Description: London ; New York, NY : Kogan Page, 2021. | Includes bibliographical references and index. |
Identifiers: LCCN 2020048960 (print) | LCCN 2020048961 (ebook) | ISBN 9781789662627 (paperback) | ISBN 9781789662641 (hardback) | ISBN 9781789662634 (ebook)
Subjects: LCSH: Business logistics. | Sustainable development
Classification: LCC HD38.5 .H459 2021 (print) | LCC HD38.5 (ebook) | DDC 658.7–dc23

Typeset by Integra Software Services, Pondicherry
Print production managed by Jellyfish
Printed and bound by CPI Group (UK) Ltd, Croydon CR0 4YY

CONTENTS

LIST OF FIGURES AND TABLES

Figures

Tables

ABOUT THE CONTRIBUTORS

Marvin Auf der Landwehr

Marvin Auf der Landwehr holds an MSc in Strategic Business Development with further postgraduate studies in digital transformation, urban logistics, business process analysis, simulation development and innovation management. After having worked for several years as Country Manager within an organization that specialized in e-commerce and digital business strategies, he possesses relevant knowledge and experiences in designing and implementing new business strategies and fostering business innovation. Currently, he works as Research Assistant and PhD candidate at the Hochschule Hannover in Germany, where he particularly engages in developing, assessing and evaluating innovation models related to urban logistics in general and last-mile fulfilment in particular.

Lydia Bals

Lydia Bals is Professor of Supply Chain and Operations Management at University of Applied Sciences Mainz since 2014 and an external Post Doctoral Research Fellow at EBS Universität since 2019. She is also affiliated with Copenhagen Business School for research since 2008. She works as an independent consultant, moderator and speaker. Until the end of 2013 she was Head of the Department Global Procurement Solutions (eg procurement strategy, sustainability, controlling, source2contract and purchase2pay processes, methods, tools and systems, benchmarking and excellence) at Bayer CropScience (BCS) AG. She also steered the international procurement solutions network in Germany, the United States/Canada, France, India, China and Brazil. Prior to joining BCS she worked as a Project Manager at Bayer Business Consulting, Germany, the in-house consulting unit of Bayer, driving projects in the functional areas of sales, research and development, controlling and procurement in various countries (including Spain, Mexico, Brazil, Turkey, Italy and France). She teaches purchasing and supply management, operations, logistics and supply chain management courses. She has published in the *Journal of Operations Management*, *Journal of Supply Chain Management*, *Journal of Purchasing and Supply Management*, *Journal of International Management* and other academic outlets.

Michael Dircksen

Michael Dircksen is Professor for International Distribution Logistics at the University of Applied Sciences in Münster, Germany. In addition, he has a Guest Professorship at the Universidad de La Sabana in Bogotá, Colombia. He regularly presents his research work at international congresses and writes and contributes to articles and books. Michael Dircksen has completed a Diploma in Business Administration and an MSc in Logistics. In his academic career at the University of Applied Sciences, he was able to collect practical experience in several countries including Germany, Ecuador, Japan, Nigeria and Saudi Arabia. After he finished his PhD he was a team leader at a 4PL logistics provider and is responsible for the planning of international transport networks considering air, sea, rail and road transports.

Klaus Fischer

Klaus Fischer is Professor for Business Administration and Sustainability Management at WBH University for Applied Sciences in Darmstadt. After his studies in business and chemical engineering, he worked at third-party funded research institutes on various topics in the fields of corporate sustainability and sustainable regional development. He received a doctorate on corporate sustainability governance in 2015 and held a Professorship for Sustainability and Strategic Management at FOM University of Applied Sciences from 2017 to 2020.

Guido Grunwald

Guido Grunwald is Professor of Business Administration, especially marketing and market research, in the Faculty of Management, Culture, and Technology at the Osnabrück University of Applied Sciences. His research interests include buyer behaviour, sustainability and relationship marketing, and more specifically communication and product policy in the face of consumer risks and negative publicity. Prior to his professorship in 2014, he worked as Senior Lecturer and Researcher in the dual higher education sector and conducted market research and consulting projects for small and medium-sized enterprises. As an Economist at the Federal Institute for Occupational Safety and Health in Dortmund he dealt with the development of socioeconomic analysis procedures under the EU Chemicals Regulation (REACH) and was a German representative in the Forum of the European Chemicals Agency (ECHA) in Helsinki. He is the author of numerous books and articles published in national and international peer-reviewed journals, including the *Journal of Environmental Law and Policy* (ZfU), *Corporate Reputation Review*, *International Journal of Retail and Distribution Management*, *Journal for Business, Economics and Ethics* (ZfWU) and the *Journal of Leadership and Organization* (ZfO).

Igor Ivanov

Igor Ivanov is a Research and Transfer Officer at the Ludwigshafen University of Business and Society. Prior to this he studied business, social and organizational psychology at the Ruhr-University Bochum and Heidelberg University. He was a Research Assistant at the University of Mannheim where his work and publications focused on the perception of politicians and political ideology.

Harry Müller

Harry Müller is Professor for General Business Administration, especially accounting and investment management, at Ludwigshafen University of Business and Society. He holds a Bachelor of Arts in history and economics, a Master of Science in business administration and was graduated Dr. rer. pol. at the University of Münster with a thesis about controlling of research performance and academic rankings. After four years of professional occupation in the financial sector, he was appointed as Professor in Ludwigshafen in 2017. In his teaching and research, he focuses on empirical accounting research, sustainability accounting and university management.

Martin Müller

Martin Müller is Chair for Sustainable Corporate Management at University of Ulm, Germany since 2008. He completed his PhD thesis in 2000 at the University of Halle-Wittenberg. Between 2001 and 2004 he was Senior Lecturer and 2005 to 2008 he was Associate Professor for Production and Environment at University of Oldenburg (Germany). His research interests include sustainable management, sustainable supply chain management and corporate social responsibility.

Stephanie Rabbe

Stephanie Rabbe is an economist and social scientist with a PhD in strategic sustainability management and holds the Chair of Entrepreneurship at HAWK University of Applied Sciences and Arts in Hildesheim since 2014.

There she is also responsible for the entire academic start-up support. Her research areas include strategy, entrepreneurship, innovation and sustainability, especially in start-ups. She teaches interdisciplinary and practice-oriented business administration for start-ups with a focus on ideas and business model development. In 2004, Stephanie Rabbe founded a start-up herself and still runs it today. She is also a Partner of Digital Pioniere UG, a management consultancy for digital transformation.

Carsten Reuter

Carsten Reuter is Full Professor of Procurement and Quality Management at Aschaffenburg University of Applied Sciences, Germany and a Visiting Professor at Université Catholique de Louvain, Belgium. Previously, he worked as a Consultant at Porsche Consulting and as Team and Project Leader at the Fraunhofer Center for Applied Research on Supply Chain Services. He studied at the University of Hamburg and the University of Nuremberg and received his PhD from the European Business School, Germany. Carsten's research interests include supply chain management, procurement and operations management, with a strong focus on sustainability and platform economy. His research has been published in, among others, the *Journal of Operations Management*, *Journal of Supply Chain Management*, *Journal of Purchasing and Supply Management*, *International Journal of Production Economics* and *Journal of Cleaner Production*.

Kristan A Schneider

Kristan A Schneider is Full Professor for Modelling and Simulation at Hochschule Mittweida. He studied mathematics at the University of Vienna from 1999–2002. Population-genetic modelling with applications in theoretical ecology was the topic of his PhD thesis, which was completed in 2005. Afterwards he continued to work at the Department of Mathematics at the University of Vienna as postdoctoral fellow and assistant professor. From 2009 to 2011 he was employed at the School of Life Sciences at Arizona State University and the Biodesign Institute at ASU, where he engaged in modelling infectious diseases, particularly in malaria. He received the Venia Legendi in mathematics at the University of Vienna in 2010. He is a recognized expert in mathematical modelling and statistics with application in various fields, including malaria, COVID-19, ecology and economics. He has established numerous collaborations with public health authorities including the Centers for Diseases Control and Prevention, the US Navy and the Indian Council for Medical Research. Currently, he is engaging in strategic partnerships with several countries in Sub-Saharan Africa to strengthen the knowledge exchange between Germany and Africa in the scope of the UN Global Sustainability Goals.

Julia Schwarzkopf

Julia Schwarzkopf is Professor for Sustainability Management at the HTW Berlin Business School. After various positions in science (including at the Potsdam Institute for Climate Impact Research) and business, she received her doctorate from the ETH Zurich on corporate climate strategies. Subsequently, the sociologist and environmental scientist worked in the field of sustainable supply chain management for a DAX-30 company before accepting the position at the HTW Berlin in April 2017. She is interested in opportunities for sustainable action by selected economic actors, especially in and along supply chains.

Marcus Sidki

Marcus Sidki is Professor of Economics and Statistics at Ludwigshafen University of Applied Sciences in Ludwigshafen, Germany. There, he heads the research group of public and non-profit enterprises and serves as Scientific Head of the university's Department of Research, Cooperation and Entrepreneurship. His research interests lie in the field of political economics and public finance. Before joining the university in 2015, he gained practical experience working in the banking industry for more than seven years. He holds a diploma in economics from the University of Heidelberg and a PhD from the German University of Administrative Sciences Speyer. He is Visiting Professor at the University of Landau and was appointed a Fellowship at the Liberal Institute of the Friedrich Naumann Foundation in 2020.

Valérie Swaen

Valérie Swaen is Full Professor of Marketing and Corporate Social Responsibility (CSR) at the Louvain School of Management, UCLouvain, Belgium, and at IESEG School of Management, France. Since September 2019, she is the President of the Louvain Research Institute in Management and Organizations, LouRIM, UCLouvain. She is also the head of the Louvain CSR network that gathers and supports researchers and practitioners who seek to put responsible leadership and sustainable production and consumption at the heart of their research and strategy. In this context, she holds (or held) different corporate chairs in CSR and sustainability (with Engie, essenscia, Proximus, Solvay, and Spadel). Prof Swaen's research interests include consumer behaviour, CSR and, more specifically, stakeholders' reactions to CSR communication. She has published papers in international journals such as *Journal of Management*, *Journal of Management Studies*, *Journal of Organizational Behavior*, *Journal of Business Ethics*, and *Marketing Letters*, among others.

Christoph von Viebahn

Christoph von Viebahn began teaching business informatics in 2005 at the School of International Business and Ship Management, Applied University of Bremen, and at the FOM University, following positions in IT and logistics consulting focusing on the maritime supply chain. In 2008, he was appointed Managing Director of the regional consortium SEIS and the assumption of responsibility for the project by the Bertelsmann Stiftung. Since 2012, he works as Professor in the field of business informatics at the University of Applied Sciences, Hannover, where he is responsible for the specialization in supply chain management and the basics of business administration. In teaching, he built up the subject of simulation in the field of business informatics.

PREFACE

Wealth has its price. As the standard of living for many people around the world rises, so does the consumption of resources. The highly industrialized countries have a particularly poor record: for example, the average German consumes no less than 16.1 tons of raw materials per year. That is twice as much as the global average and 10 per cent more than the European average. At the same time, Germans produce 412 million tons of waste every year. That corresponds to almost five tons of waste per person.

This worrying trend is a global one. Developing countries and emerging economies are largely relying on growth-linked industrialization and are using the same means as developed countries to provide their growing populations with an acceptable standard of living. Based on the current state of manufacturing technology, the production of steel, aluminium, plastics and cement alone will cause about 800 gigatons of CO_2 by the end of the 21st century. This means that the emissions just from these four material flows would account for the total global emissions permissible if the two-degree target is to be achieved.

The scientific community, governments and civil society are therefore faced with the question: How can we pursue prosperity today without depriving future generations of the foundations of an existence worth living?

The Sustainable Development Goals set out by the United Nations are the blueprint for achieving a better and more sustainable future for all. They address the global challenges we face, including those related to poverty, inequality, climate change, environmental degradation, peace and justice. The 17 goals are all interconnected, and, so that no one is left behind, it is important that we achieve them all by 2030, including Goal 12: Ensure sustainable consumption and production patterns. This goal also addresses issues related to supply chain management for sustainability by stating that 'sustainable consumption and production aims at doing more and better with less', net welfare gains from economic activities can increase by reducing resource use, degradation and pollution along the whole lifecycle, while increasing quality of life. There also needs to be a significant focus on supply chain operations, involving everyone from producer to final consumer. This includes educating consumers on sustainable consumption and lifestyles, providing them with adequate information through standards and labels and engaging in sustainable public procurement, among other things.

Based on this paradigm, this book focuses in particular on 'the importance of supply chain management for sustainability in global value chains' and addresses accompanying challenges in three main sub-areas:

Part One: Ethical principles of sustainable value chain management

Part Two: Measuring sustainability in global value chains

Part Three: Actions to continuously improve sustainability in global value chains

The book contributes to this pressing issue by describing current trends in industry, business and society and presenting research results in the areas of cross-company requirements for social and ethical sustainability principles, aspects of corporate governance to promote sustainability by measuring and managing business processes, and action-oriented aspects for the continuous implementation of best practices to further promote and foster sustainability in global value chains.

ACKNOWLEDGEMENTS

The chapters in this book were written within the scope of a project funded by the Deutsche Forschungsgemeinschaft (DFG, German Research Foundation) – 417752672 on the topic of supply chain management for sustainability in global value chains. We would like to thank the DFG for its support throughout the project and for the opportunity to advance the current research topics. We are also grateful to all authors for their valuable contributions and insights into their current research towards making the world a more sustainable place for present and future generations.

LIST OF ABBREVIATIONS

ADC	average diversity curve
AR	action research
C2C	cradle-to-cradle
CA	cooperative awareness
CC	cooperative capabilities
CE	circular economy
CEP	courier, express, and parcel
CN	cooperative necessity
CO	cooperation opportunities
CPFR	collaborative planning, forecasting, and replenishment
CQ	communication quality
CSR	corporate social responsibility
DFG	Deutsche Forschungsgemeinschaft
EPI	environmental performance indicator
ETF	empty trip factor
FCL	full container load
GDP	gross domestic product
GSCM	green supply chain management
GVC	global value chain
HCT	high-capacity transport
IPT	information processing theory
LCL	less container load
LF	loading factor
LSP	logistics service provider
MNC	multinational corporation
MNE	multinational enterprise
OEM	original equipment manufacturer
PSM	purchasing and supply management
PSS	product-service systems
ROI	return on investment
SCM	supply chain management
SDG	sustainable development goal
SME	small and medium-sized enterprise
SSCM	sustainable supply chain management

TBL	triple bottom line
TCO	total costs of ownership
TDC	total diversity curve
TEU	twenty foot equivalent unit
VCM	value creation module
WBCSD	World Business Council for Sustainable Development
WCED	World Commission on Environment and Development

Introduction 01

About the book

MICHAEL HENKE, HOLGER KOHL AND DENIS DAUS

This book summarizes the results of a project academy initiated by the German Research Foundation – Deutsche Forschungsgemeinschaft (DFG) and details the state of research on the topic of sustainability in supply chains.

DFG is the self-governing organization for science and research in Germany. Established in 1951, it promotes science in all its facets and supports research projects in all scientific disciplines. In addition, the DFG advises parliaments and authorities on scientific issues and maintains the links between research and foreign science and industry. The core task of the DFG is the competitive selection of the best research projects by scientists at universities and research institutes as well as their funding. Therefore, special attention is paid to the promotion of young scientists, who can apply for the funding of knowledge-led research projects on the topics they have selected from one discipline or using interdisciplinary approaches. DFG funding thus guarantees a high-quality differentiation within the German science system and at the same time helps to shape the European research area.

In this light, the DFG launched a project academy on the subject of 'sustainability in global value chains' in April 2018, funded over a period of two years. The aim of this project academy is to offer professors the opportunity to start conducting research projects at an early stage in their careers. Participants gain insights into the application formalities for funding and the implementation of research projects. In order to ensure a professional coverage of the value chain, the participants are experts in their respective fields of purchasing, logistics, production, supply chain management (SCM), sustainability and business ethics.

In the course of the project academy the professors were able to present their research ideas as well as gain insights into important aspects in the application process and assessment of the applications, the management of research projects and the DFG funding. The meetings throughout the project academy duration were characterized by an inspiring exchange about research opportunities and cooperation possibilities as well as diverse ideas on how our world can be improved from a sustainability perspective.

The lively exchange of all participants and collaborative development of the individual research ideas resulted in the cooperative and interdisciplinary research topics that are presented in this book. Following the project academy, the participants developed further their respective research proposals and submitted them to DFG for funding.

The editors of this book, Prof Dr Michael Henke, professor at the chair of enterprise logistics at the University of Dortmund and head of the Fraunhofer Institute for Material Flow and Logistics IML, and Prof Dr-Ing Holger Kohl, head of the Department of Sustainable Business Development at the TU Berlin and head of the corporate management division at the Fraunhofer Institute for Production Systems and Design Technology IPK, coordinate and head the project academy.

The importance of supply chain management for sustainability in global value chains 02

HOLGER KOHL, MICHAEL HENKE AND DENIS DAUS

Since the beginning of the Industrial Revolution and the associated increase in welfare, society is heavily based on the consumption of products and services in the currently dominant linear model of economic development. This model is also described as the 'take–make–dispose' approach and is based on the imperative of continuous economic growth that comes with an increased use of natural resources. Since these natural resources are for the most part exhaustible and non-renewable, the current situation constitutes a natural barrier to economic growth (Skawińska and Zalewski, 2018: 218). With ever-increasing wealth and forecasted population growth (United Nations, 2019), the Earth is confronted with huge sustainability challenges, which causes a myriad of problems for society, the economy, and especially for the environment. These problems constitute, for example, rising CO_2 concentration in the atmosphere with the related greenhouse effect, pollution of soil, shortage of water, increasing amounts of communal and industrial waste, and the aforementioned scarcity of natural resources with the effect of increasing prices or fluctuating markets (Bouchery *et al*, 2017: 15; Lee *et al*, 2012). This situation is not a new phenomenon, as environmental issues, a development towards sustainability and a reconciliation between economy and ecology have been the topic of political debate since the 1960s. In order to counteract the negative consequences of resource depletion and to promote the sustainable use of natural resources, the concept of sustainable development was created in 1970 (Banaitė and Tamošiūnienė, 2016). The concept was extended by the World Commission on Environment and Development (WCED) with regards to three interdependent dimensions of well-being, namely economic, social and environmental (WCED, 1987), and became a political objective of the European Union in the Treaty of Amsterdam in 1999 (Duran *et al*, 2015). It is now a comprehensive concept published in the UN Agenda for Sustainable Development ('Agenda 2030'), which defines 17 intersectional sustainable development goals and 169 targets in order to implement sustainable development (United Nations, 2015).

Sustainable development is at its core a concept that enables the needs of present generations to be met while at the same time securing the same level of welfare for future generations (Ibrahim *et al*, 2015). This notion remains valid today and is becoming increasingly important in the current socio-economic debate. However, the theory of sustainable development is a relatively new paradigm in management research and is continuously expanding due to challenges in the yet prevailing linear model of economic development. Challenges, such as socio-economic and ecological imbalances, changing aims and methods or the economic crises in the 21st century, therefore require new management approaches on the way to sustainability. The necessity to adapt sustainability principles in practice becomes more and more obvious. A traditional linear supply chain is based on the concept that resources are extracted from the geosphere and biosphere, and the manufactured products, which are at the end of their life, as well as packaging materials and wastes from multiple stages of the supply chain, are disposed of in landfill (Farooque *et al*, 2019: 884–85). If these kind of linear business models cannot be adapted, the depletion of virgin resources will continue to increase, accelerating its associated negative consequences (Ellen MacArthur Foundation, 2015: 16). Against this background, the United Nations highlights the importance of the supply chain management (SCM) function within the business sector to foster more sustainable products and processes (UNGC, 2015). A transition away from a linear approach to the more sustainable design and management of supply chains requires attention to be turned to a reduction of the pace of growth and consumption, a consideration of external environmental costs and mechanisms as well as to technological solutions for recycling and closed-loop production processes (Skawińska and Zalewski, 2018). Several researchers and proponents of the de-growth movement endorse an end to the prevalent ideology of growth as a way to rectify environmental issues and to be conscious about finite resources and our limits (Washington, 2015; Vieira, 2016; Jackson, 2017). The impact of industrialization on the environment is evident. Supply chains with their different tasks and stakeholders play a significant part in it, eg by consuming enormous amounts of resources and energy as well as creating wastes in the form of scrap during production and after usage of the product. Hence, it is essential to implement more sustainability into supply chains.

This outline demonstrates the need for enhanced sustainability principles in supply chains and their integration by means of appropriate SCM approaches. The research themes presented in this book address this need by looking at it from different disciplines. In the first instance, an understanding of the term sustainability in the context of supply chains and related state of research is necessary.

Sustainability concepts in supply chain research have been examined by several authors in the past (Linton *et al*, 2007; Seuring and Müller, 2008; Srivastava, 2007; Kleindorfer *et al*, 2005). An evaluation of 60 sustainability definitions and concepts shows that a range from one to eight different sustainability dimensions is covered in literature (Tremmel, 2004). Over time, the concept of the three pillars of sustainability (economic, social, environmental) – also referred to as the triple bottom line (TBL) (Elkington, 1999) – has prevailed and is widely accepted in academia. This goes along with the concept of sustainable development defined by the WCED. These dimensions of sustainable development stand in complex interdependency to each other, incorporating synergies between them (Cornescu and Adam, 2014).

Existing sustainability concepts do not give the same priority to the three dimensions of sustainability (Andes *et al*, 2019: 11). In the context of performance and sustainability management in supply chains, this is underlined by the finding that only a little research has so far been done in relation to all three sustainability dimensions (Isaksson, 2018). The economic and environmental dimensions are frequently discussed in literature. Social or ethical aspects are, however, less represented. Nonetheless, the social discussion on the necessity for the long-term preservation of the environment is intensified by increasingly scarce resources, the increasing burden on the environment and the increased environmental awareness of consumers as well as their demand for social responsibility (BMUB, 2016: 9 ff; European Union, 2012: 35 ff.). Also, for companies, the pressure to build up effective sustainability competences and address social responsibility in operations, purchasing and SCM is continuously increasing. Economic and environmental sustainability in combination with special attention to employee orientation is therefore gaining importance in companies (Brugger, 2010: 26; Seuring and Müller, 2008: 1699).

To support companies in acquiring comprehensive competences in sustainability and enable them to manage it, a myriad of international standards and frameworks are available for measuring and promoting sustainable development (Andes *et al*, 2019: 315 ff.). Only a small portion of them (eg PAS 1044, VDI 4070, DIN ISO 26000) offers a holistic view on sustainability and takes into account all three aspects of sustainability. The other frameworks each address only one aspect of sustainability. For example, the economic evaluation is supported by *DIN EN ISO 14051*, *VDI 4405*, *4400* or *4491*. Social aspects are underrepresented. However, the framework *Social Accountability 8000* considers the evaluation of the social component and in recent years a large number of standards have emerged that serve as guidelines and reference systems for the fulfilment of social responsibility in SCM (Andes *et al*, 2019: 27). Other frameworks and guidelines refer to an ecologically oriented assessment of sustainability performance (eg *EMAS*, the entire *ISO 14000* series, *GHG Protocol*, *DIN ISO 50001* or *VDI 4600*). Although the frameworks represent recommendations through large, complex collections of indicators for sustainability and its performance, they are difficult to manage and operationalize. A methodological guideline and a derivation of appropriate measures, recommendations for action or best practices are missing.

In the area of scientific methods, only a few approaches include all levels of sustainability performance in their assessment, for example the concept for the sustainability-oriented design of integrated production systems (Bergmann, 2010), the Sustainability Performance Management Audit (Kuhn and Pischke-Malkus, 2012), the Indicators of Sustainable Production (Veleva and Ellenbecker, 2001) or the Sustainability Balanced Scorecard (Deegen, 2001). Again, these methods do not provide suggestions for improvement or the derivation of recommendations and best practices.

Sustainable manufacturing and value creation in global networks

Industrial production plays a particularly important role in the implementation of sustainability in supply chains (Bretzke and Barkawi, 2012, 56 ff;

Wirth *et al*, 2011: 691). Most industrial production processes and the production-logistics environment in the manufacturing industry are not sustainable due to high CO_2 or other process-related emissions during production, transport, storage and transhipment processes. This is amplified by a lack of consideration of social aspects, eg during the implementation of production-organizational concepts, as well as a strong focus on technological performance and an inadequate economic assessment (Bretzke and Barkawi, 2012: 2; Gregori and Wimmer, 2011: 23 f.). The products and services responsible for issues in sustainability are at the same time key objects in addressing the present sustainability challenges, eg in terms of a more sustainable production and consumption approach. As a consequence, the principle of sustainable production along the entire supply chain is clearly moving into focus. Producing enterprises are increasingly called upon to respond with sustainable management in their supply chains (Wirth *et al*, 2011: 691 ff; Wildemann, 2018: preamble I).

From a company's point of view, the connection between sustainability and corporate success has been examined in greater detail by several researchers. There is evidence that sustainability offers a long-term competitive advantage for corporations (Campbell, 2007) and that sustainable acting is a chance for companies since it represents a differentiating factor. However, other research concludes that there are only negative effects for competitiveness through sustainability (Halme and Niskanen, 2001). Either way, if industrialized countries want to maintain the current level of wealth and secure or even increase welfare for future generations, the goal should be a sustainable value creation along global supply chains as well as sustainable supply chain management (SSCM).

To do so, a more specific view on the aspect of value creation and higher-level architecture of value creation networks is helpful.

Value creation and value creation modules

The value of an object, in contrast to ethical or aesthetic value, describes the relation between an object and a subject. It can be understood as use and exchange value and represents the current potential of being used and its potential of being useful in the future compared to other objects (Wenke, 1987). But the technological value and its use are diverse. According to the VDI 3780 criteria this can be, for instance, functionality, safety, prosperity as the satisfaction of demand or economy in terms of profitability and efficiency, but also personal development, societal or environmental quality or health (Verein Deutscher Ingenieure eV, 2000). In addition to the functionality, the value of products and services can be aspects that stimulate human emotions, like the image of a product. In combination with societal development, the meaning of value also modifies and shows a shift from a purely economic to a more holistic valuation. Referring to that, Ueda (2009) proposed the creation of a new concept of sustainable value that is commensurate with the present challenges (Ueda *et al*, 2009).

In an industrial context, value creation is the activity to shape the value of a product, product part or raw material. It can be divided into primary/main activities, causing direct increase in value, and secondary/auxiliary activities, causing indirect increase in value (Porter, 2000). To achieve this, five different factors, closely interlocked with each other, are necessary. Seliger (2007) defines them as product, process, equipment, organization and human, which describe the 'what', 'how', 'by what', 'where and when' and 'who' of each value creation activity. The Value Creation Module (VCM) is the totality of these factors on a specific observation level and is illustrated in Figure 2.1 (Seliger, 2007).

The observation level, and therefore the scope of a value creation module, can be from a manufacturing tool and operation, value creating cells and systems, a whole factory to a national and international entrepreneurial conglomerates. All of these value creation modules can be interpreted not only in economical but also in an ecological and a social dimension. For instance, the resource effectiveness and efficiency of a value creation module has influence on the ecological dimension as well as health and qualification influence on the social dimension (Seliger, 2007). All of these generated effects of value creation modules on the three dimensions of sustainability can be measured by sustainability assessment methods (Bonvoisin, 2017).

Figure 2.1 The Value Creation Module

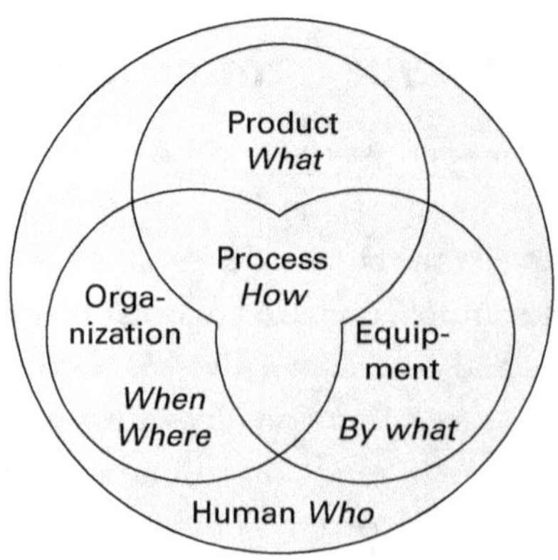

SOURCE Seliger (2007)

Process chains and vertical and horizontal integration

The creation of value is organized by process chains that are generically structured into suppliers, a focal company or action, and consumers (Porter, 2000). According to that, each value creation module is linked in the value-added chain to other modules, which is illustrated in Figure 2.2. For a single module, upstream activities represent the supply network, whereas downstream located activities can be seen as the distribution network. This combination into a process chain represents the vertical dimension of value creation. The redundant horizontal dimension is the parallelism of modules and process chains and represents various products or comprehensive capacities. From an

Figure 2.2 Process chains with horizontal and vertical integration

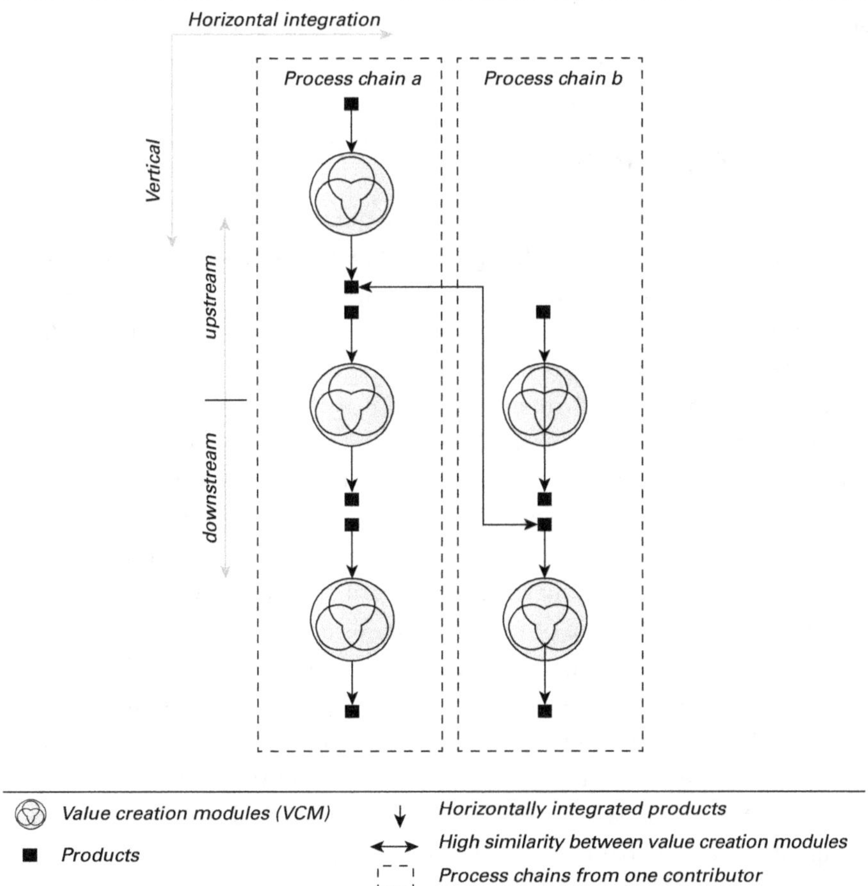

SOURCE Heyer (2014)

entrepreneurial point of view, the objective has to be to get own specific value as a contribution integrated into a larger value creation network, while, from a top-down perspective, entrepreneurs try to purchase elements to enrich their production system (Seliger, 2011).

By a growing number of products and variants, producing companies are facing an increasing complexity. To survive in global competition, enterprises focus more on their core competencies. As a result, they divide the value chain increasingly into high-specified enterprises and organize themselves in global value networks. This dynamic of cooperation and competition drives the integration of modules into networks. The challenge for the management is to maintain a balance between broad technological knowledge as future potentials and the concentration of economically required core competencies. From a cross-company perspective, the challenge is how to negotiate about own and partner's activities in value creating networks and how to use the dynamics of cooperation and competition as a tool for sustainable value creation (Seliger, 2012).

Value creation networks

The consideration of sustainable manufacturing can be divided into four major research layers: manufacturing technologies, product development, value creation networks and the global manufacturing impact. A value creation network is the connection of value creation modules into process chains with interconnections on a defined observation level. It addresses the organization of companies and manufacturing networks. Referring to the four sustainability layers, the degree of sustainability is not only defined by the product design but also by lots of choices made in the value creation network that are not accessible to the product development team (Bonvoisin, 2017).

'A guiding question of research is how the dynamics of competition and cooperation in globalized markets can be utilized by innovative technology to cope with the challenge of rationally required mankind's sustainable development on Earth' (Seliger, 2012). Figure 2.3 describes the architecture of value creation networks as an approach to coping with the challenge. The core of value creation modules, defined by scope and value creation factors, is created to be evaluated regarding their impact on the three dimensions of sustainability. All value creation modules are integrated by cooperation and competition into global process chains and networks.

But next to the value creation modules themselves and their specific impact or effect on the dimensions of sustainability, the organization and

Figure 2.3 Approach to cope with the challenges

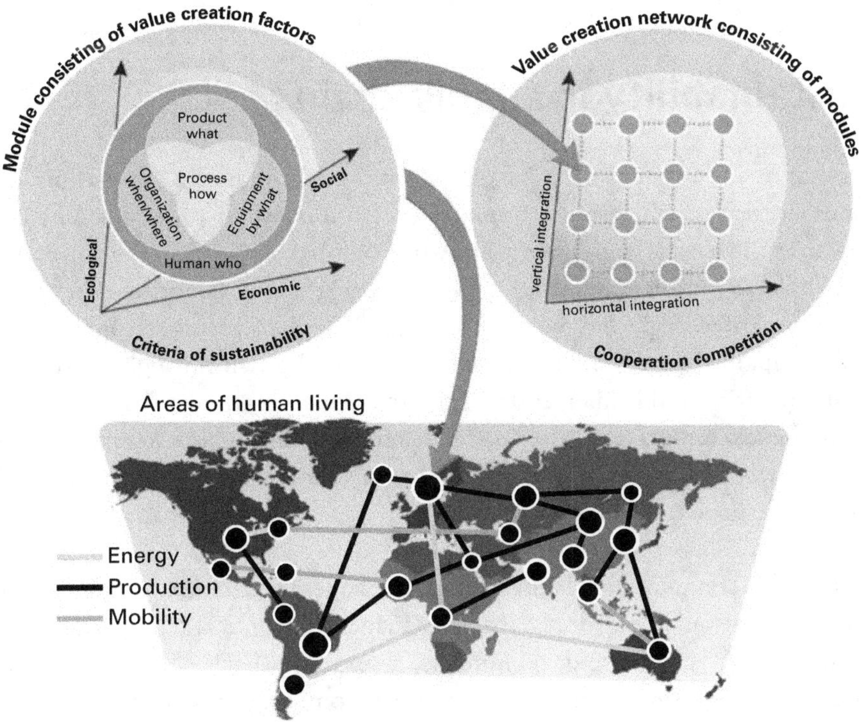

SOURCE Bonvoisin (2017)

connection of the modules are the core of interest. The location of value creation modules and the combination of sites also have effects on sustainability dimensions by the influence of regional structures and by logistics. For instance, next to the transportation distance between the sole modules, the transportation systems that were used have to be part of the consideration. Furthermore, the re-manufacturability of a product is not only defined by the design itself, but also by the existing infrastructure and organization within the value creation network (Bonvoisin, 2017).

Taking this into consideration, new approaches to ensure the development of organizational infrastructure regarding sustainable products and production are required. In relation to that, Bonvoisin (2017) quotes the multi-objective and integrated value creation planning as two critical aspects. One challenge lies in the coordination of an independently managed organization with individual profit maximization behaviour, with more integrated planning. The other is to integrate several dimensions into the decision-making process in pursuit of connection value creation modules (Bonvoisin, 2017).

Sustainability in supply chains

As one of the consequences of globalization, a company's internal added value decreases, which puts supply chains in a constant process of change towards increasing complexity and more global networks (Linton *et al*, 2007; Carter and Rogers, 2008). In these global networks production processes are often dispersed, which results in the global creation of value. This is accompanied by an environmental and social burden throughout supply chains (Seuring and Müller, 2008). Since the global creation of value together with the awareness for sustainable behaviour throughout entire supply chains increases, it becomes obvious that sustainability cannot be handled by a single firm. It is, rather, a supply chain issue because globally connected supply chains are progressively competing with each other (Li *et al*, 2006). Within this context, there is the need to implement sustainable management and cooperation along supply chains (Miemczyk *et al*, 2012).

With regards to these developments, several approaches and terminologies have emerged in supply chain literature promoting a major shift towards sustainability, for example sustainable supply chain management (SSCM) (Carter and Easton, 2011; Touboulic and Walker, 2015; Leszczynska and Maryniak, 2017), green supply chain management (GSCM) (Srivastava, 2007; Chakraborty, 2010; Abu Seman, 2012; Malviya and Kant, 2015), closed-loop supply chains (Schenkel *et al*, 2015; Govindan *et al*, 2015; Souza, 2013), or circular economy (CE) (Geissdoerfer *et al*, 2018; Manavalan and Jayakrishna, 2019; Mayer *et al*, 2019). Although these concepts have different foci, some are often used interchangeably (Gurtu *et al*, 2015). This misconception becomes obvious when looking exemplarily at the published definitions of SSCM and GSCM concepts.

Most definitions for SSCM, for example, explicitly address all three dimensions of the TBL. On the contrary, none of the available definitions on GSCM mention social aspects and they barely consider the economic dimension. Instead, the focus of GSCM is mostly on environmental issues. The SSCM approach can be seen as an extended view of GSCM (Ahi and Searcy, 2013). From a business perspective, the GSCM approach could motivate organizations to cooperate with green raw material suppliers as key partners in order to reinforce green resources and green activities (Chen and Huang, 2019a: 17).

In the field of SSCM, there is already significant research evidence on how individual business functions can improve their respective environmental performance (Gurtu *et al*, 2017; Beske and Seuring, 2014). An adoption of SSCM concepts was helpful for organizations to create a blended business and environmental value (Park *et al*, 2010). However, adequate integration both across functional areas and along several stages of the value chain does not yet exist (Wilhelm *et al*, 2016), although this is a basic prerequisite for the design of sustainable value chains. It is therefore necessary to overcome the predominant functional thinking. With regards to the TBL, SSCM research rarely provides a comprehensive view since the economic, environmental and social dimensions often are not covered altogether or not equally (Ahi and Searcy, 2013).

Considering the scope of SSCM, Figure 2.4 provides an overview of previous research understanding of SSCM tasks, especially in terms of environmental and social sustainability in supply chains.

Figure 2.4 Framework for environmental and social supply chain sustainability actions

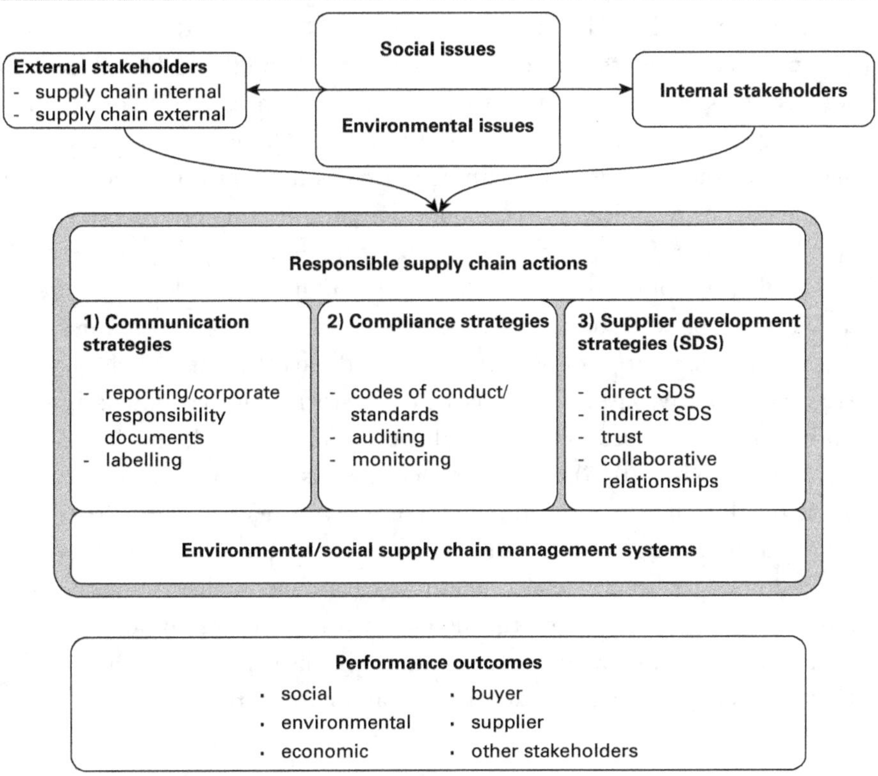

SOURCE Schulze and Bals (2018)

Closed-loop supply chains are designed to bring back products and packaging materials to the producer for value recovery and thus improve environmental performance (Guide and Wassenhove, 2006). Compared to conventional manufacturing, this approach can significantly save materials, labour and energy as well as reduce waste (Toffel, 2004). Nevertheless, since closed-loop concepts focus on the original (producer's) supply chain and do not include other adjunct channel members, the extent of value recovery is limited. As a consequence, closed-loop supply chains still generate large amounts of wastes because it is rarely feasible to circulate all wastes or by-products within the same supply chain. A so-called circular supply chain, on the other hand, reaches beyond the limitations of closed-loop supply chains because it can recover value from waste by collaborating with organizations within the industrial sector or from different industrial sectors (Weetman, 2017). After a series of concepts, such as zero waste or green economy, the term circular economy (CE) has been established in literature describing closed-loop approaches more thoroughly (Kopnina, 2018).

The concept of CE can be seen as a result of the development of sustainability approaches (Banaitė and Tamošiūnienė, 2016). CE explicitly focuses on circulation of materials that are produced, used and discarded in the system of industrial production (Murray *et al*, 2017). It furthermore clearly distinguishes between the biological (regenerative) and the technical (restorative) cycles of a product and thus significantly enhances GSCM and SSCM by the regenerative dimension. On the one hand, biological materials become part of the biosphere and can be reused as inputs for production. On the other hand, technical materials are designed for material recovery, eg through repair, refurbishing, remanufacturing and recycling (Weetman, 2017). This conception stems from the field of industrial ecology and shows that CE might be well suited to mimic the circular cycles of the natural ecosystem with regards to product design, use and reuse (Mont and Heiskanen, 2015). Exemplarily, natural resources are transformed into products and the by-products can be used as resources for other industries (Zhu *et al*, 2010). Lacy and Rutqvist (2015) even state that a transition to a CE may be the biggest revolution and opportunity for how we organize production and consumption in the global economy. The concept represents a big opportunity for companies to create a competitive advantage by disrupting the way we produce and consume, eg through innovative business models, digital technologies and circular capabilities. It is a radical paradigm shift in the relationships between markets, customers and natural resources.

Similarly, the cradle-to-cradle (C2C) approach is gaining broad attention as a solution to many of the environmental and natural resource challenges by transforming industries from a polluting and resource depleting system into a sustainable system of production. Contrary to focusing on the reduction of environmental impact of a product or process, the idea of C2C is to remove harmful impacts and replace them with beneficial elements (Nielsen and Brunoe, 2015). Furthermore, in contrast to the linear industrial system, where products at the end of their life are disposed of in landfill or incinerated, polluting the environment, C2C tries to imitate the metabolism of nature in which all waste from plants and animals is recycled to create new life (McDonough and Braungart, 2002). Eventually it fosters the creation of a CE.

Sustainable sourcing

Until now we have seen that researchers have analysed different strategies and concepts companies can use to integrate sustainability aspects into their supply chains, especially under consideration of the TBL perspective. The establishment of environmental and social standards as well as implementation of corporate sustainability requires not only the involvement of several departments, but also of the organization's suppliers. The purchasing function is specifically relevant for an organization's overall sustainability (Tate *et al*, 2010). This is primarily due to its position where the material flows into the company begin and because each organization can be only as sustainable as its upstream supply chain (Krause *et al*, 2009).

From a sourcing perspective, procurement companies are often made responsible for social or ecological effects resulting not only from their own actions, but also from the behaviour of their suppliers and partners within the entire supply chain (Hartmann and Moeller, 2014; Kovács, 2008). This makes it necessary for the purchasing function to develop comprehensive sustainable sourcing strategies. Hence, SSCM together with sustainable sourcing have become an important research stream in academia and management practice (Quarshie *et al*, 2016; Zimmer *et al*, 2016). In combination with sourcing, SSCM includes procurement and supplier management functions, eg sustainability-oriented supplier selection and auditing or supplier collaboration and development (Hollos *et al*, 2012; Leire and Mont, 2009). Close supplier relationships are important in daily activities because the poor performance (in economic, environmental and social terms) of suppliers reflects in large part on the focal company. As a consequence, the reputation of the focal company suffers and sales volumes decline more than on the suppliers' side (Handfield *et al*, 2005).

From this perspective, purchasing and supply management (PSM) has been established in order to avoid unethical behaviour and reputational damage (Carter, 2004). Nevertheless, studies have shown that managers have difficulties in incorporating sustainability dimensions in decision making and feel undecided in terms of proper decision making about how to manage ethical behaviour in their respective organizations in order to withstand the external pressure and their stakeholders' requirements.

An appropriate sourcing strategy that considers sustainability aspects should be chosen based on the prevalent buying settings as well as the diverse sustainability challenges and supply chains of the respective company (Lampel *et al*, 2014). At the same time, corporate activities need to be in line with the ethical requirements of the internal and external stakeholders of a company in order to ensure economic sustainability (Kleindorfer *et al*, 2005). Purchasing activities need to be extended towards taking account of other stakeholders and increasing internal cooperation in order to overcome functional silos (Tassabehji and Moorhouse, 2008). These competencies become more important as the implementation of corporate sustainability progresses (Worthington *et al*, 2008).

When sourcing from emerging markets, companies outsource certain activities and cooperate with suppliers abroad. This is, however, a challenge because many companies from emerging markets face sustainability issues. Difficulties comprise eg a lack of legal regulations, educated labour, technology or proper infrastructure. If outsourcing companies want to comply with sustainability and ethical behaviour imposed by their stakeholders, they need to carefully screen and choose suppliers based on multiple criteria. In literature related to supplier assessment there is a lack of decision support systems that integrate sustainability criteria with conventional criteria, eg price or quality. Thus, it is crucial to develop sustainable SCM practices in order to integrate operational, organizational and sustainability perspectives (Roth *et al*, 2008).

As with the previously described different sustainability concepts in supply chain research, available research in the field of sustainable sourcing and sourcing decisions does not consider all dimensions of the TBL to a comprehensive extent. Researchers consider either social (Leire and Mont, 2009) or environmental (Min and Galle, 2001) aspects. Within the social dimensions the focus is, for example, on relationships between suppliers and buyers (Svensson and Bååth, 2008), prevention of child labour (Winstanley *et al*, 2002), or the establishment of codes of conduct (Mamic, 2005). From the environmental perspective the focus is, for example, on purchasing's role in facilitating recycling, reuse and reduction of resource consumption (Min and Galle, 1997), or connecting sourcing to strategic aspects, such as product development or risk management (Handfield *et al*, 2005; Vachon and Klassen, 2006). In the field of corporate social responsibility (CSR), more comprehensive concepts have been developed by combining both environmental and social criteria (Carter, 2004, 2005). Schneider and Wallenburg (2012) advanced this research by addressing different ways in which sustainable sourcing can be implemented based on the company-specific emphasis on the three dimensions of the TBL. Nevertheless, a profound insight into the interdependencies between social and environmental aspects is not evident and a connection with economic performance remains absent (Harwood and Humby, 2008; Simpson *et al*, 2007). Also, the majority of available sourcing methodologies are either cost-oriented or ad hoc, without the proper tools and techniques required to deal with sustainability (Hatami-Marbini *et al*, 2017).

Sustainable logistics

Literature on logistics and supply chain disciplines shows increasing awareness of sustainable development (SD) and sustainable logistics operations. The logistics function plays a particularly critical role in organizations' supply chain operations and their long-term sustainability strategies because it is essential for identifying inefficiencies and reducing carbon footprint (Dey *et al*, 2011). Sustainable logistics is an essential topic for the development of SSCM since it includes many corresponding subjects, such as type of transport, infrastructure, or operational management practices, that should be considered in establishing environmentally friendly transportation systems (Al-Odeh and Smallwood, 2012). Key areas of interest therein are, for example, CSR (Keating *et al*, 2008), environmental logistics (Wu and Dunn, 1995), green logistics (McKinnon, 2010; Aronsson and Huge Brodin, 2006), the environmental impact of freight transport, and sustainable warehousing and storage (Grant *et al*, 2017), and some of these terms are also used interchangeably in the literature (Abbasi and Nilsson, 2012). In addition, different authors have proposed environmental practices that focus in particular on logistics from the perspective of purchasing management (Bowen *et al*, 2001) as well as SCM (Sheu *et al*, 2005). Especially due to the global increase of production and international transportation of goods between countries, environmental issues constitute a major concern for transport and logistics (Dey *et al*, 2011).

With regard to evaluation of logistics activities, economic evaluation has been the traditional focus for many logistics enterprises. Under this scheme, green logistics received increasing attention because of less quantifiable environmental and social aspects. Hence, El-Berishy *et al* (2013) point out that environmental responsibility cannot be dissociated from economic development. Under consideration of the TBL, decision making in logistics represents an increasingly complex task for companies because decisions need to be made at strategic, tactical and operational levels (Qaiser *et al*, 2017). An analysis of literature under the TBL umbrella has shown that most publications in the field of sustainable logistics neglect the integration of both environmental and social aspects. Instead, these papers often focus solely on green and environmental issues (Dutta *et al*, 2020). Logistical activities can have positive socio-economic effects, such as supporting a growing wealth, but can also have negative consequences on the environment and societies. For example, logistical activities are still dependent on fossil fuels, that emit greenhouse gases when burned, and contribute to the depletion of non-renewable natural resources. This in turn has negative consequences for the environment and health and safety of individuals, and pollutes land and water. To overcome this, SD of logistics requires economic and social benefits while decreasing the negative consequences on the environment (Abbasi and Nilsson, 2016). This is, however, a challenging task because logistical activities present several economic, environmental and social challenges, for example in terms of globalization, urbanization, global warming, migration or aging of the population (Abbasi and Nilsson, 2016). A solution approach is delivered, for example, by Dutta *et al* (2020) who has developed a model of decision making that incorporates social aspects next to environmental and economic aspects. Also, Rashidi and Cullinane (2019) incorporate environmental and social aspects in logistics in order to promote a sustainable logistics management system.

The management of the described challenges and sustainable logistics operations needs to incorporate environmental management principles (Ubeda *et al*, 2011). For instance, managers must make appropriate decisions about the mode of transportation and put more emphasis on clean vehicle technology (Dey *et al*, 2011). It is evident that managers have increased awareness of environmental issues for several reasons. On the one hand, there is an emphasis on transportation of goods in sustainable logistics systems (Grant *et al*, 2017). This means that the need for transportation of products is increasing, resulting in more greenhouse gas emissions, which in turn contributes to global warming and facilitates economic disasters (Evangelista *et al*, 2018). Suggested counter-measures aim to prioritize consolidation of shipments when planning and programming flows, or choose less polluting forms of transportation (McKinnon, 2010; Schade and Schade, 2005).

On the other hand, this development calls for more sustainable logistics services (Govindan *et al*, 2019). In this context, cooperation between manufacturers and retailers as well as outsourcing of logistical activities to logistics service providers (LSPs) requires special attention as an alternative to the dominant value chain perspective. This is also due to the limitation of SCM research, where the focus is on the manufacturer or retailer (Huemer, 2012). LSPs play a particularly important role in creating trust and value in supply chains (Marasco, 2008). This viewpoint provides the potential to make logistics more environmentally friendly. However, in the context of LSPs, little attention has been paid to associated sustainability aspects (Lieb and Lieb, 2010; Wolf and Seuring, 2010) and to the integration of the TBL (Abbasi and Nilsson, 2016).

Lu and Bock (2016) examine the field of sustainable logistics from a comprehensive perspective taking into account the entire supply chain. The authors point out the main challenges that influence modern logistics and supply chains and cluster them according to five themes: supply chain strategy and management, information and communication technology for logistics and related business models, vertical and horizontal collaboration, intelligent hubs, and policies for sustainable logistics. The development of sustainable logistics and implementation of innovations therein requires a deep understanding of the accompanying implementation processes, underlying critical factors, challenges and actors involved (Björklund and Forslund, 2018). Accordingly, in times of emerging digital technologies, such as the idea of 'Industry 4.0' coined in Germany in 2011, industries are aiming to progress operational excellence through advancing the developments of Industry 4.0 technologies (Mangla *et al*, 2019). Hence, the integration of Industry 4.0 with SSCM and sustainable logistics in particular is examined by several authors and has resulted in instructive suggestions considering technical, organizational and social aspects (Dev *et al*, 2020; Grzybowska *et al*, 2020).

Sustainability is an interdisciplinary topic

Compared to different sustainability management approaches used in the 21st century, the authors Skawińska and Zalewski (2018) propose that the concept of CE is best suited to meet the prerequisites of SD in the most accurate way. In comparison to the concepts SSCM or GSCM, CE goes one step further by reducing the need for virgin materials and increasing the circulation of resources within supply chains (Genovese *et al*, 2017). A holistic approach can be undertaken with the CE concept because circular thinking is systematically applied to all supply chain functions and stages as well as to manufactured products and services. Moreover, in circular supply chains, organizations collaborate with each other within and across sectors in order to maximize the utility of goods and materials. This is a promising vision for SCM since performance in resource efficiency and profitability together with minimum negative environmental, economic and social consequences can be achieved at the same time (Farooque *et al*, 2019: 884). Nevertheless, many parts of the value chain, such as manufacturing, distribution or sales are rarely involved in the concept of CE (Kalmykova *et al*, 2018: 199) and its integration into SCM is still unclear (Aminoff and Kettunen, 2016). Depending on different views of stakeholders, industries or countries, there is also differentiation in the perceived risks of resource scarcity and the appropriate responses to mitigate these risks. Despite that, a common ground has evolved that only a change in the current way of resource consumption and better resource efficiency can ensure a sufficient supply of natural resources, protect biodiversity and enable sustainable growth for the global population (Frodermann, 2018: 1). The discussion around sustainability in SCM has indeed pointed out restorative cycles, while regenerative aspects are still missing in this context. Against this background, there is a need to enhance existing sustainability concepts in SCM towards a more circular thinking in all supply chain stages and functions, and at the same time minimize the negative environmental, economic and social impacts (Farooque *et al*, 2019).

When looking from the political angle, the required policies to foster sustainability concepts are not always in place. Chen and Huang (2019a) therefore suggest emphasizing sustainability policies to enhance green willingness and capabilities in the daily operations of businesses as well as to increase investments in order to progress future SD. This is also crucial for green business model innovations or the lifecycle management of products and services (Chen and Huang, 2019b). As supply chains are the origin of a large share of environmental impacts, they also include great potential for reducing or avoiding considerable risks to the environment as well as to the companies themselves. A growing expectation to recognize one's own social responsibilities, eg related to one's supply chain, is the result of tighter relationships between companies and suppliers due to globalization. Therefore, these topics are also addressed at the political level (Weiss *et al*, 2017). Despite the variety of research streams and approaches to tackle sustainability issues, Pagell and Shevchenko (2014) point out that a holistic integration of sustainability along global supply chains continues to be a current challenge across industries and sectors. For example, encouraging less consumption stands in contrast to today's dominant thinking of neoliberal economic growth (Kopnina and Blewitt, 2014).

The political, industrial and supply chain perspectives illustrate the necessity for increasingly interdisciplinary research over several stages of the supply chain and for consideration of all three sustainability dimensions on an equal basis. Based on definitions of GSCM and SSCM as well as publications in the field of sustainability, Ahi and Searcy (2013) find that research in the area of sustainability is a highly interdisciplinary matter. Also Skawińska and Zalewski (2018) suggest that the sustainability approach has to be interdisciplinary because it needs to take into account the natural barriers of growth (due to depleting resources), the drawbacks of the current (mostly linear) economies, ethical aspects, or cultural norms and values.

This book makes a contribution towards this goal by introducing interdisciplinary research in the field of sustainability in global value chains. We examine this overarching topic by conceptualizing three research questions (see Figure 3.1).

References

Abbasi, M and Nilsson, F (2012) Themes and challenges in making supply chains environmentally sustainable, *Supply Chain Management: An international journal*, **17** (5), pp 517–30

Abbasi, M and Nilsson, F (2016) Developing environmentally sustainable logistics, *Transportation Research Part D: Transport and Environment*, **46**, pp 273–83

Abu Seman, NA (2012) Green supply chain management: A review and research direction, *International Journal of Managing Value and Supply Chains*, **3** (1), pp 1–18

Ahi, P and Searcy, C (2013) A comparative literature analysis of definitions for green and sustainable supply chain management, *Journal of Cleaner Production*, **52**, pp 329–41

Al-Odeh, M and Smallwood, J (2012) Sustainable supply chain management: Literature review, trends, and framework, *IJCEMInternational Journal of Computational Engineering and Management*, **15** (1), pp 85–90

Aminoff, A and Kettunen, O (2016) Sustainable supply chain management in a circular economy: Towards supply circles, in *Sustainable Design and Manufacturing 2016: Smart Innovation, Systems and Technologies*, ed R Setchi, R J Howlett, Y Liu and P Theobald, Vol 52, Springer International Publishing, Cham, pp 61–72

Andes, L, Lützkendorf, T and Ströbele, B (2019) Methodensammlung zur Nachhaltigkeitsbewertung Grundlagen, Indikatoren, Hilfsmittel, Karlsruhe Institut für Technologie KIT, Karlsruhe

Aronsson, H and Huge Brodin, M (2006) The environmental impact of changing logistics structures, *The International Journal of Logistics Management*, **17** (3), pp 394–415

Banaitė, D and Tamošiūnienė, R (2016) Sustainable development: The circular economy indicators selection model, *Journal of Security and Sustainability Issues*, **6** (2), pp 315–23

Bergmann, L (2010) *Nachhaltigkeit in Ganzheitlichen Produktionssystemen*, Zugl: Braunschweig, Techn. Univ., Diss., 2009, *Schriftenreihe des Instituts für Werkzeugmaschinen und Fertigungstechnik der TU Braunschweig*, Vulkan-Verl, Essen

Beske, P and Seuring, S (2014) Putting sustainability into supply chain management, *Supply Chain Management: An international journal*, **19** (3), pp 322–31

Björklund, M and Forslund, H (2018) Exploring the sustainable logistics innovation process, *Industrial Management and Data Systems*, **118** (1), pp 204–17

BMUB (2016) *Deutsches Ressourceneffizienzprogramm II: Programm zur nachhaltigen Nutzung und zum Schutz der natürlichen Ressourcen*, 1st edn, Berlin

Bonvoisin, J (2017) Field of research in sustainable manufacturing, in *Sustainable Manufacturing: Challenges, Solutions and implementation perspectives, sustainable production, life cycle engineering and management*, ed R Stark, G Seliger and J Bonvoisin, Springer Open, Cham, Switzerland, pp 3–20

Bouchery, Y, Corbett, CJ, Fransoo, J C and Tan, T (eds) (2017) *Sustainable Supply Chains: A research-based textbook on operations and strategy*, Springer Series in Supply Chain Management, Vol 4, Springer International Publishing, Cham, SL

Bowen, FE, Cousins, PD, Lamming, RC and Farukt, AC (2001) The role of supply management capabilities in green supply, *Production and Operations Management*, **10** (2), pp 174–89

Bretzke, W-R and Barkawi, K (2012) *Nachhaltige Logistik*, Springer Berlin Heidelberg, Berlin, Heidelberg

Brugger, F (2010) *Nachhaltigkeit in der Unternehmenskommunikation: Bedeutung, Charakteristika und Herausforderungen*, Zugl: Lüneburg, Univ, Diss, 2010, 1 Aufl, Gabler Verlag / Springer Fachmedien Wiesbaden GmbH Wiesbaden, Wiesbaden

Campbell, JL (2007) Why would corporations behave in socially responsible ways? An institutional theory of corporate social responsibility, *Academy of Management Review*, **32** (3), pp 946–67

Carter, CR (2004) Purchasing and social responsibility: A replication and extension, *The Journal of Supply Chain Management*, **40** (4), pp 4–16

Carter, CR (2005) Purchasing social responsibility and firm performance, *International Journal of Physical Distribution and Logistics Management*, **35** (3), pp 177–94

Carter, CR and Easton, LP (2011) Sustainable supply chain management: Evolution and future directions, *International Journal of Physical Distribution and Logistics Management*, **41** (1), pp 46–62

Carter, CR and Rogers, DS (2008) A framework of sustainable supply chain management: Moving toward new theory, *International Journal of Physical Distribution and Logistics Management*, **38** (5), pp 360–87

Chakraborty, S (2010) Concise chronological road map of evolving green supply chain management concepts: A review, *The IUP Journal of Supply Chain Management*, **4**, pp 7–25

Chen, T-Y and Huang, C-J (2019a) A two-tier scenario planning model of environmental sustainability policy in Taiwan, *Sustainability*, **11** (8), p 2336

Chen, Z and Huang, L (2019b) Application review of LCA (life cycle assessment) in circular economy: From the perspective of PSS (product service system), *Procedia CIRP*, **83**, pp 210–17

Cornescu, V and Adam, R (2014) Considerations regarding the role of indicators used in the analysis and assessment of sustainable development in the EU, *Procedia Economics and Finance*, **8**, pp 10–16

Deegen, T (2001) *Ansatzpunkte zur Integration von Umweltaspekten in die Balanced Scorecard*, Zugl: Lüneburg, Univ, Dipl-Arb, 2001, CSM Center for Sustainability Management, Lüneburg

Dev, NK, Shankar, R and Qaiser, FH (2020) Industry 40 and circular economy: Operational excellence for sustainable reverse supply chain performance, *Resources, Conservation and Recycling*, **153**, p 104583

Dey, A, LaGuardia, P and Srinivasan, M (2011) Building sustainability in logistics operations: A research agenda, *Management Research Review*, **34** (11), pp 1237–59

Duran, DC, Artene, A, Gogan, LM and Duran, V (2015) The objectives of sustainable development: Ways to achieve welfare, *Procedia Economics and Finance*, **26**, pp 812–17

Dutta, P, Mishra, A, Khandelwal, S and Katthawala, I (2020) A multiobjective optimization model for sustainable reverse logistics in Indian E-commerce market, *Journal of Cleaner Production*, **249**, p 119–348

El-Berishy, N, Rügge, I and Scholz-Reiter, B (2013) The interrelation between sustainability and green logistics, *IFAC Proceedings Volumes*, **46** (24), pp 527–31

Elkington, J (1999) *Cannibals With Forks: The triple bottom line of 21st century business*, Capstone, Oxford

Ellen MacArthur Foundation (2015) [accessed 23 September 2020] *Towards a Circular Ecnomy: Business rationale for an accelerated transition* [Online] https://www.ellenmacarthurfoundation.org/assets/downloads/TCE_Ellen-MacArthur-Foundation_9-Dec-2015.pdf (archived at https://perma.cc/V8WY-DAH8)

European Union (2012) *Confronting Scarcity: Managing water, energy and land for inclusive and sustainable growth, European report on development*, 32011/12, Publ Off, Luxembourg

Evangelista, P, Santoro, L and Thomas, A (2018) Environmental sustainability in third-party logistics service providers: A systematic literature review from 2000–2016, *Sustainability*, **10** (5), p 1627

Farooque, M, Zhang, A, Thürer, M, Qu, T and Huisingh, D (2019) Circular supply chain management: A definition and structured literature review, *Journal of Cleaner Production*, **228**, pp 882–900

Frodermann, L (2018) *Exploratory Study on Circular Economy Approaches: A comparative analysis of theory and practice, Wirtschaftsethik in der globalisierten Welt*, Springer Fachmedien Wiesbaden, Wiesbaden

Geissdoerfer, M, Morioka, SN, Carvalho, MM de and Evans, S (2018) Business models and supply chains for the circular economy, *Journal of Cleaner Production*, **190**, pp 712–21

Genovese, A, Acquaye, AA, Figueroa, A and Koh, SL (2017) Sustainable supply chain management and the transition towards a circular economy: Evidence and some applications, *Omega*, **66**, pp 344–57

Govindan, K, Soleimani, H and Kannan, D (2015) Reverse logistics and closed-loop supply chain: A comprehensive review to explore the future, *European Journal of Operational Research*, **240** (3), pp 603–26

Govindan, K, Kadziński, M, Ehling, R and Miebs, G (2019) Selection of a sustainable third-party reverse logistics provider based on the robustness analysis of an outranking graph kernel conducted with ELECTRE I and SMAA, *Omega*, **85**, pp 1–15

Grant, DB, Wong, CY and Trautrims, A (2017) *Sustainable Logistics and Supply Chain Management: Principles and practices for sustainable operations and management*, Kogan Page, London

Gregori, G and Wimmer, T (eds) (2011) *Grünbuch der nachhaltigen Logistik: Handbuch für die ressourcenschonende Gestaltung logistischer Prozesse*, 1 Aufl, BVL Bundesvereinigung Logistik, Wien

Grzybowska, K, Awasthi, A and Sawhney, RS (2020) *Sustainable Logistics and Production in Industry 4 0: New opportunities and challenges, EcoProduction*, Springer, Cham

Guide, VDR and Wassenhove, LN (2006) Closed-loop supply chains: An introduction to the feature issue (Part 1), *Production and Operations Management*, **15** (3), pp 345–50

Gurtu, A, Searcy, C and Jaber, MY (2015) An analysis of keywords used in the literature on green supply chain management, *Management Research Review*, **38** (2), pp 166–94

Gurtu, A, Searcy, C and Jaber, MY (2017) Sustainable supply chains, in *Green Supply Chain Management for Sustainable Business Practice: Premier reference source*, ed M Khan, M Hussain and MM Ajmal, Vol 2, Business Science Reference, Hershey, PA, pp 1–26

Halme, M and Niskanen, J (2001) Does corporate environmental protection increase or decrease shareholder value? The case of environmental investments, *Business Strategy and the Environment*, **10** (4), pp 200–14

Handfield, R, Sroufe, R and Walton, S (2005) Integrating environmental management and supply chain strategies, *Business Strategy and the Environment*, **14** (1), pp 1–19

Hartmann, J and Moeller, S (2014) Chain liability in multitier supply chains? Responsibility attributions for unsustainable supplier behavior, *Journal of Operations Management*, **32** (5), pp 281–94

Harwood, I and Humby, S (2008) Embedding corporate responsibility into supply: A snapshot of progress, *European Management Journal*, **26** (3), pp 166–74

Hatami-Marbini, A, Agrell, PJ, Tavana, M and Khoshnevis, P (2017) A flexible cross-efficiency fuzzy data envelopment analysis model for sustainable sourcing, *Journal of Cleaner Production*, **142**, pp 2761–79

Heyer, S (2014) *Community-Based Design of Process Chains for Manufacturing and Recycling*, Dissertation, Technische Universität Berlin, *Berichte aus dem Produktionstechnischen Zentrum Berlin*, Fraunhofer Verlag, Stuttgart

Hollos, D, Blome, C and Foerstl, K (2012) Does sustainable supplier co-operation affect performance? Examining implications for the triple bottom line, *International Journal of Production Research*, **50** (11), pp 2968–86

Huemer, L (2012) Unchained from the chain: Supply management from a logistics service provider perspective, *Journal of Business Research*, **65** (2), pp 258–64

Ibrahim, FI, Omar, D and Mohamad, NHN (2015) Theoretical review on sustainable city indicators in Malaysia, *Procedia – Social and Behavioral Sciences*, **202**, pp 322–29

Isaksson, R (2018) Revisiting the triple bottom line, in *Sustainable Development and Planning X, Siena, Italy, 9/4/2018 – 9/6/2018*, ed G Passerini and N Marchetini, WIT Press, Southampton, pp 425–36

Jackson, T (2017) *Prosperity Without Growth: Foundations for the economy of tomorrow*, 2nd edn, Routledge, London, New York

Kalmykova, Y, Sadagopan, M and Rosado, L (2018) Circular economy: From review of theories and practices to development of implementation tools, *Resources, Conservation and Recycling*, **135**, pp 190–201

Keating, B, Quazi, A, Kriz, A and Coltman, T (2008) In pursuit of a sustainable supply chain: Insights from Westpac Banking Corporation, *Supply Chain Management: An international journal*, **13** (3), pp 175–79

Kleindorfer, PR, Singhal, K and Wassenhove, LN (2005) Sustainable operations management, *Production and Operations Management*, **14** (4), pp 482–92

Kopnina, H (2018) Circular economy and cradle to cradle in educational practice, *Journal of Integrative Environmental Sciences*, **15** (1), pp 119–34

Kopnina, H and Blewitt, J (2014) *Sustainable Business: Key issues, key issues in environment and sustainability*, Taylor and Francis, Hoboken

Kovács, G (2008) Corporate environmental responsibility in the supply chain, *Journal of Cleaner Production*, **16** (15), pp 1571–78

Krause, DR, Vachon, S and Klassen, RD (2009) Special topic forum on sustainable supply chain management: Introduction and reflections on the role of purchasing management, *Journal of Supply Chain Management*, **45** (4), pp 18–25

Kuhn, A and Pischke-Malkus, S (eds) (2012) *Das Sustainability Performance Management Audit: Ein Modell zur Messung und Optimierung der Nachhaltigkeitsleistung eines Unternehmens*, Zugl: Dortmund, Techn Univ, Diss, 2012, *Fabrikorganisation*, Verl Praxiswissen, Dortmund

Lacy, P and Rutqvist, J (2015) *Waste to Wealth: The circular economy advantage*, Palgrave Macmillan, Basingstoke

Lampel, J, Mintzberg, H, Quinn, JB and Ghoshal, S (2014) *The Strategy process: Concepts, contexts, cases*, 5th edn, Pearson Education, Harlow

Lee, BJ, Preston, F, Kooroshy, J, Bailey, R and Lahn, G (2012) *Resources Futures*, Royal Inst of Intern Affairs, London

Leire, C and Mont, O (2009) The implementation of socially responsible purchasing, *Corporate Social Responsibility and Environmental Management*, **6** (5), pp 27–39

Leszczynska, A and Maryniak, A (2017) Sustainable supply chain: A review of research fields and a proposition of future exploration, *International Journal of Sustainable Economy*, **9** (2), p 159

Li, S, Ragu-Nathan, B, Ragu-Nathan, TS and Subba Rao, S (2006) The impact of supply chain management practices on competitive advantage and organizational performance, *Omega*, **34** (2), pp 107–24

Lieb, KJ and Lieb, RC (2010) Environmental sustainability in the third-party logistics (3PL) industry, *International Journal of Physical Distribution and Logistics Management*, **40** (7), pp 524–33

Linton, JD, Klassen, R and Jayaraman, V (2007) Sustainable supply chains: An introduction, *Journal of Operations Management*, **25** (6), pp 1075–82

Lu, M and Bock, J De (2016) *Sustainable Logistics and Supply Chains: Innovations and integral approaches*, *Contributions to management science*, Springer, Cham

Malviya, RK and Kant, R (2015) Green supply chain management (GSCM): A structured literature review and research implications, *Benchmarking: An international journal*, **22** (7), pp 1360–94

Mamic, I (2005) Managing global supply chain: The sports footwear, apparel and retail sectors, *Journal of Business Ethics*, **59** (1–2), pp 81–100

Manavalan, E and Jayakrishna, K (2019) An analysis on sustainable supply chain for circular economy, *Procedia Manufacturing*, **33**, pp 477–84

Mangla, SK, Sharma, YK, Patil, PP, Yadav, G and Xu, J (2019) Logistics and distribution challenges to managing operations for corporate sustainability: Study on leading Indian diary organizations, *Journal of Cleaner Production*, **238**, p 117620

Marasco, A (2008) Third-party logistics: A literature review, *International Journal of Production Economics*, **113** (1), pp 127–47

Mayer, A, Haas, W, Wiedenhofer, D, Krausmann, F, Nuss, P and Blengini, GA (2019) Measuring progress towards a circular economy: A monitoring framework for economy-wide material loop closing in the EU28, *Journal of Industrial Ecology*, **23** (1), pp 62–76

McDonough, W and Braungart, M (2002) *Cradle to Cradle: Remaking the way we make things*, 1st edn, North Point Press, New York

McKinnon, AC (ed) (2010) *Green Logistics: Improving the environmental sustainability of logistics*, Kogan Page, London

Miemczyk, J, Johnsen, TE and Macquet, M (2012) Sustainable purchasing and supply management: A structured literature review of definitions and measures at the dyad, chain and network levels, *Supply Chain Management: An international journal*, **17** (5), pp 478–96

Min, H and Galle, WP (1997) Green purchasing strategies: Trends and implications, *International Journal of Purchasing and Materials Management*, **33** (2), pp 10–17

Min, H and Galle, WP (2001) Green purchasing practices of US firms, *International Journal of Operations and Production Management*, **21** (9), pp 1222–38

Mont, O and Heiskanen, E (2015) Breaking the stalemate of sustainable consumption with industrial ecology and a circular economy, in *Handbook of Research on Sustainable Consumption*, ed LA Reisch, Elgar Publishing, Cheltenham, pp 33–48

Murray, A, Skene, K and Haynes, K (2017) The circular economy: An interdisciplinary exploration of the concept and application in a global context, *Journal of Business Ethics*, **140** (3), pp 369–80

Nielsen, K and Brunoe, TD (2015) Cradle to cradle products, modularity and closed loop supply chains, in *Advances in Production Management Systems: Innovative production management towards sustainable growth – IFIP WG 57 International Conference, APMS 2015, Tokyo, Japan, September 17–19, Proceedings, IFIP Advances in Information and Communication Technology*, ed S Umeda, Vol 459, Springer, Cham, pp 689–96

Pagell, M and Shevchenko, A (2014) Why research in sustainable supply chain management should have no future, *Journal of Supply Chain Management*, **50** (1), pp 44–55

Park, J, Sarkis, J and Wu, Z (2010) Creating integrated business and environmental value within the context of China's circular economy and ecological modernization, *Journal of Cleaner Production*, **18** (15), pp 1494–501

Porter, ME (2000) *Wettbewerbsvorteile: Spitzenleistungen erreichen und behaupten*, 6 Überarbeitete Auflage, Campus-Verlag, Frankfurt/Main

Qaiser, FH, Ahmed, K, Sykora, M, Choudhary, A and Simpson, M (2017) Decision support systems for sustainable logistics: A review and bibliometric analysis, *Industrial Management and Data Systems*, **117** (7), pp 1376–88

Quarshie, AM, Salmi, A and Leuschner, R (2016) Sustainability and corporate social responsibility in supply chains: The state of research in supply chain management and business ethics journals, *Journal of Purchasing and Supply Management*, **22** (2), pp 82–97

Rashidi, K and Cullinane, K (2019) Evaluating the sustainability of national logistics performance using data envelopment analysis, *Transport Policy*, **74**, pp 35–46

Roth, AV, Tsay, AA, Pullman, ME and Gray, JV (2008) Unraveling the food supply chain: Strategic insights from China and the 2007 recalls, *The Journal of Supply Chain Management*, **44** (1), pp 22–39

Schade, B and Schade, W (2005) Evaluating economic feasibility and technical progress of environmentally sustainable transport scenarios by a backcasting approach with ESCOT, *Transport Reviews*, **25** (6), pp 647–68

Schenkel, M, Krikke, H, Caniëls, MCJ and van der Laan, E (2015) Creating integral value for stakeholders in closed loop supply chains, *Journal of Purchasing and Supply Management*, **21** (3), pp 155–66

Schneider, L and Wallenburg, CM (2012) Implementing sustainable sourcing: Does purchasing need to change? *Journal of Purchasing and Supply Management*, **18** (4), pp 243–57

Schulze, H and Bals, L (2018) Implementing sustainable supply chain management: A literature review on required purchasing and supply management competences, in *Social and Environmental Dimensions of Organizations and Supply Chains: Tradeoffs and synergies, greening of industry networks studies*, ed M Brandenburg, GJ Hahn andT Rebs, Vol 38, Springer, Cham, pp 171–94

Seliger, G (2007) *Sustainability in Manufacturing: Recovery of resources in product and material Cycles*, Springer-Verlag, Berlin, Heidelberg

Seliger, G (2011) Sustainability engineering by product-service systems, in *Glocalized Solutions for Sustainability in Manufacturing*, ed J Hesselbach and C Herrmann, Springer-Verlag, Berlin, Heidelberg, pp 22–28

Seliger, G (2012) Sustainable manufacturing for global value creation, in *Sustainable Manufacturing: Shaping global value creation*, ed G Seliger, Springer-Verlag, Berlin, Heidelberg, pp 3–8

Seuring, S and Müller, M (2008) From a literature review to a conceptual framework for sustainable supply chain management, *Journal of Cleaner Production*, **16** (15), pp 1699–710

Sheu, J-B, Chou, Y-H and Hu, C-C (2005) An integrated logistics operational model for green-supply chain management, *Transportation Research Part E: Logistics and transportation review*, **41** (4), pp 287–313

Simpson, D, Power, D and Samson, D (2007) Greening the automotive supply chain: A relationship perspective, *International Journal of Operations and Production Management*, **27** (1), pp 28–48

Skawińska, E and Zalewski, RI (2018) Circular economy as a management model in the paradigm of sustainable development, *Management*, **22** (2), pp 217–33

Souza, GC (2013) Closed-loop supply chains: A critical review, and future research, *Decision Sciences*, **44** (1), pp 7–38

Srivastava, SK (2007) Green supply-chain management: A state-of-the-art literature review, *International Journal of Management Reviews*, **9** (1), pp 53–80

Svensson, G and Bååth, H (2008) Supply chain management ethics: Conceptual framework and illustration, *Supply Chain Management: An international journal*, **13** (6), pp 398–405

Tassabehji, R and Moorhouse, A (2008) The changing role of procurement: Developing professional effectiveness, *Journal of Purchasing and Supply Management*, **14** (1), pp 55–68

Tate, WL, Ellram, LM and Kirchoff, JF (2010) Corporate social responsibility reports: A thematic analysis related to supply chain management, *Journal of Supply Chain Management*, **46** (1), pp 19–44

Toffel, MW (2004) Strategic management of product recovery, *California Management Review*, **46** (2), pp 120–141

Touboulic, A and Walker, H (2015) Theories in sustainable supply chain management: A structured literature review, *International Journal of Physical Distribution and Logistics Management*, **45** (1/2), pp 16–42

Tremmel, J (2004) Nachhaltigkeit – definiert nach einem kriteriengebundenen Verfahren, *GAIA – Ecological Perspectives for Science and Society*, **13** (1), pp 26–34

Ubeda, S, Arcelus, FJ and Faulin, J (2011) Green logistics at Eroski: A case study, *International Journal of Production Economics*, **131** (1), pp 44–51

Ueda, K, Takenaka, T, Váncza, J and Monostori, L (2009) Value creation and decision-making in sustainable society, *CIRP Annals*, **58** (2), pp 681–700

UNGC (2015) [accessed 23 September 2020] *Supply Chain Sustainability: A practical guide for continuous improvement* [Online] https://www.unglobalcompact.org/docs/issues_doc/supply_chain/SupplyChainRep_spread.pdf (archived at https://perma.cc/EC8X-TSNB)

United Nations (2015) [accessed 23 September 2020] *Transforming Our World: The 2030 agenda for sustainable development* [Online] https://www.un.org/ga/search/view_doc.asp?symbol=A/RES/70/1&Lang=E (archived at https://perma.cc/Z9L6-54GS)

United Nations (2019) *World Population Prospects 2019: Ten key findings*, Department of Economic and Social Affairs, Population Division

Vachon, S and Klassen, RD (2006) Extending green practices across the supply chain, *International Journal of Operations and Production Management*, **26** (7), pp 795–821

Veleva, V and Ellenbecker, M (2001) Indicators of sustainable production: Framework and methodology, *Journal of Cleaner Production*, **9** (6), pp 519–49

Verein Deutscher Ingenieure eV (2000) *VDI Richtlinie 3780: Technikbewertung – Begriffe und Grundlage* No VDI 3780, Beuth Verlag, Berlin

Vieira, P (2016) Is overpopulation a growth? The pathology of permanent expansion, *Oxford Literary Review*, **38** (1), pp 67–83

Washington, H (2015) *Demystifying Sustainability: Towards real solutions*, Routledge, London

WCED (World Commission on Environment and Development) (1987) *Report of the World Commission on Environment and Development: Our common future*, Oxford University Press, Oxford

Weetman, C (2017) *A Circular Economy Handbook for Business and Supply Chains: Repair, remake, redesign, rethink*, 1st edn, Kogan Page, London

Weiss, D, Hajduk, T and Knopf, J (2017) *Step-by-Step Guide to Sustainable Supply Chain Management: A practical guide for companies*, Federal Ministry for the Environment, Nature Conservation, Building and Nuclear Safety (BMUB), Berlin

Wenke, K-G (1987) *Theorie der Wertschöpfung und der Wertschöpfungsrechnung*, Dissertation, Universität Mainz

Wildemann, H (2018) *Nachhaltigkeit in der Supply Chain: Leitfaden für unternehmensübergreifendes Wertschöpfungsmanagement, Leitfaden*, Vol 109, 8 Auflage, TCW, Transfer-Centrum für Produktions-Logistik und Technologie-Management GmbH et Co KG, München

Wilhelm, MM, Blome, C, Bhakoo, V and Paulraj, A (2016) Sustainability in multi-tier supply chains: Understanding the double agency role of the first-tier supplier, *Journal of Operations Management*, **41** (1), pp 42–60

Winstanley, D, Clark, J and Leeson, H (2002) Approaches to child labour in the supply chain, *Business Ethics: A European review*, **11** (3), pp 210–23

Wirth, S, Schenk, M and Müller, E (2011) Fabrik – Ort innovativer und kreativer Wertschöpfung, *ZWF Zeitschrift für wirtschaftlichen Fabrikbetrieb*, **106** (10), pp 691–94

Wolf, C and Seuring, S (2010) Environmental impacts as buying criteria for third party logistical services, *International Journal of Physical Distribution and Logistics Management*, **40** (1/2), pp 84–102

Worthington, I, Ram, M, Boyal, H and Shah, M (2008) Researching the drivers of socially responsible purchasing: A cross-national study of supplier diversity initiatives, *Journal of Business Ethics*, **79** (3), pp 319–31

Wu, H-J and Dunn, SC (1995) Environmentally responsible logistics systems, *International Journal of Physical Distribution and Logistics Management*, **25** (2), pp 20–38

Zhu, Q, Geng, Y and Lai, K-h (2010) Circular economy practices among Chinese manufacturers varying in environmental-oriented supply chain cooperation and the performance implications, *Journal of Environmental Management*, **91** (6), pp 1324–31

Zimmer, K, Fröhling, M and Schultmann, F (2016) Sustainable supplier management: A review of models supporting sustainable supplier selection, monitoring and development, *International Journal of Production Research*, **54** (5), pp 1412–42

Interdisciplinary research work in the field of SSCM 03

MICHAEL HENKE, HOLGER KOHL AND DENIS DAUS

The project academy focuses on a comprehensive analysis of how global value chains need to be designed and managed in order to overcome conflicting goals and implement sustainability. Thus, under the overall theme 'Sustainability in Global Value Chains', three sub-topics are formulated. Figure 3.1 depicts the three research questions that serve as the basis for the interdisciplinary research topics in this book.

These research questions build on each other logically: only when ethical and conceptual foundations have been analysed is it possible to define various measurement models in order to implement them in practice and prove their effectiveness.

With respect to social demands, which are expressed in this context in the form of increasingly stringent and diverse regulations, new approaches are needed that simultaneously target several levels of supply chains. Companies that take a pioneering role and act proactively in this area on their own initiative could thus anticipate such regulations and use new developments as opportunities instead of reactively managing them as potential risks. This approach would be entirely in line with an ethical, value-based assumption of responsibility in global supply chains (Boyd *et al*, 2007). The three research questions are described in more detail below.

Figure 3.1 Research questions in the field of sustainability in global value chains

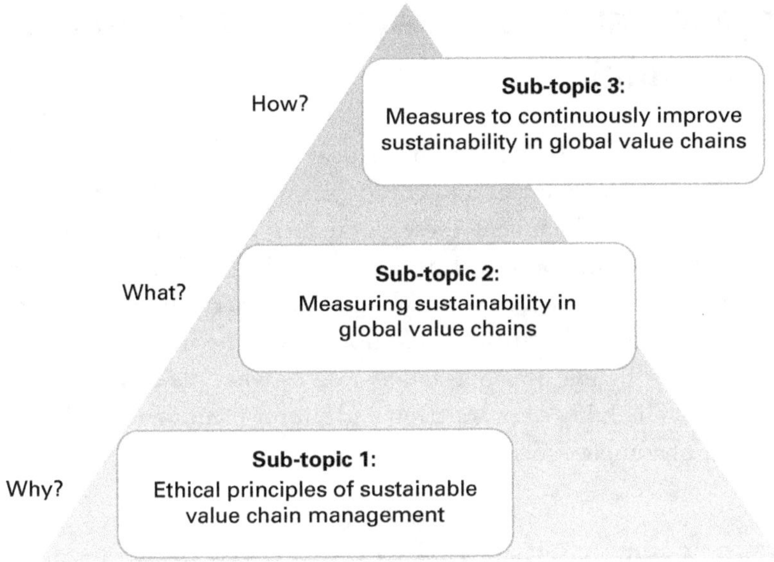

Which ethical aspects of the sustainability concept have to be considered as framework conditions?

This subtopic examines *ethically correct behaviour* and what it means in the context of global value chains. The aim is to explore whether these ethical values are manifested mainly in certification and standardization frameworks of international institutions or whether a more fundamental approach to ethical principles is necessary. In this respect, it must be clarified to what extent global standards can be enforced in geographically diversified value chains and by whom such standards should be defined, demanded and reviewed. In addition, we want to investigate the question of how multinational companies can fill governance gaps in so-called *failed states* or *crisis regions* in an economically responsible way.

Which parameters and activities should be improved and how can progress be made measurable?

The focus of this subtopic is on the critical parameters for comparability between industries, countries and companies as well as the exploration of new approaches to document these parameters. It should be clarified to what extent indicators of SSCM have been applied in Germany so far, and how they can be classified in comparison with other countries with regard to the implementation status. In addition, it will be investigated to what extent these key figures are collected as well as what the relationship is between the sustainability of production and supply chains and the behaviour or reaction of complex social, economic systems.

Which actions are viable to achieve sustainable value chains and anchor them more effectively in practice?

This subtopic aims to clarify the question of whether best practice solutions can be found, which allow the development of dynamic capabilities within companies and value chains that enable autonomous and continuous improvement of sustainability performance. In addition, possibilities should be discussed of how measures to improve sustainability performance can be successfully integrated into practice and which structural and relational characteristics of the value chains and actors can be supportive for their dissemination. The aim is furthermore to find out how value chains can be made more sustainable overall, ie beyond the direct supplier, which governance mechanisms are available to local companies with regard to the control of subcontractors and how an efficient, effective and resilient supply chain network can be developed. Ultimately, this subtopic addresses the classification of the role of digitization, especially big data analysis and artificial intelligence, in defining measures to improve sustainability.

Reference

Boyd, DE, Spekman, RE, Kamauff, JW and Werhane, P (2007) Corporate social responsibility in global supply chains: A procedural justice perspective, *Long Range Planning*, 40 (3): 341–56

PART ONE
Ethical principles of sustainable value chain management

It was only at the turn of the millennium that the inclusion of both ecological and social criteria in SCM increased (Handfield *et al*, 2002). This applies in particular to global SCM with a focus on emerging and developing countries (Lobel, 2006). A vivid example of the dimensions and impacts of this issue is that the United Nations Educational, Scientific and Cultural Organization (UNESCO) estimate that some 2.1 billion people lack access to clean and readily available drinking water at home. For the people concerned, this often results in poor health and living conditions, malnutrition, and a poor outlook for education and employment (UNESCO WWAP, 2019: 35). These circumstances facilitate social conflicts and even violence, which in turn leads to human displacement and migration (Miletto *et al*, 2017). While technological solutions along supply chains can address economic and environmental aspects of water saving and distribution, these solutions are not necessarily affordable or geographically accessible for those most affected by the water problem. This often eco-efficient motivation of scientific research (less water consumption = more cost savings) leads to short-sighted, primarily technical-economic considerations of these problems, which do not take sufficient account of the negative social impacts they can have.

A similar view emerges with regard to the problem of so-called 'conflict minerals' (Hofmann *et al*, 2018). These raw materials are mined and processed in crisis regions in such a way that non-governmental, criminal actors or terrorists benefit from the trade with these materials. The earnings are used to finance violent conflicts, especially in the Democratic Republic of Congo and its neighbouring states, under which the civilian population of these states suffers (Global Witness, 2013). Although this problem has been known since the reporting on 'blood diamonds' from Sierra Leone and Angola in the 1990s and is clearly related to the supply chain, it has received little attention in scientific (western) research because it lacks the obvious economic relevance (Rotter *et al*, 2014; Hofmann *et al*, 2018).

Within the framework of the project academy, the ethical foundations of the management of sustainable value chains will therefore be increasingly addressed as a foundation. At the same time, this area of work forms the basis for further joint research.

References

Global Witness (2013) Breaking the links between natural resources and conflict: The case for EU regulation: A civil society position paper, Global Witness

Handfield, R, Walton, SV, Sroufe, R and Melnyk, SA (2002) Applying environmental criteria to supplier assessment: A study in the application of the Analytical Hierarchy Process, *European Journal of Operational Research*, **141** (1), pp 70–87

Hofmann, H, Schleper, MC and Blome, C (2018) Conflict minerals and supply chain due diligence: An exploratory study of multi-tier supply chains, *Journal of Business Ethics*, **147** (1), pp 115–41

Lobel, O (2006) Sustainable capitalism or ethical transnationalism: Offshore production and economic development, *Journal of Asian Economics*, **17** (1), pp 56–62

Miletto, M, Caretta, MA, Burchi, FM and Zanlucchi, G (2017) *Migration and its Interdepencies with Water Scarcity, Gender and Youth Employment*, United Nations Educational, Scientific, and Cultural Organization, Paris

Rotter, JP, Airike, P-E and Mark-Herbert, C (2014) Exploring political corporate social responsibility in global supply chains, *Journal of Business Ethics*, **125** (4), pp 581–99

UNESCO WWAP (2019) [accessed 23 September 2020] *Leaving No One Behind: The United Nations world water development report 2019*, UNESCO [Online] https://unesdoc.unesco.org/ark:/48223/pf0000367306 (archived at https://perma.cc/EPT3-ETTX)

04

Start-ups as relevant supporters and initiators of sustainability attributes in global value chains of the future

STEPHANIE RABBE, CHRISTOPH VON VIEBAHN AND MARVIN AUF DER LANDWEHR

Introduction

How will sustainable start-ups have a noticeable influence on global value chains or supply chains in the future?

The economic relevance of start-ups is increasing. They invent new services and innovative business models, disrupt established markets as well as industry sectors, boost the digitalization and influence cooperation in global value chains or supply chains. This chapter focuses on start-ups with a sustainable entrepreneurial mindset and exploits their intended as well as their actual effects on value chains or supply chains. In terms of goals, intentions, results and impacts, sustainable start-ups are equally oriented towards social, ecological and economic attributes. These attributes determine the development and implementation of innovations. Their suppliers and logistics partners must cope with their high expectations to support their sustainable business activities. The chapter aims to develop approaches to operationalize these expectations by examining the ecological dimension (eg reduction of emissions), the economic dimension (eg scalability of solutions, purchasing decisions) and the social dimension (eg forms of cooperation and competition) of sustainable start-ups in value chains or supply chains, using case studies or conceptual considerations. The objective of this chapter is to gain insight into the question 'How will sustainable start-ups have a noticeable influence on global value chains or supply chains in the future?'

A special context is the observation that companies, especially small and medium-sized enterprises (SMEs), cooperate within their sector in established value chains and that their ability to act jointly with asymmetric partners outside their own sector can be regarded as a key competence in the future. Interviews and case studies show that science and business notice a striking *cooperation gap* in the operational design of cooperation, the origin of which seems to stem from the factual and perceived asymmetry of the partnerships. It is therefore important to discuss the extent to which sustainable strategies of established companies and start-ups are based on cooperation with each other.

Framework

Asymmetric partnerships between start-ups and SMEs: A predetermined breaking point

Established companies are faced with the challenge of opening up their innovation processes to external impulses in order to actively use their corporate environment to increase their own innovation potential (ZEW, 2016). According to the Community Innovation Survey, 63.7 per cent of German companies pursued innovation activities between 2014 and 2016. Of these, a large proportion (60.8 per cent) implemented innovations of a technological or non-technological nature and are regarded as so-called *innovative companies*. As the number of employees increases, the proportion of innovative companies rises from 54.9 per cent for smaller companies to 74.2 per cent for medium-sized companies and 89.6 per cent for large companies. In particular, SMEs focus on either technological or non-technological innovation activities (IfM Bonn, 2019). Som (2015) states that, for example, SMEs cooperate in established value chains within their sector and anticipates their ability to cooperate with asymmetric partners outside their own sector as a future key competence. In the case study with Runamics, this contribution therefore focuses on a sustainable start-up as an asymmetric partner outside the industry for cooperation and innovation for SMEs (RKW, 2018; Deloitte, 2017).

According to prevailing opinion, start-ups act as technology input for value chains and disruptors of traditional business models. They are active drivers of cross-cutting issues such as sustainability or digitization and act as transfer channels from science and universities (Plöger, 2016). Some 67.1 per cent of start-ups cooperate with established companies (Kollmann *et al*, 2018). Their goals are a simplified market and customer access, proof of concept as well as image gains and technology expertise (Deloitte, 2017). Their motives for cooperation are technical (joint research and development), economic (cost reduction) or organizational (exchange of experience) (Deloitte, 2017). Cooperation takes place in pilot projects (50.3 per cent), in marketing (47.9 per cent) and in research and development (44.5 per cent) (Kollmann *et al*, 2018).

In Kühmayer's *Leadership Report 2017*, start-ups are still regarded as 'innovation pioneers' (Kühmayer, 2016) but in his *Leadership Report 2019* disillusionment sets in and the focus is once again on the 'heroes of medium-sized businesses' (Kühmayer, 2018). The state of the art is also divided in two fragments: optimistic contributions define cooperation between SMEs and start-ups as a promising success factor based on suitable cooperation models, trust and balanced expectations (Wrobel *et al*, 2017); critical studies counter this fear of cooperation with a lack of experience (*KMU-Report Berlin*, 2018) and untapped potential (Kollmann *et al*, 2016). Problems include the identification of the right partners, a 'generation conflict' (Kuckertz and Allmendinger, 2017), different corporate structures and culture (Löher *et al*, 2017), a lack of commitment on the part of management, and unwanted dependence on third parties (*KMU-Report Berlin*, 2018). For some SMEs, cooperation with start-ups represents an examination of their attractiveness as a participation or purchase option, which leads to a one-sided view from the investment perspective (RKW, 2018).

Objective

Creating awareness of cooperation

A solution for dealing with the imbalance can be the creation of *cooperative awareness* as a success factor of strategy formation. Here, the chapter contributes to future research of asymmetric partnerships (Wrobel *et al*, 2017) and offers a first conceptual attempt at an explanation with the assumption of an insufficiently pronounced awareness of cooperation and approaches to its improvement. The frame of reference is the so-called *strategic awareness* (Gibb and Scott, 1985), the inadequately developed strategic awareness, which is used as an explanation of the planning gap that is assumed to exist in SMEs (Rabbe and Schulz, 2007). This is the reason for the high complexity of the problem, because sustainability is an important strategic issue for sustainable start-ups that they can only place appropriately in cooperation if it has a similarly high strategic significance for their partners. For example, a distinctive strategic competence together with an appropriate cooperative competence on both sides of a partnership can promote the influence of sustainable start-ups on the value chains of the future. In this chapter, the conceptual considerations of cooperative awareness are followed by an explanation of the methodological approach and the Runamics case study.

Cooperative awareness

Gibb and Scott (1985) describe *strategic awareness* as the sum of *strategic necessity*, *strategic ability*, *environmental awareness* and *management time*. The assumed planning gap is considered a consequence of a lack of strategic awareness.

If one considers quantitative and qualitative deficiencies in the cooperation behaviour between stabilized companies and start-ups as reasons for the cooperation gap, an analogous analysis would be appropriate. We define *cooperative awareness* (CA) as the sum of the recognized necessity of SMEs and start-ups to cooperate with each other (*cooperative necessity*, CN), their *cooperative capabilities* (CC), the perception of *cooperation opportunities* (CO) and the *communication quality* (CQ) for initiating and realizing cooperation (Figure 4.1).

Figure 4.1 Cooperative awareness

CA = CN + CC + CO + CQ

Implications

In order to close the cooperation gap and create cooperative awareness, initial implications can be formulated for the positive effect of the individual components and for the development of a cooperative awareness.

Cooperative necessity

To raise awareness of the need for cooperation, hub initiatives, for example, aim to be an interface for innovation partners and to inform about synergies between established companies and start-ups. They collect contacts and create docking points to relevant networks. However, there is a lack of low-threshold, local or regional formats and suitable channels. Original marketing campaigns or targeted project funding could contribute to visibility.

Cooperative capabilities

The development of modern teaching and training formats should aim to ensure that the participants come together in teams and develop their own qualification needs based on their cooperation project (cf. Tiimiakatemia). Therefore, they use various modules, lecturers act as coaches and have the task of moderating the processes in a target-oriented way and accompanying them in an inspiring way. Thus, the foundations are laid for the exchange of experience and hierarchy-free learning between one another, and stabilizing competences are specifically trained.

Wrobel (2017) refers, for example, to the cooperation phases 'Learn, Match and Partners', which take into account the various levels and depths of cooperation (Wrobel *et al*, 2017). These different phases require different skills. In order to enable both partners to cooperate, an analogous solution to Heyse and Erpenbeck's (2009) competence atlas is conceivable, which extends this approach and considers different cooperation competences as well as their learnability.

Cooperation opportunities

In order to create cooperation opportunities for start-ups, hub initiatives facilitate access to a network of investors or customers, enable a professional to increase the reach of own idea and often offer online contact with experts. For companies, they open up access to start-ups and their agile innovation potential. In order to exploit this potential, network formats with a focus on joint innovation projects and active exchange are conceivable. Research and university-related projects offer the first digital and analogue platforms to initiate this exchange.

Communication quality

The starting point for promising cooperation is the consistent and sensitive management of expectations throughout the phases of cooperation.

Currently, a wide variety of innovation platforms are being developed which, with the help of digital technologies and communication methods, attempt to stimulate and accelerate creative solution processes, but thus only address performance-oriented success factors. However, there is no target-oriented moderation and effective accompaniment of joint innovation processes. The stability-oriented perspective of the success factors requires an intensive examination of aspects such as trust, culture, similarity, common goal formulation, commitment or flexible organization. A solution approach includes systematic consulting concepts to support upcoming cooperation that is yet to be implemented; for example, role plays, team building on partner level and joint strategy development, in order to understand the culturally conditioned, diverging viewpoints of the counterpart.

The sustainability of this first conceptual explanatory approach and the effectiveness of the implications will now be examined with the help of the case study.

Methodology

To identify the impact of start-ups on sustainability attributes within global value chains and to discover the relevance of cooperation awareness on both sides of an (asymmetric) partnership, we pursue a transdisciplinary research approach by means of a case study. In general, it is difficult to clearly distinguish sustainability-related problems, because they neither have a precisely defined target state nor provide any information about potential challenges and obstacles between the actual and the target state. Such problems, also referred to as 'ill-defined problems', serve as a typical starting point of the case study approach and require knowledge at three levels – understanding, comprehension, explanation (Scholz and Tietje, 2002: 26ff).

In the context of this study, we employ the definition of Robert K Yin (2009: 17f), which suggests that the decision analysis and evaluation is a central element of the case study approach, where, based on several sources of evidence whose data converge in a triangular manner, a contemporary phenomenon is empirically studied in its real context. In general, a distinction can be made between an integrated and a holistic case study design (Scholz and Tietje, 2002: 9f). While the latter is characterized by a qualitative research approach, integrated case studies encompass more than one unit of analysis and support both qualitative and quantitative evaluations (Bortz and Döring, 1995).

To answer our research hypothesis, we investigate the start-up Runamics and its value chain architecture, which was selected as the case study object in the course of a theoretical sampling based on content-related criteria for sustainability-oriented value creation. Due to its unique organizational and holistic focus on sustainable value creation, the start-up provides an ideal framework for our research and promises unrivalled insights into the initiation of sustainability attributes along global value chains. After all, case-study-based research is not about representative population samples, but about entities whose characteristics are likely to provide comprehensive insights into the subject of the research (Dul and Hak, 2008).

In line with the prior-presented definition, the examination of the company's impact on the sustainability of its stakeholders constitutes an 'ill-defined problem'. Additionally, Runamics can be regarded as a representative study object for investigating the impact of start-ups on sustainability attributes in global value chains, so that the complexity of the problem can be considered in appropriate substantive depth (Yin, 2009: 47). Hence, we have chosen an integrated single case approach. Our methodological process model in relation to design and implementation of the case study and the interactions of the individual phases is shown in Figure 4.2 and derived from the principles given by Scholz and Tietje (2002), Zaugg (2007) as well as Yin (2009).

To analyse the specific impact of Runamics on sustainability attributes, we use the classic value chain architecture of Porter (2008). Since young start-up companies mainly focus on primary business activities (Raith, 2014), within the framework of our study, the following business areas are

Figure 4.2 Methodical process model regarding the holistic case study development

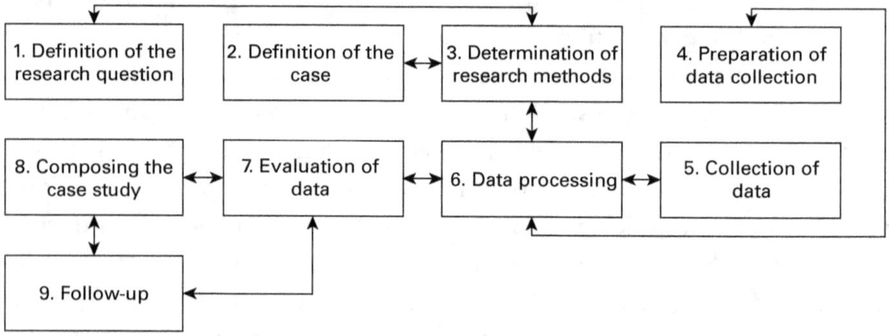

considered: inbound logistics; operations; marketing and sales; outbound logistics; and customer service. In contrast, supporting activities such as human resources, enterprise infrastructure, technology development, and procurement play a subordinate role as they are usually not, or only to a very limited extent, present in start-up organizations, and are therefore not examined in this case study (Figure 4.3).

Data acquisition

In order to collect the required information regarding the affected value chain elements in the case study, a two-hour expert interview was conducted

Figure 4.3 Case study object according to Porter's value chain architecture

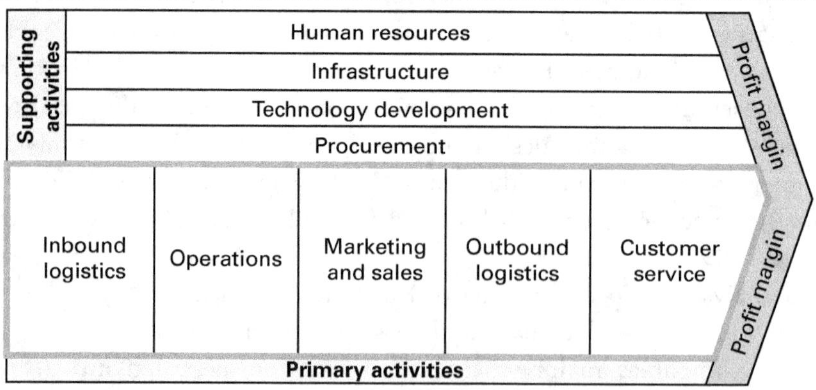

SOURCE Porter (2008)

with the founder of the start-up Runamics. While the company and its general context provide the framework for this study, a total of five subordinate cases have been identified, namely the primary businesses activities presented by Porter (2008). The advantage of this approach is that it does not aim to individually compare the sub-cases with each other, but analyses their variations, expressions, interactions and effects (Easton, 1995). By examining the specific variations in a single environment, a more comprehensive overview can be provided, ultimately facilitating an individual high-quality contribution to the overall case.

In addition to the role of the value chain members and the individual influence of the start-up on sustainability attributes, the expert interview also addressed the characteristics of the primary business activities as well as the general value creation process. The specific questions for the interview were developed in line with the guidelines of Meuser and Nagel (2009) and are based on issues related to value chain oriented sustainability (Geibler, 2010; Walther, 2010; Schulz, 2012; Mersiowsky *et al*, 2019). The individual suppliers were indirectly integrated into the data acquisition phase by adding an additional dimension to the supplier perspective and asking the buying company about the suppliers' representatives, actions, behaviours, points of view, etc. To ensure high data quality and validity, a detailed record and description of the entire expert interview was sent to the interviewee for re-validation. For the interpretation and evaluation of the accepted record fragments, we utilized the qualitative, summarizing content analysis according to Mayring (2010). Accordingly, the transcription material was paraphrased, generalized and reduced in content to solely represent essential statements regarding the given investigation cases. To further increase the internal validity, both transcriptional material and content analysis results were discussed, compared and, where necessary, adapted to the consensus throughout the research team. This dedicated process avoided content inconsistencies and ensured a higher overall data quality. Ultimately, the resulting data sources were used to describe and evaluate the impact of Runamics on the individual sustainability attributes of its value chain members.

Case study analysis

In the subsequent section, the results of the within-case analysis as well as the cross-case analysis concerning the identified sub-cases are presented.

Descriptive case presentation: Within-case analysis

Founded in 2019, Runamics is a start-up organization that emphasizes sustainable value creation and product development, both in terms of entrepreneurial as well as strategic focus. Distribution lines exclusively include running, fitness and sportswear products featuring a minimal proportion of plastics and microfibres. Although the aim of the start-up is the highest degree of sustainability regarding the ecological, economic and social dimension, it faced a major and problematic decision immediately after its foundation. Since sportswear needs to satisfy a high range of application requirements, it is currently not possible for some products (for example, tights and leggings) to completely dispense artificial raw materials and synthetic fibres such as spandex. For this reason, currently, products with a minimal plastic content are sold. Nevertheless, the company's long-term goal is to intensely support sustainability research in the textile industry in order to be able to sell 100 per cent plastic-free sportswear in the near future.

Along the value chain of Runamics, in addition to raw material suppliers and spinning mills/yarn suppliers, an essential role is also played by fabric manufacturers (embroidery/weaving mills), haberdashery suppliers, sewing companies, fulfilment partners and courier services. The entire value chain as well as the interdependencies of their entities and the respective activity spectrum are shown in Figure 4.4.

With regard to inbound logistics, Runamics is essentially confronted with the fact that the entire sustainability topic has a very low priority for many suppliers, which means that requirements for raw and semi-finished materials are often negligently disregarded or that generally there is no interest in a business relationship. The economic dimension (profitability of the business model) is especially challenged by many suppliers. In addition, due to comparatively low purchase quantities and the size of the start-up, there is only slight cooperation pressure. Although an increasing proportion of society demanded sustainably produced clothing in the decades prior to 2019, sustainable value creation in the textile industry is still often underestimated and disregarded.

In order to increase its impact on inbound logistics as a small company, Runamics skipped communication in the first stage of the value creation process (raw materials) and directly contacted established, international, textile-fibre processing spinning mills. Subsequently, the networks and connections of the spinning mills were utilized to find suitable raw material suppliers and fabric manufacturers. Through this approach, Runamics was able to improve

Figure 4.4 Exemplary representation of the primary activities within the value chain of the start-up Runamics

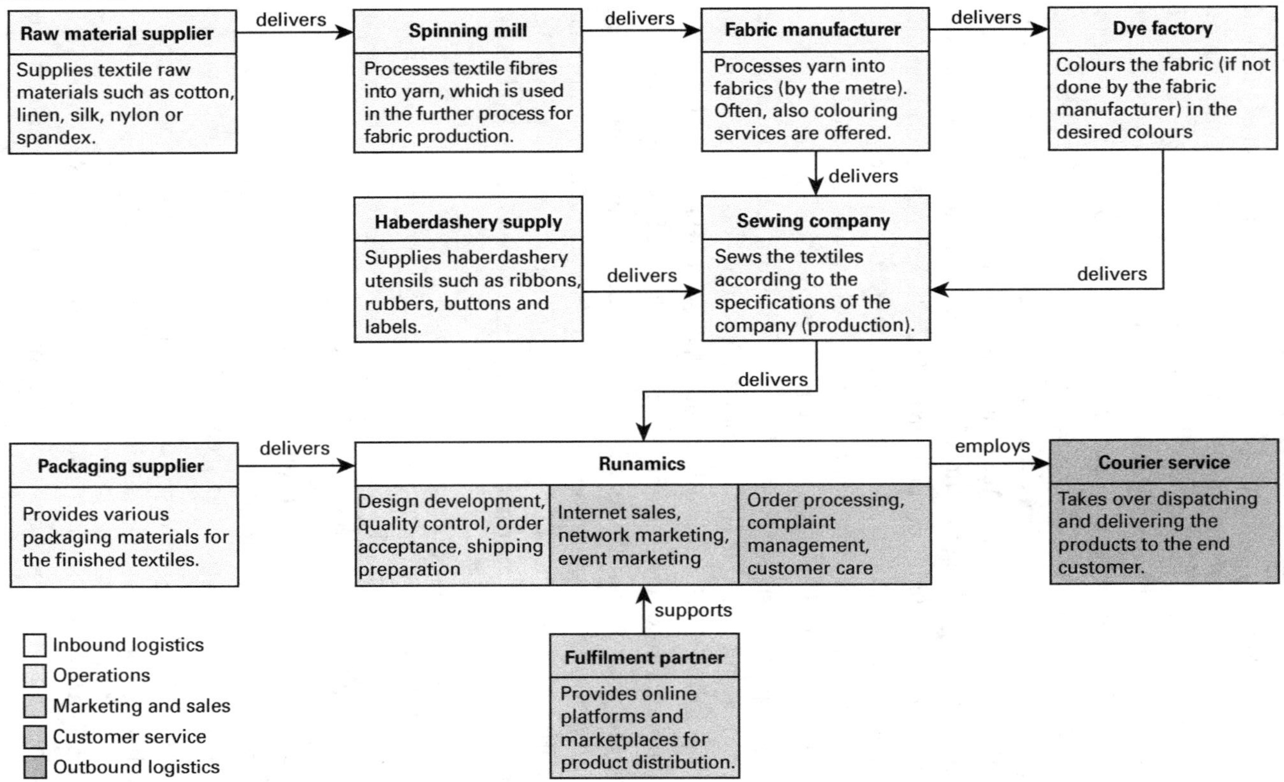

the willingness of suppliers to cooperate, so that the sustainability claim of the company could be enforced, both in terms of ecological raw materials, economic value creation and social cooperation. The search for and cooperation with a suitable fabric manufacturer has proven to be particularly difficult and tedious, since the fabric manufacturer is required to have its own concept for sustainable production and product development as well as to include plastic-free/low-plastic materials in its portfolio. Due to a lack of expertise in dealing with sustainably produced textiles, many suppliers are unable to meet the requirements of the start-up. For example, plastic-free prototypes are wrapped in poly bags and packed several times, which ultimately is contrary to the idea of sustainability. Accordingly, Runamics is working hard to maximize transparency along the entire value chain to ensure ecologically valuable products and sustainable production cycles, while avoiding cooperation problems due to cultural differences and communication issues. If no agreement can be reached on environmentally friendly inbound logistics, the start-up generally desists from cooperation with the respective player.

Packaging materials are sourced directly from Germany and are both plastic-free and reusable. In addition, the company abstains from multiple packaging for individual products and has established a packaging system with minimal amounts of empty space, resulting in less packaging materials being required overall. Here, the selection and sustainability awareness of the suppliers is much more pronounced, so that no additional sustainability demands are set by the start-up. The primary activities of operations, marketing and sales, and customer service are all carried out by Runamics itself and include:

- the development of product designs, quality control of raw materials, semi-finished and final products, acceptance of customer orders, packaging and shipping preparation (operations);
- the distribution of the products via the Runamics website as well as a dedicated fulfilment partner, network marketing with high-profile personalities (influencers) and event marketing (marketing and sales);
- the handling of customer orders, claim and complaint management as well as general customer service (customer service).

In all sub-areas, sustainable value creation is taken into account in all dimensions. Accordingly, for example partners for network marketing are also selected in line with the company philosophy and only used as distribution partners if they share the sustainability requirements and mindset of the organization. Sales activities are supported by a fulfilment partner who respects the demands and claims of Runamics and has a major focus on sustainable value creation. The recycling of packaging materials, the use of ecological raw materials and climate-neutral shipping processes are important criteria for choosing a suitable sales partner. While large, established companies such as Amazon are not considered as an additional distribution channel due to their own demands and a lack of sustainability claims, they are occasionally deployed as additional sales platform. However, in this case, shipping and distribution is still handled by Runamics, while the platform is exclusively used as a sales point.

The final customer is ultimately supplied by an external courier service, which is selected on the basis of the compensation programmes. Due to the economic pressure on start-ups, currently it is not possible for the organization to base courier choices on more comprehensive selection criteria for sustainable deliveries. Existing compensation programmes already meet many of the company's requirements and are attractive from an economic as well as an ecological point of view. However, in the future, Runamics plans to evaluate individual sustainability components such as empty runs and transport modes and subsequently make a selection based on a sound component analysis.

Supportive activities such as recruitment and infrastructure are not yet relevant due to the size of the enterprise. Nevertheless, Runamics' strategic alignment already envisages sustainability-related requirements for these activities as the company progresses. These requirements include, among other things, aspects such as short journeys and service routes when it comes to recruitment as well as climate-friendly energy supply of the office facilities.

Cross-case analysis

In the previous section, we presented the case study and analysed the specific sub-cases, also taking into account individual peculiarities of the respective instances. In addition, information and large amounts of data from the expert interview were summarized and structured by means of the case study report to prepare for cross-case analysis. The results of the sub-cases are now combined on a higher level of abstraction and generalized. Finally, the outcomes are used to derive hypotheses that generally explain the impact of start-ups on sustainability in global value chains.

In the field of inbound logistics, there is an indirect influence on the ecological value creation of the raw material and yarn suppliers by determining product and process requirements using the fabric supplier. However, since there is usually no contact with the suppliers, the transparency along the value chain is limited at this point. In addition, fabric suppliers are generally not willing to disclose their own suppliers. Nevertheless, in order to still ensure sustainable product development, spinning mills complying with the requirements can be described and analysed in order to cooperate with their fabric manufacturer network. At first glance, cooperation between suppliers and start-ups may appear to be an economically attractive option, but since there is no pronounced cooperation necessity among suppliers, cooperation capabilities and cooperation quality take a back seat. The suppliers' cooperative awareness in inbound logistics with regard to sustainability attributes is therefore rather deficient. The cooperation awareness of the spinning mills with regard to the sustainability requirements of the start-up results from a positive development of all its components. In particular, the indirect use of the spinning mills' relationships influences the suppliers' willingness to cooperate. This increases the quality of cooperation with the spinning mills, which share the sustainability requirements of the start-up.

The fabric manufacturer, who acts as a direct business partner and supplies pulp in the form of piece goods, can usually be directly influenced by the company's sustainability requirements and is guided by the expectations of the customer in terms of product composition, quality, treatment and refinement. However, due to the lack of transparency, sustainability along early stages of the value chain cannot be guaranteed. Vertically positioned manufacturers also take over the dyeing processes so that statements about the sustainability of this production step can be controlled and coordinated more easily. Due to the scaling possibilities and the larger selection of specialized dyeing companies, additionally integrating separate dyeing factories into the value chain can make sense when a certain company size and purchase quantity has been reached.

Due to the large selection and strong competitive pressure in the haberdashery industry, there is a great influence on the sustainability attributes of the haberdashery suppliers. The same applies to fulfilment partners and courier services. Sewing plants, which are, together with the material suppliers, the most important partners in inbound logistics, are difficult to influence in their added value creation, even in direct partnerships. Especially in an international context, working conditions and linguistic barriers play a major role. Moreover, economic business parameters must be taken into account, since this processing step represents the largest cost factor for the end product. Thus, at this point the impact of the start-up on sustainable value creation is less important than the selection of global partners who meet the respective requirements with regard to the economic, ecological and social dimensions.

Conclusion

Sustainability in value chains as the result of cooperation awareness

Depending on how strong the influence of the start-up is on the individual activities within the value-added chain architecture, their role as relevant carriers, supporters and initiators of sustainability attributes in global value chains increases. However, a sustainable entrepreneurial mindset generally creates a value-added chain that has a high degree of sustainability, since suppliers who do not meet the requirements of the start-up are not integrated into the architecture or stimulated by rigorous demands for sustainable value creation at all levels. The extent to which influence can be exercised by small and young companies depends primarily on the nature of the cooperation partners and their business model.

The interpretation of the cooperation awareness of the respective partners in the dimensions described above can be performed based on the collected information. In this way, evaluations of the cooperation behaviour are possible which, if positive, force the penetration of the value-added chains with sustainability attributes.

If sustainability-relevant concepts and ideals are shared, there is generally more transparency and readiness to adapt. In addition, the size of the cooperation partners plays an important role. While corporations and large companies generally have little cooperative awareness or willingness to work with start-ups, and cannot be influenced by sustainability requirements, SMEs and family-owned businesses are, despite a lack of sustainability concepts within the textile industry, prepared to adopt sustainability attributes required by start-ups and adapt to their added-value creation requirements. For SMEs and family-owned businesses, it can be a viable strategy for the future to deal more intensively with their cooperation awareness and, above all, the development of cooperation skills (cooperative capabilities) in order to generate long-term and sustainable competitive and innovative advantages through cooperation with start-ups.

References

Bortz, J and Döring, N (1995) *Forschungsmethoden und Evaluation*, Springer, Berlin and Heidelberg

Deloitte (2017) [accessed 23 September 2020] *Shake it up: Kooperationen zwischen Mittelstand und Start-up* [Online] https://www2.deloitte.com/content/dam/Deloitte/de/Documents/Mittelstand/Deloitte-Erfolgsfaktoren-Mittelstand-Kooperationen%20Start-ups2017.pdf (archived at https://perma.cc/Z6VX-ZA23)

Dul, J and Hak, T (2008) *Case Study Methodology in Business Research*, Butterworth-Heinemann, Oxford

Easton, G (1995) *Case Research as a Methodology for Industrial Networks: A realist apologia, IMP Conference (11th)*, IMP

Geibler, J v (2010) *Nachhaltigkeit in globalen Wertschöpfungsketten: Nicht-staatliche Standards als Steuerungsinstrument im internationalen Biomassehandel*, Ruhr-Univ., Diss., 2009. Bochum and *Wirtschaftswissenschaftliche Nachhaltigkeitsforschung: Vol. 12*. Metropolis, Marburg

Gibb, A and Scott M (1985) Strategic awareness, personal commitment and the process of planning in the small business, *Journal of Management Studies*, 22 (6), pp 612ff

Heyse, V and Erpenbeck, J (2009) *Kompetenztraining. Informations- und Trainingsprogramme*, Schaeffer-Poeschel, Stuttgart

IfM Bonn (2019) [accessed 23 September 2020] *Mittelstand im Einzelnen* [Online] https://www.ifm-bonn.org/statistiken/mittelstand-im-einzelnen/#accordion=0&tab=6 (archived at https://perma.cc/JB84-NUT9)

KMU-Report Berlin (2018) Berlin

Kollmann, T, Stöckmann, C, Hensellek, S and Kensbock, J (2016) *Deutscher Startup Monitor 2016: Der perfekte Start*, Berlin and Essen

Kollmann, T, Hensellek, S, Jung, PB and Kleine-Stegemann, L (2018) *Deutscher Startup Monitor 2016: Neue Signale, klare Ziele*, Berlin and Essen

Kuckertz, A and Allmendinger, M (2017) *Den „Generationenkonflikt" durch richtige Kooperation überwinden – Was Start-ups von Großunternehmen erwarten*, Research Brief, Hohenheim

Kühmayer, F (2016) *Leadership Report 2017*, Frankfurt

Kühmayer, F (2018) *Leadership Report 2019*, Frankfurt

Löher, J, Paschke, M and Schröder, C (2017) *Kooperationen zwischen etabliertem Mittelstand und Start-ups*, IfM-Materialien (258), IfM, Bonn

Mayring, P (2010) [accessed 23 September 2020] Qualitative Inhaltsanalyse, in *Handbuch Qualitative Forschung in der Psychologie*, ed G Mey and K Mruck, pp 601–13, VS Verlag für Sozialwissenschaften, Wiesbaden [Online] https://doi.org/10.1007/978-3-531-92052-8_42 (archived at https://perma.cc/C964-QYC7)

Mersiowsky, I, Bösch, U and Feigenbutz, G (2019) [accessed 23 September 2020] *Wertschöpfungskettenorientierte Betrachtung der Digitalisierung im Mittelstand*, in *FOM-Edition. Strategie und Transformation im digitalen Zeitalter (48)*

ed MH Dahm and S Thode, Springer Fachmedien, Wiesbaden, pp 327–47 [Online] https://doi.org/10.1007/978-3-658-22032-7_19 (archived at https://perma.cc/E9BT-F6LT)

Meuser, M and Nagel, U (2009) [accessed 23 September 2020] *Das Experteninterview — konzeptionelle Grundlagen und methodische Anlage*, in *Methoden der vergleichenden Politik- und Sozialwissenschaft*, ed S Pickel, G Pickel, HJ Lauth and D Jahn, (27) 1: 465–79, VS Verlag für Sozialwissenschaften, Wiesbaden [Online] https://doi.org/10.1007/978-3-531-91826-6_23 (archived at https://perma.cc/JY5R-USDF)

Plöger, I (2016) *Die Bedeutung von Innovationen durch Start-ups für die deutsche Industrie und der Beitrag des BDI*, Fachforum Berlin, November 2016

Porter, ME (2008) *Competitive Advantage: Creating and sustaining superior performance*, 2nd edn, Free Press, Riverside

Rabbe, S and Schulz A (2007) *Strategisches Management in KMU – Unternehmer zwischen „Planungslücke" und „strategic awareness"*, in *Planung in kleinen und mittleren Unternehmen*, ed JA Meyer, Jahrbuch der KMU-Forschung und Praxis 2017: 19ff., Eul, Lohmar and Köln

Raith, M (2014) [accessed 23 September 2020] *Wertschöpfung und Businessplanung*, in *Integrated Design Engineering*, ed S Vajna, (27) pp 527–538, Springer, Berlin and Heidelberg [Online] https://doi.org/10.1007/978-3-642-41104-5_18 (archived at https://perma.cc/CC89-BU5Y)

RKW (2018): *Mittelstand meets Startup*, RKW, Eschborn

Scholz, RW and Tietje, O (2002) *Embedded Case Study Methods: Integrating quantitative and qualitative knowledge*, Sage Publications, Thousand Oaks, CA

Schulz, O (2012) [accessed 23 September 2020] Nachhaltige ganzheitliche Wertschöpfungsketten, in *Corporate Social Responsibility*, ed A Schneider and R Schmidpeter: 271–84, Springer, Berlin and Heidelberg [Online] https://doi.org/10.1007/978-3-642-25399-7_18 (archived at https://perma.cc/2K3R-JF7W)

Som, O (2015) *Innovationsverhalten von KMU – Aktuelle Herausforderungen und Entwicklungsperspektiven*, Vortrag, DIHK, Berlin

Tiimiakatemia® (2019) [accessed 23 September 2020] Team academy approach [Online] https://tiimiakatemia.com/en/ (archived at https://perma.cc/S5KW-BKKK)

Walther, G (2010) [accessed 23 September 2020] *Nachhaltige Wertschöpfungsnetzwerke: Überbetriebliche Planung und Steuerung von Stoffströmen entlang des Produktlebenszyklus*, Techn. Univ. Braunschweig, Habil.-Schr., 2009 (1. Aufl.), *Produktion und Logistik*. Gabler, Wiesbaden [Online] https://doi.org/10.1007/978-3-8349-8643-6 (archived at https://perma.cc/B4J3-JHA7)

Wrobel, M, Schildhauer, T and Preiß, K (2017) *Kooperationen zwischen Startups und Mittelstand. Learn. Match. Partner*, Alexander von Humboldt Institute for Internet and Society, Berlin

Yin, RK (2009) *Case Study Research: Design and methods*, 4th edn, *Applied Social Research methods series (5)*, Sage, Los Angeles

Zaugg, RJ (2007) *Fallstudien-Methodik: Fälle schreiben und lösen*, Gabler, Wiesbaden

ZEW (2016) [accessed 23 September 2020] *Innovativer Mittelstand* [Online] http://ftp.zew.de/pub/zew-docs/gutachten/InnovativerMittelstand2025ZEWPrognos2016.pdf (archived at https://perma.cc/LST5-WY7Z)

Global value chain sustainability governance 05

Implications for management research and practice

KLAUS FISCHER

Introduction

Global value chains are increasingly receiving attention regarding their impacts on global sustainability. In political and economic sciences, management research and practice as well as in the public discourse about corporate social responsibility and sustainable development, the role of dominant chain actors as multinational corporations (MNCs) is controversially discussed in that context.

In a positive sense, multinationals can contribute to filling governance gaps, for example concerning human rights, decent work, prevention of corruption and environmental protection by (co-)creating, implementing and monitoring sustainability standards in their global value chains. Critically seen, their role and motives concerning sustainability policies in value chains can be questioned in the light of seeking the lowest costs of production and procurement.

However, acting as dominant players beyond the limitations of national governance, multinational corporations take an essential role as actors of private governance in and through their global value chains. As scholars from different disciplines state, this role leads to the necessity of a rethinking of traditional governance concepts in management research and practice.

In order to come to a more differentiated view on forms of governance relating to global value chains and the sustainability context, this chapter aims to detail the first steps of conceptualizing 'global value chain sustainability governance'. Thereby, defining elements and theoretical bases of global value chain sustainability governance, as well as implications for management theory and practice, will be discussed.

Research focus

MNCs take quite an ambivalent role in global value chains regarding corporate responsibility and sustainable development. On the one hand, they systematically seek economic advantages through global purchasing, production, and investment activities. By benefiting from low sustainability standards in industrially developing and emerging countries, they earn increasing criticism from civil society and political actors on exactly these practices (Soundararajan *et al*, 2019). On the other hand, MNCs' activities can also contribute to filling gaps of governance through global value chains by designing, implementing and controlling standards in fields such as human rights, working conditions, corruption, and environmental protection.

Thereby, the limitations of governance through nation states in a globalized economy and concerning complex transnational challenges of sustainability are well-discussed in political science and shed light on alternative forms of governance beyond and without nation state (Zürn, 2008). Consequently, MNCs' role in governance and implementing goals of sustainable development gained interest from political science, economics, and management theory (Aras and Crowther, 2010; Benn and Dunphy, 2013; Idowu *et al*, 2015) as well as in the global sustainability discourse reflected by the UN Agenda 2030 (United Nations, 2015).

MNCs as the lead firms of global value chains are seen as important actors of global governance (Matten *et al*, 2010; Tihany *et al*, 2014), also and in particular in areas of limited statehood (Börzel and Deitelhoff, 2018). This focus on a changing role of business for governance materializes in different theoretical, political and managerial concepts, for example in business ethics and corporate social responsibility (Sethi, 2008), sustainable supply chain management (Gold *et al*, 2009) or conceptional advancements of corporate governance (Mason and Simmons, 2014) and corporate citizenship (Matten *et al*, 2010).

However, the politicization of corporations is also critically discussed. The fundamental question in this context is whether corporations should, at all, provide collective goods and common welfare beyond doing business, as they are not politically mandated and legitimized for those tasks by the societies concerned (Palazzo and Scherer, 2008; Willke and Willke, 2008). When looking at their ambivalent role, the question arises why MNCs should contribute to increasing sustainability standards at all (Lee and Gereffi, 2015), which might endanger their economic profits from globalization. And if they do, which interests are behind their commitment and what does this mean for an appropriate design of copororate policies and management tools?

Recognizing the growing relevance of MNCs as global governance actors, it is thus necessary to further discuss the governance processes that are emerging from their interactions in global value chains. Starting from an outline of general chain governance, the characteristics of global value chain (GVC) sustainability governance will be worked out in this chapter. Therefore, the focus lies on illustrating the relevant governance actors, structures and processes as well as the intended output of these forms of governance.

Additionally, implications for management research and practice will be discussed. Here, theoretical approaches that might induce further theorizing and empiric research on GVC sustainability governance will be presented, as well as suggestions for further developments of management concepts.

The global value chain concept

'Global value chains' has evolved to a well-established term in the debates referring to globalization, global supply chains, and international trade and development (Gereffi, 2019; World Bank Group, 2019). As a phenomenon of the modern era of globalization, GVCs are characterized by value creation activities across several national borders, embodying intermediate trade-flows between the participating supplier and buyer countries (World Bank Group, 2017).

Their far-reaching implications for the economies and countries involved led to growing attention on GVCs in the scientific and political debate in recent decades. In their first *Global Value Chain Development Reports* of 2017 and 2019, the World Bank and other co-publishing partners look back on the development of GVCs since the middle of the 1990s and emphasize their high potential for economic development and poverty eradication worldwide.

Although there are first indications for consolidating growth rates, GVCs hold a significant share of about two-thirds of global trade in value-added terms. They are thus an essential vehicle for the participation of developing countries in world markets (World Bank Group, 2017; World Bank Group, 2019).

A global value chain emerges from the value creation activities that are globally performed to bring a product or service from conception through different phases of production to end-users and beyond. They comprise activities of product design, production, sales and marketing, and final consumption, but also disposal and recycling after use (Gereffi and Fernandez-Stark, 2011).

The GVC concept is thus broader than that of global supply chains, allowing a more lifecycle-oriented perspective. Supply chain concepts typically conclude at the stage of end-users and initially emphasize logistics aspects (Richey *et al*, 2010). However, their scope has significantly widened in recent years. Thus, relevant contributions for discussing sustainability aspects of global value creation are referring to 'sustainable' or 'green' supply chain management (Seuring and Müller, 2008; Abu Seman *et al*, 2012). Additionally, it has to be mentioned, that although the scope of GVCs goes (theoretically) beyond the phase of consumption, the main focus of chain governance still lies at the upstream parts of the chain, that is, from raw material extraction up to the brand and original equipment manufacturers or retailers. Subsequent phases of consumption, disposal and possible recycling activities are not yet often addressed. In this chapter, no further distinctions shall thus be made between global 'supply' or 'value' chain concepts. Both are relevant for conceptualizing GVC sustainability governance and will be referred to.

Independent from the terms used, global value or supply chains emerge because they improve the competitive advantages of the firms involved. For MNCs, this means reducing production costs and outsourcing non-core manufacturing or service activities, as well as getting access to necessary resources and knowledge (Gereffi *et al*, 2005). An important governing role in GVCs is taken by so-called 'lead firms', which coordinate and drive relevant processes in the chain (Lee and Gereffi, 2015). They can be original equipment manufacturers and brand companies delivering products to final consumers or powerful and dominant suppliers. Although lead firms were mainly located in western countries for a long time, 'rising power firms' or 'emerging-market multinationals' are gaining more and more importance (Lee and Gereffi, 2015; Hendriks, 2017).

For a further discussion of governance in GVCs, it should be kept in mind that these chains are as diverse as the industries and countries in which they are located. Thereby, all phases of value creation can potentially be dispersed to different countries around the globe and be performed by various firms and actors, also including those from informal sectors. Further differences result from the industry-specific production processes and technologies used. For example, global agricultural value chains are much less complex than those of high-tech manufacturing goods. GVCs of the textile and apparel sector are rather short and linear, while the supply chains of the electronics and automotive industry tend to be complex networks.

Besides the aforementioned processual and geographic varieties, there also exist different types of supplier–producer relationships. These depend on whether the chain is particularly buyer- or supplier-driven (Gereffi and Lee, 2016). For example, in the buyer-driven apparel and footwear sector, brand manufacturers or retail buyers are governing how the chain works, mainly driven by cost factors. In supplier-driven chains, quite big and powerful suppliers are more dominant due to decreasing manufacturing depth of original equipment manufacturers, as in the automobile or electronics industry. However, this power structure can shift along with the different tier levels of GVCs, which is further increasing governance complexity.

All in all, various forms of influence and interactions between value chain actors emerge from these constellations (Lee and Gereffi, 2015; Gereffi *et al*, 2005; Fischer, 2017). This variety requires a more in-depth discussion of value chain governance, in particular when its sustainability impacts are discussed, as this further increases the complexity of the discourse. Consequently, GVC sustainability governance will be further conceptualized, starting from the succeeding presentations of overall governance and chain governance concepts.

The governance concept

Governance is an umbrella term used in various disciplines and contexts, coming along with different intentions and objectives. This variety is both a blessing and a curse. On the one hand, it allows us to explore and describe complex phenomena of steering, influence and management while building a bridge between the respective disciplines and contexts involved. Those are traditionally the economic and sociological neo-institutionalism, political science as well as political concepts such as global or good governance. Governance thus delivers a particular 'lingua franca' necessary to explore and develop adequate transdisciplinary concepts and solutions for complex phenomena of steering in reality (Fischer, 2017).

On the other hand, there is the risk that governance becomes a positively connoted but empty signifier standing for a couple of meanings in different contexts (Offe, 2008). In academia, politics and management practice, 'governance' often refers to overarching and necessary, but not further specified approaches of managing and steering social systems towards improvement. According to the respective context, this refers to governing societies effectively in a post-nation-state era, to the set-up and design of institutions for handling agency problems or to ensure the good conduct of corporations or even of statehood, as in the political concept of good governance and the respective programmes of the World Bank (World Bank, 1992).

For benefiting from the potentials of the governance concept, it is thus necessary to clarify the theoretical propositions, objectives and intentions underlying the very different contexts in which the term is used. Keeping that in mind, the concept of value chain governance is first of all briefly outlined in the following section. As will be shown, value chain governance traditionally refers to new institutional economics, aiming to achieve efficient transactions in the chain and coping with agency problems (Gereffi *et al*, 2005).

Conceptualizing global value chain sustainability governance

An outline of general chain governance

The primary function of chain governance can be described as balancing the self-interest of autonomous firms (as decision makers) in the chain with their existing interdependencies aiming at improving overall chain performance (Richey *et al*, 2010). Looking at the early conceptualization by Humphrey and Schmitz (2001), one can argue that governance in a value chain always arises when some firms or actors in the chain work according to parameters set by others. From a governance-theoretical point of view, supply chain actors are thus divided into 'governors' (in the sense of standard-setters) and 'governed' (standard-taking organizations).

Beyond logistic aspects, these parameters could address overall product quality, but also the design of the production processes and work systems involved, linked with sustainability objectives, as amongst others labour and environmental standards. Concerning the relevant mechanisms behind,

Humphrey and Schmitz (2001) define value chain governance as 'inter-firm relationships and institutional mechanisms through which *non-market co-ordination* of activities in the chain is achieved' (p 5, author's italics). Gereffi *et al* (2005) finally deduced five basic types of chain governance, which do not exclude market coordination and cover the whole range from market (arm's length transactions), over modular, relational, and captive network governance, up to hierarchy.

Concerning its theoretical foundation, the classical concept of value chain governance mainly refers to new institutionalism (Gereffi *et al*, 2005). Theorizing chain governance is seen as a necessary extension of the governance dichotomy of 'market and hierarchy' in transaction cost economics (Williamson, 1979). The governance setting shall be designed optimally to minimize transaction costs and to overcome agency problems endangering the collective success of the chain. Thereby, the nature of transactions in the chain defines which form of governance is adequate (Lee and Gereffi, 2015).

GVC sustainability governance

Although the above-presented general chain governance concept delivers the first base for conceptualizing GVC sustainability governance, it is still too narrow a framework. A closer look at its overarching context shows that GVC sustainability governance differs in several aspects from the 'core concept' of value chain governance:

- Its overall intention refers to global political sustainability goals going far beyond the individual as well as collective target system of the chain actors.
- The underlying processes of governance are embedded in the bigger context of global sustainability governance. They are thus not limited to the sphere of the value chain, requiring compatibility with overarching governance theories, structures and assessment criteria.
- Compared with classical value chain governance, which mainly addresses the internal actors of the chain around a lead firm, a multitude of different stakeholder groups is involved in and affected by GVC sustainability governance.

In order to take these differences into account, GVC sustainability governance is conceptualized in this section. Therefore, the intended governance output, the actors involved, as well as the different modes of governance – in the sense of varying governance structures and processes – will be presented.

Governance output

As shown in the previous sections, GVC sustainability governance refers to global political sustainability goals reaching far beyond the individual as well as collective target systems of the chain actors. Discussing the role of MNCs and other value chain parties as actors of sustainability governance thus requires us to look at the bigger context in the light of *avoiding the negative effects* of GVC activities, such as environmental degradation, corruption, health and safety issues or human and workers' rights abuses, and, additionally, in the light of *increasing the positive effects*, such as economic participation, community building and investment in social capital.

Consequently, the *intended output* of GVC sustainability governance is to contribute effectively to the implementation of global sustainability objectives as currently materialized in the 17 UN Sustainable Development Goals (SDGs) (United Nations, 2015). Due to the high interdependency of the goals, it is hard to define which of them are most likely to be impacted by GVCs. Trade activities, foreign direct investments and various related production processes in GVCs influence the social, economic and environmental development of the participating actors and countries in diverse manners (Fischer, 2020). GVC activities can thus have positive as well as negative impacts on all of the 17 fields that are addressed by the SDGs. At least from a corporate social responsibility point of view, all of them are of potential relevance for multinational actors engaged in global value creation (Schönherr *et al*, 2017).

However, a closer look at the goals and their sub-targets allows seven SDGs to be identified to which the possible sustainability contributions and impacts of GVCs mainly refer (Fischer, 2020):

- Goal 1: End poverty in all its forms everywhere.
- Goal 4: Ensure inclusive and equitable quality education and promote lifelong learning opportunities for all.
- Goal 8: Promote sustained, inclusive and sustainable economic growth, full and productive employment and decent work for all.
- Goal 9: Build resilient infrastructure, promote inclusive and sustainable industrialization and foster innovation.
- Goal 10: Reduce inequality within and among countries.

- Goal 12: Ensure sustainable consumption and production patterns.
- Goal 17: Strengthen the means of implementation and revitalize the Global Partnership for Sustainable Development.

Regardless of concretely referring to SDGs, the potential positive or negative impacts of GVCs on their participating actors, such as workers, firms or whole sectors and countries, have already been discussed for a couple of years. This debate comprises the two poles of, on the one hand, a possible 'race to the bottom' (Singh and Sammit, 2004; Olney, 2013) or 'immiserizing growth' (Kanbur, 2019; Bhagwati, 1968), and, on the other, the concept of economic, social and environmental upgrading (Barrientos *et al*, 2011; Gereffi and Lee, 2016).

For conceptualizing the intended output of GVC sustainability governance, the latter mentioned concepts of upgrading are of particular interest. Their core idea is 'the process by which economic actors – nations, firms and workers – move from low-value to relatively high-value activities in global production networks' (Gereffi, 2019: 197), leading to economic, social and even environmental benefits (Golini *et al*, 2018; Marchi *et al*, 2013).

Thereby, the upgrading concept initially emerges from striving for long-term competitiveness of value chains and has thus initially not a sustainability perspective in the narrow sense (Bush *et al*, 2015). Its underlying paradigm of global competitiveness may consequently influence the perspective on governance processes. This needs to be kept in mind when discussing 'upgrading processes' in the context of global sustainability, and thus with a different notion behind.

Governance structures and processes

As a result of their profound discussion of sustainability governance in global value chains and networks, Bush *et al* (2015) distinguish three different ideal types of governing: governance *in* chains, governance *of* chains, and governance *through* chains. These different modes also adequately exemplify the diversity of GVC sustainability governance. In order to describe the different underlying governance structures and processes of GVC sustainability governance, these three ideal types are referred to in the following discussion.

'Governance *in* chains' as defined by Bush *et al* (2015) mainly refers to the functionalist perspective of logistics and supply chain management, enlarged by the integration of sustainability issues. It comes along with a business administration point of view, focusing on the approaches of sustainable supply chain management (SSCM), which comprise management systems of monitoring, measuring and controlling sustainability issues along the chain, such as codes of conduct, supplier (self) assessments, audits and supplier development (Seuring and Müller, 2008). At the centre of consideration are thus the chain-internal firms (in particular the lead firms) and their efforts to improve the social and environmental performance in the chain as part of their rather individual CSR activities. Consequently, sustainability governance *in* chains means 'to create efficient control over suppliers to minimize environmental and social risks' (Bush *et al* 2015: 11). This mode of governance can be seen as an expansion of the institutionalist chain governance approach presented above. In this sense, non-compliance with sustainability norms increases transaction costs (as due to stakeholder sanctions or a questioned 'licence to operate') and the challenge of enforcing sustainability standards in the chain can be understood as an agency problem.

Just as with 'governance *in* chains', 'governance *of* chains' mainly focuses on chain-internal processes of vertical governance (Bush *et al*, 2015). Here, however, the underlying paradigm is not business administration and a (sustainable) supply chain management point of view, but political economy. Governance *of* chains is thus not driven by initiatives of CSR management at a single firm level, but deals further with the power asymmetries between lead firms and suppliers. Here, the question of how governance arrangements facilitate economic and social upgrading of the participating chain actors and countries is of central relevance. These reflections are highly compatible with a global sustainability governance perspective as they deal with the positive or negative side effects of global labour division and value creation.

Finally, 'governance *through* chains' addresses a broader level that captures the interaction between the value chain with 'a wider set of networked actors and activities that collectively steer sustainable production and consumption practices' (Bush *et al* 2015: 13). Beyond chain-internal firms as the central actors of governance 'in' and 'of' chains, key players are externals here, such as civil society actors, multi-stakeholder organizations. Their interactions lead to horizontal forms of governance (Gereffi and Lee, 2016), which are, however, closely interrelated with the vertical processes of governance *in* and *of* chains presented above. While for the latter governance forms, the input and requirements from externals were translated by the internal chain actors and transferred to governance processes, in the case of governance *through* chains, the external stakeholders are directly participating in shaping the governance arrangements.

These three modes of governance provide a useful analytical framework for GVC sustainability governance and elucidate the different approaches and theories behind them. Their sharp distinction is, however, rather conceptual as the boundaries seem to be blurring in reality. Thus, intra-firm governance and tools of SSCM (referring to the type 'governance *in* chains') are inseparably linked to inter-firm coordination in the chain (referring to 'governance *of* chains'). Instruments such as codes of conduct, supplier selection policies or business-to-business audits exemplarily show that both forms cannot be separated. Additionally, the current state of the corporate social responsibility (CSR) debate already goes beyond mere responsibility for the side-effects of core business activities. Aspects such as creating shared value for stakeholders and society at large (European Commission, 2011) and community involvement and development (ISO, 2010) have been basic elements of CSR policy concepts in recent years. They are closely linked to aspects of upgrading and vertical governance, again building a bridge between governance *in*, *of*, and *through* chains.

Governance actors

As already mentioned with regard to the structures and processes of GVC sustainability governance, relevant governance actors can be found inside as well as outside the value chain. Vertical forms of governance describe influences and interrelations *between chain-internal actors* such as buyer and supplier companies (Gereffi and Lee, 2016). They are traditionally driven by the framing of new institutionalism, dealing with the optimization of transaction costs in the chain.

Going beyond the traditional focus of Humphrey and Schmitz (2001), one needs to consider that value chain parameters can also be defined and controlled by external actors. Those can be government institutions, international organizations such as the International Labour Organization or the Organisation for Economic Co-operation and Development, and actors of civil society such as non-governmental organizations (Messner, 2003). They are leading to horizontal forms of GVC sustainability governance in the sense of interactions *between actors internal and external to the value chain* (Gereffi and Lee, 2016), as referred to in the case of governance *through* chains above. These external actors are primarily not focusing on parameters for efficient coordination in the chain, but are instead setting normative parameters such as environmental and social standards from the political agenda of global sustainability. Their intentions and resulting governance processes thus lie beyond the analytical mindset of economic institutionalism.

Implications for management research and practice

Integrating different theoretical perspectives and concepts

Tihany *et al* (2014) and Bush *et al* (2015) propose an array of possible research questions concerning a broader conceptualization of governance in management research or rather with regard to sustainability governance of global value chains. They thereby suggest a rethinking of governance, exceeding classical approaches that are based on new institutionalism and managerial functionalism.

This call for a more diverse and transdisciplinary perspective concerning governance in management and global value chain research is relevant for further conceptualizing and exploring GVC sustainability governance, too. Accordant with the bridging character of the governance concept, exploring GVC sustainability governance can benefit from a combination of complementary theoretical perspectives and approaches – presupposing that they do not base this on incommensurable propositions.

Without claiming to be complete, Table 5.1 shows some relevant theories and governance approaches from different disciplinary foci that could induce further research in the field of GVC sustainability governance.

The theories and concepts listed all provide elements for defining, analysing and describing phenomena of GVC sustainability governance. They thereby represent complementary and not contradictory perspectives that could be used to raise new research avenues and integrate formerly isolated considerations:

- Organizational sociology focuses, amongst others, on the phenomena of isomorphism and decoupling in light of organizational legitimacy (Meyer and Rowan, 1977; DiMaggio and Powell, 1983). Such theories can help to explain strong isomorphisms between corporate sustainability practices in the value chain and a divergence between formal CSR structures and de facto organizational activities of chain actors (Hiß, 2004, 2006; Fischer, 2017).
- New institutional economics explore which institutional settings are most efficient for reducing transaction costs (Williamson, 1979; Jensen and Meckling, 1976), leading to respective governance arrangements in value chains, such as contracts or codes of conduct in light of agency theory.

Table 5.1 Conceptualizing theories and approaches for GVC sustainability governance

<table>
<tr><th rowspan="2"></th><th colspan="4">Disciplinary focus</th></tr>
<tr><th>Organizational sociology</th><th>New institutional economics</th><th>Management research, business ethics</th><th>Political theory</th></tr>
<tr><td>Function of governance or governance research</td><td>Ensuring the legitimacy of organizational activities and structures</td><td>Increasing economic efficiency and minimizing transaction costs</td><td>Ensuring compliance of business activities with stakeholder requirements and moral standards</td><td>Providing collective goods and contributing to the common welfare</td></tr>
<tr><td rowspan="3">Relevant theories and concepts (examples)</td><td>Institutional isomorphism</td><td>Agency theory</td><td>Stakeholder theory and CSR</td><td>Normative political theory</td></tr>
<tr><td></td><td colspan="3">Political economy</td></tr>
<tr><td colspan="2"></td><td colspan="2">Normative political theory</td></tr>
<tr><td rowspan="3">Corresponding governance approaches</td><td colspan="3">Corporate governance</td><td></td></tr>
<tr><td colspan="2"></td><td colspan="2">Global governance</td></tr>
<tr><td colspan="4">Economic governance</td></tr>
</table>

- Management research and business ethics provide concepts dealing with a broader understanding of corporate governance. They are referring to stakeholder requirements and moral as well as resource-orientated obligations of firm behaviour (Sacconi, 2004; Wieland, 2008; Aras and Crowther; 2009), which can be transferred to the GVC context, too. Combined with stakeholder theory, the resource dependence approach (Pfeffer and Salancik, 2003) can, for example, give answers concerning dominating stakeholder interests in the design of CSR policy and governance arrangements in GVCs (Fischer and Jentsch, 2019).
- Political theory and political economy deal, amongst others, with the politicization of non-state actors as companies and their role in a global governance context (Palazzo and Scherer, 2008; Börzel and Deitelhoff, 2018). Thereby, in particular, questions about the legitimacy of state and non-state government processes (Jacob *et al*, 2018) are relevant with regard to exploring GVC sustainability governance.
- The aforementioned theories and concepts finally correspond with different scientific and political governance approaches, such as economic and global governance (Dixit, 2008; Fuchs, 2007). In the sense of a multi-level concept, they are linked with the perspective on governance at a firm or value chain level (Fischer, 2017).

Considering governance aspects in stakeholder management

Stakeholder concepts play an important role in sustainability management research and practice. By taking an actor-specific perspective, they allow explanation of the emergence of organizational sustainability policies and management tools that reflect different stakeholder requirements (Fischer, 2017). Stakeholder theory is modelling the systemic embedding of an organization in its surrounding environment, constituted by mutual relations and interdependencies between actor groups. It thus delivers a theoretical precondition for integrating the sustainability concept into management theory and practice. 'Stakeholders' are a conceptual signifier for the needs and requirements of current as well as future generations concerning the economic activities of a corporation (Freeman, 2007).

Concerning GVCs and accordant sustainability management approaches, two different kinds of stakeholder groups are most relevant: first, those that are holding lead firms responsible for possible sustainability grievances in

GVCs, such as NGOs, political institutions and – to a certain extent – business-to-business and business-to-consumer companies; second, those that are affected by global value creation activities, but are not powerful enough to enforce their claims, such as low-skilled workers at upstream supplier sites or local communities in the Global South.

Despite – or maybe due to – this variety, stakeholder integration in modern CSR management concepts remains quite fuzzy concerning the types and ways of their involvement (Fischer and Jentsch, 2019). In the light of sustainability governance, it is, for example, essential to distinguish whether the groups involved are supplying critical resources to the integrating company, or not (Garvare and Johansson, 2010).

In further research as well as in the layout of stakeholder management instruments, aspects influencing governance processes and outcomes should thus be considered more deeply:

- Which kinds of stakeholder types are predominantly integrated, which are missing?
- What is the real intention of stakeholder integration? Does it aim to keep the licence to operate from powerful stakeholders, to increase corporate reputation, or to improve the sustainability impacts of value creation activities?
- To what extent are the stakeholders integrated, and what would increase the effectiveness concerning sustainability achievements? Are they only informed or actively consulted, and do cooperation or even delegation exist, in order to gain knowledge and join resources for problem solving?

Scrutinizing the legitimacy and effectiveness of sustainability management approaches

GVC sustainability governance refers to the normative and political concept of sustainable development. Consequently, assessment criteria for relevant management approaches need to be adapted to this political context, too. Thereby, the intended output of GVC sustainability governance refers to overall upgrading processes and sustainability impacts, and its actors are taking a rather public and politicized role. This sheds light on questions of legitimacy and effectiveness of these forms of governance and its constituting processes, such as SSCM practices from lead firms (as codes of conduct, audits, supplier selection and development).

Table 5.2 Input, throughput and output legitimacy in the context of GVC sustainability governance

	Guiding questions	Requirements	Measures
Input legitimacy	Which actors are de facto influencing the design and implementation of governance processes and management instruments, and to what extent? How is the inclusion of the actors 'governed' guaranteed (eg workers and firms in the Global South)?	Inclusiveness, participation	Measures of comprehensive stakeholder integration such as local stakeholder dialogues or nation-specific surveys
Throughput legitimacy	Are there fair and transparent procedures of decision making, considering the will of the respective 'demos' (societies) addressed?	Transparency, publicness, equity	Use of new instruments (such as crowdsourcing) in the sense of political deliberation Public participation at the design stage of governance and management instruments (eg assessment tools, materiality matrices)
Output legitimacy	Which de facto social, environmental, and economic impacts are achieved? Could value chain participants realize upgrading opportunities?	Effectiveness	Impact assessment measures such as (social) lifecycle assessment and sustainability performance measurement

SOURCE Adapted from Fischer and Jentsch, 2019

Because non-state actors are per se not democratically legitimized, they lack input legitimacy in a classical sense. It is thus often argued that the legitimacy of non-governmental governance should be assessed by looking at its results and outcomes instead (Geibler, 2013). At first glance, this focus on output legitimacy seems to be an adequate way of assessing new forms of governance: positive outcomes make them broadly acceptable and thus legitimate. However, this would presuppose that the legitimizing 'demos' (in the sense of people) is identical to the governed, as it is the case in nation states (Schmelzle, 2008).

When looking at the various actors and processes of GVC sustainability governance, it becomes clear that this coincidence does not per se exist here. Divergent groups of stakeholders (see above) are influencing and influenced by GVC sustainability governance, taking the role of the 'governors' or the 'governed'. As in the case of other forms of non-public governance, it remains to some extent unclear for whom governance measures serve and consequently to whom the governing bodies need to answer (Schmelzle, 2008). Concerning GVC sustainability governance, this could be western stakeholder groups demanding minimum social and environmental standards, or those groups that are ultimately affected by adverse conditions.

Within future management research and practice, possible trade-offs concerning the legitimacy and effectiveness of respective management approaches should thus be further explored. Table 5.2 provides a first reference framework for that, containing relevant guiding questions, requirements, and measures that address the elements of input, throughput, and output legitimacy. This framework could be referred to when exploring and designing management approaches for GVC sustainability governance.

Conclusion

Exploring the role of global value chains and their actors in the light of sustainability governance has revealed that a much broader understanding of 'chain governance' is necessary than is traditionally conceptualized in economic theory and management practice. Different system levels and their interrelations need to be considered when drawing the bigger picture of global sustainability and possible contributions from GVCs. Those include the levels of a single worker or value chain actor, that of corporations and global production networks, up to a national and global perspective. Therefore, established concepts and terms such as SSCM, value chain governance and corporate social responsibility need to be reframed to some extent, as well as their underlying theories and governance approaches. As argued in this chapter, combining and integrating different disciplinary approaches under the conceptual umbrella of governance can be fruitful for further exploring that topic and suggesting new research avenues. However, this should not be practised as an end in itself or lead to an arbitrary eclecticism, but should develop synergies between commensurable approaches. For example, combining complementary views as that of institutionalism and power theories can help us to understand the behaviour of governance actors in value chains better. Alternatively, adapting classical requirements from political science to non-governmental governance processes can enable the development of more comprehensive criteria for designing and assessing sustainability management approaches in value chains. Generally speaking, there is much room for further conceptualizing GVC sustainability governance and thus for further theoretic as well as empiric research in this field. One primarily important issue would be to intensify the research on the effectiveness and impacts of the manifold 'CSR toolbox instruments' used for addressing the sustainability of global value creation.

References

Abu Seman, NA, Zakuan, N, Jusoh, A and Ahrif, MS (2012) Green supply chain management: A review and research direction, *International Journal of Managing Value and Supply Chains*, **3** (1), pp 1–18

Aras, G and Crowther, D (2009) Corporate governance and corporate social responsibility in context, in *Global Perspectives on Corporate Governance and CSR*, ed G Aras and D Crowther, Gower, Farnham, pp 1–41

Aras, G and Crowther, D (eds) (2010) *A Handbook of Corporate Governance and Social Responsibility*, Gower, Farnham

Barrientos, S, Gereffi, G and Rossi, A (2011) Economic and social upgrading in global production networks: A new paradigm for a changing world, *International Labour Review*, **150** (3/4), pp 319–40

Benn, S and Dunphy, DC (eds) (2013) *Corporate Governance and Sustainability: Challenges for theory and practice*, Routledge, London

Bhagwati, JN (1968) Distortions and immiserizing growth: A generalization, *The Review of Economic Studies*, **35** (4), pp 481–85

Börzel, TA and Deitelhoff, N (2018) Business, in *The Oxford Handbook of Governance and Limited Statehood*, ed T Risse, TA Börzel and A Draude, Oxford University Press, Oxford

Bush, SR, Oosterveer, P, Bailey, M and Mol, APJ (2015) Sustainability governance of chains and networks: A review and future outlook, *Journal of Cleaner Production*, **107**, pp 8–19

DiMaggio, PJ and Powell, WW (1983) The iron cage revisited: Institutional isomorphism and collective rationality in organizational fields, *American Sociological Review*, **48** (1), pp 147–60

Dixit, AK (2008) Economic governance, in *The New Palgrave Dictionary of Economics*, ed SN Durlauf and LE Blume, Palgrave Macmillan, London

European Commission (2011) [accessed 23 September 2020] *A Renewed EU Strategy 2011–14 for Corporate Social Responsibility*, COM (2011) 681 final [Online] http://www.europarl.europa.eu/meetdocs/2009_2014/documents/com/com_com(2011)0681_/com_com(2011)0681_en.pdf (archived at https://perma.cc/UK8X-9J6L)

Fischer, K (2017) Corporate sustainability governance, *Nachhaltigkeitsbezogene Steuerung von Unternehmen in einer globalisierten Welt*, Springer Spektrum, Wiesbaden

Fischer, K (2020) Sustainability of global value creation and supply chains, in *Human Factors for Sustainability. Theoretical perspectives and global applications*, ed A Thatcher, KJ Zink and K Fischer, CRC Press, Boca Raton, pp 237–57

Fischer, K and Jentsch, M (2019) Sustainable supply chain governance: Multinationale Unternehmen als Akteure nichtstaatlicher Governance in globalen Lieferketten, in *Nachhaltiges Beschaffungsmanagement*, ed W Wellbrock and D Ludin, Springer, Wiesbaden, pp 55–74

Freeman, RE (2007) The development of stakeholder theory: An idiosyncratic approach, in Great minds in management: The process of theory development, ed KG Smith, Oxford University Press, Oxford, pp 417–35

Fuchs, D (2007) Business and governance: Transnational corporations and the effectiveness of private governance, in Globalization: State of the art and perspectives, ed SA Schirm, Routledge, London, New York, pp 122–42

Garvare, R and Johansson, P (2010) Management for sustainability: A stakeholder theory, *Total Quality Management*, **21** (7), pp 737–44

Gereffi, G (2019) Global value chains and international development policy: Bringing firms, networks and policy-engaged scholarship back in, *Journal of International Business Policy*, **2** (3), pp 195–210

Gereffi, G and Fernandez-Stark, K (2011) *Global Value Chain Analysis: A primer*, Center on Globalization, Governance and Competitiveness, Durham, NC

Gereffi, G and Lee, J (2016) Economic and social upgrading in global value chains and industrial clusters: Why governance matters, *Journal of Business Ethics*, **133** (1), pp 25–38

Gereffi, G, Humphrey, J and Sturgeon, T (2005) The governance of global value chains, *Review of International Political Economy*, **12** (1), pp 78–104

Gold, S, Seuring, S and Beske, P (2009) Sustainable supply chain management and inter-organizational resources: A literature review, *Corporate Social Responsibility and Environmental Management*, **16** (5), pp 230–45

Golini, R, Marchi, V d, Boffelli, A and Kalchschmidt, M (2018) Which governance structures drive economic, environmental, and social upgrading? A quantitative analysis in the assembly industries, *International Journal of Production Economics*, **203** (2018), pp 13–23

Hendriks, G (2017) The sustainable development effects of investment by emerging-market multinationals: Shaping beneficial outcomes for home and host country, *Transnational Corporations*, **24** (3), pp 73–88

Hiß, S (2004) Corporate social responsibility: A myth? The example of the 'Round Table Codes of Conduct' in Germany, CSGR Working Paper No 140/04, University of Warwick, Warwick

Hiß, S (2006) *Warum übernehmen Unternehmen gesellschaftliche Verantwortung? Ein soziologischer Erklärungsversuch*, Campus Verlag, Frankfurt am Main

Humphrey, J and Schmitz, H (2001) Governance in global value chains, *IDS Bulletin*, **32** (3), pp 19–29

Idowu, SO, Frederiksen, CS, Mermod, AY and Nielsen, MEJ (eds) (2015) *Corporate Social Responsibility and Governance: Theory and practice*, Springer, Cham, Heidelberg, New York

ISO (International Organization for Standardization) (2010) *ISO 26000:2010: Guidance on social responsibility*, International Organization for Standardization, Geneva

Jacob, D, Ladwig, B and Schmelzle, C (2018): Normative political theory, in *The Oxford Handbook of Governance and Limited Statehood*, ed T Risse, TA Börzel and A Draude, Oxford University Press, Oxford

Jensen, MC and Meckling, WH (1976) Theory of the FIrm: Managerial behavior, agency costs and ownership structure, *Journal of Financial Economics*, **3** (4), pp 305–60

Kanbur, R (2019) *Immiserizing Growth: When growth fails the poor*, Oxford University Press, New York

Lee, J and Gereffi, G (2015) Global value chains, rising power firms and economic and social upgrading, *Critical Perspectives on International Business*, **11** (3/4), pp 319–39

Marchi, V de, Di Maria, E and Micelli, S (2013) Environmental strategies, upgrading and competitive advantage in global value chains, *Business Strategy and the Environment*, **22** (1), pp 62–72

Mason, C and Simmons, J (2014) Embedding corporate social responsibility in corporate governance: A stakeholder systems approach, *Journal of Business Ethics*, **119** (1), pp 77–86

Matten, D, Crane, A and Moon, J (2010) Corporations and citizenship: New perspectives on corporate power and responsibility, in *Unternehmensethik:*

Forschungsperspektiven zur Verhältnisbestimmung von Unternehmen und Gesellschaft, ed O Schumann, A Brink and T Beschorner, Metropolis, Marburg, pp 123–48

Messner, D (2003) Etablierte Weltwirtschaftsdiskurse und neue Governance-Muster in der globalen Ökonomie: Das Konzept des World Economic Triangle, in *Globale Politik. Entwicklung und Frieden in der Weltgesellschaft*, ed T Fues and J Hippler, JHW Diet, Bonn, pp 90–111

Meyer, JW and Rowan, B (1977) Institutionalized organizations: Formal structure as myth and ceremony, *American Journal of Sociology*, **83** (2), pp 340–63

Offe, C (2008) Governance: ‚Empty signifier' oder sozialwissenschaftliches Forschungsprogramm? in *Governance in einer sich wandelnden Welt*, ed GF Schuppert and M Zürn, VS Verlag, Wiesbaden, pp 61–76

Olney, WW (2013) A race to the bottom? Employment protection and foreign direct investment, *Journal of International Economics*, **91** (2), pp 191–203

Palazzo, G and Scherer, AG (2008) Corporate social responsibility, democracy, and the politicization of the corporation, *Academy of Management Review*, **33** (3), pp 773–75

Pfeffer, J and Salancik, GR (2003) *The External Control of Organizations: A resource dependence perspective*, Stanford Business Books, Stanford

Richey, RG, Roath, AS, Whipple, JM and Fawcett, SE (2010) Exploring a governance theory of supply chain management: Barriers and facilitators to integration, *Journal of Business Logistics*, **31** (1), pp 237–56

Sacconi, L (2004) *Corporate Social Responsibility (CSR) as a Model of 'Extended' Corporate Governance: An explanation based on the economic theories of social contract, reputation and reciprocal conformis*, Liuc Papers (142)

Schmelzle, C (2008) Governance und Legitimität, in *Transdisziplinäre Governanceforschung. Gemeinsam hinter den Staat blicken*, ed S De La Rosa, U Höppner and M Kötter, Nomos, Baden-Baden, pp 162–87

Schönherr, N, Findler, F and Martinuzzi, A (2017) Exploring the interface of CSR and the sustainable development goals, *Transnational Corporations*, **24** (3), pp 33–47

Sethi, SP (2008) Defining the concept of good corporate citizenship in the context of globalization: A paradigm shift from corporate social responsibility to corporate social accountability, in *Handbook of Research on Global Corporate Citizenship*, ed AG Scherer and G Palazzo, Edward Elgar, Cheltenham, pp 74–98

Seuring, S and Müller, M (2008) From a literature review to a conceptual framework for sustainable supply chain management, *Journal of Cleaner Production*, **16** (15), pp 1699–710

Singh, A and Sammit, A (2004) Labour standards and the 'race to the bottom': Rethinking globalisation and worker rights from developmental and solidaristic perspectives, *Oxford Review of Economic Policy*, **20**, pp 85–104

Soundararajan, V, Brown, JA and Wicks, AC (2019) Can multi-stakeholder initiatives improve global supply chains? Improving deliberative capacity with a stakeholder orientation, *Business Ethics Quarterly*, **29** (03), pp 385–412

Tihany, L, Graffin, S and George, G (2014) Rethinking governance in management research, *Academy of Management Journal*, **57** (6), pp 1535–43

United Nations (2015) [accessed 23 September 2020] *Transforming Our World: The 2030 Agenda for Sustainable Development* [Online] http://www.un.org/ga/search/view_doc.asp?symbol=A/RES/70/1 (archived at https://perma.cc/X4PW-GDBC)

von Geibler, J (2013) Market-based governance for sustainability in value chains: Conditions for successful standard setting in the palm oil sector, *Journal of Cleaner Production*, **56**, pp 39–53

Wieland, J (2008) Governance-Ökonomik: Die Firma als Nexus von Stakeholdern. Eine Diskussionsanregung, in *Die Stakeholder-Gesellschaft und ihre Governance. Management, Netzwerke*, ed J Wieland, Diskurs Metropolis, Marburg, pp 15–38

Williamson, OE (1979) Transaction cost economics: The governance of contractual relations, *Journal of Law and Economics*, **22** (2), pp 233–61

Willke, H and Willke, G (2008) The corporation as a political actor? A systems theory perspective, in Handbook of research on global corporate citizenship, ed AG Scherer and G Palazzo, Edward Elgar, Cheltenham, pp 552–74

World Bank (1992) *Governance and Development*, World Bank, Washington, DC

World Bank Group (2017) *Global Value Chains Development Report 2017: Measuring and analyzing the impact of GVCs on economic development*, World Bank Group, Washington, DC

World Bank Group (2019) *Global Value Chain Development Report 2019: Technological innovation, supply chain trade, and workers in a globalized world*, World Bank Group, Washington, DC

Zürn, M (2008) Governance in einer sich wandelnden Welt – eine Zwischenbilanz, in Governance in einer sich wandelnden Welt, ed GF Schuppert and G Zürn, VS Verlag, Wiesbaden, pp 553–80

PART TWO
Measuring sustainability in global value chains

Current research in the field of sustainable supply chains provides numerous results on criteria and approaches for measuring performance within the economic and ecological dimensions (Beamon, 2005; Srivastava, 2007; Tate *et al*, 2010; Gurtu *et al*, 2017: 7; Halldórsson *et al*, 2009: 89).

As early as 1997, Noci identified criteria such as 'green competence', 'environmental efficiency', 'green image' and 'lifecycle cost' that should lead to higher ecological performance along the entire value chain. Green *et al* (1998) then derived ecological criteria for supplier selection decisions in international research in order to enable a 'greener' value chain. Humphreys *et al* (2003) presented a combination of qualitative and quantitative performance criteria by integrating environmental criteria into the supplier selection process. A comprehensive overview of the literature on measurement and evaluation criteria in SCM along the entire value chain was presented by Seuring and Müller (2008) and Miemczyk *et al* (2012). However, the economic and environmental aspects are still more frequently given high priority so that the social aspects (Hutchins and Sutherland, 2008; Müller and Stölzle, 2016; Yawar and Seuring, 2017; Mota *et al*, 2015: 16) and holistic consideration of all three sustainability dimensions (Carter and

Rogers, 2008; Edgeman and Eskildsen, 2014) often remain unconsidered in research and practice.

In addition, it is unclear how the relevant key figures can be consistently collected and logically aggregated across the entire supply chain so that sustainability performance can be displayed at the end product level across the various stages of the supply chain. As a result, there is a great need for further research to measure the sustainability performance of supply chains in order to initiate future optimization measures and effectively demonstrate their impact. The following research topics address these needs and make a major contribution to closing the research gap.

References

Beamon, BM (2005) Environmental and sustainability ethics in supply chain management, *Science and Engineering Ethics*, **11** (2), pp 221–34

Carter, CR and Rogers, DS (2008) A framework of sustainable supply chain management: Moving toward new theory, *International Journal of Physical Distribution and Logistics Management*, **38** (5), pp 360–87

Edgeman, R and Eskildsen, J (2014) Modeling and assessing sustainable enterprise excellence, *Business Strategy and the Environment*, **23** (3), pp 173–87

Green, K, Morton, B and New, S (1998) Green purchasing and supply policies: Do they improve companies' environmental performance? *Supply Chain Management: An international journal*, **3** (2), pp 89–95

Gurtu, A, Searcy, C and Jaber, MY (2017) Sustainable supply chains, in *Green Supply Chain Management for Sustainable Business Practice: Premier reference source*, vol 2, ed M Khan, M Hussain and MM Ajmal, Business Science Reference, Hershey, PA, USA, pp 1–26

Halldórsson, Á, Kotzab, H and Skjøtt-Larsen, T (2009) Supply chain management on the crossroad to sustainability: A blessing or a curse? *Logistics Research*, **1** (2), pp 83–94

Humphreys, PK, Wong, YK and Chan, FTS (2003) Integrating environmental criteria into the supplier selection process, *Journal of Materials Processing Technology*, **138** (1–3), pp 349–56

Hutchins, MJ and Sutherland, JW (2008) An exploration of measures of social sustainability and their application to supply chain decisions, *Journal of Cleaner Production*, **16** (15), pp 1688–98

Miemczyk, J, Johnsen, TE and Macquet, M (2012) Sustainable purchasing and supply management: A structured literature review of definitions and measures at the dyad, chain and network levels, *Supply Chain Management: An international journal*, **17** (5), pp 478–96

Mota, B, Gomes, MI, Carvalho, A and Barbosa-Povoa, AP (2015) Towards supply chain sustainability: Economic, environmental and social design and planning, *Journal of Cleaner Production*, **105**, pp 14–27

Müller, M and Stölzle, W (2016) Socially responsible supply chains: A distinct avenue for future research? in *Supply Management Research: Aktuelle Forschungsergebnisse 2015*, ed R Bogaschewsky, M Eßig, R Lasch and W Stölzle, *Advanced Studies in Supply Management*, vol 18, 1 Auflage, Springer Gabler, Wiesbaden, pp 121–51

Noci, G (1997) Designing green vendor rating systems for the assessment of a suppliers environmental performance, *European Journal of Purchasing and Supply Management*, **3** (2), pp 103–14

Seuring, S and Müller, M (2008) From a literature review to a conceptual framework for sustainable supply chain management, *Journal of Cleaner Production*, **16** (15), pp 1699–710

Srivastava, SK (2007) Green supply-chain management: A state-of-the-art literature review, *International Journal of Management Reviews*, 9 (1), pp 53–80

Tate, WL, Ellram, LM and Kirchoff, JF (2010) Corporate social responsibility reports: A thematic analysis related to supply chain management, *Journal of Supply Chain Management*, **46** (1), pp 19–44

Yawar, SA and Seuring, S (2017) Management of social issues in supply chains: A literature review exploring social issues, actions and performance outcomes, *Journal of Business Ethics*, **141** (3), pp 621–43

Sustainability controlling in integrated value chains 06

HARRY MÜLLER

Abstract

The current practices in sustainability accounting and corporate social responsibility (CSR) communication with stakeholders struggle to provide a comprehensive picture of environmental costs across the different companies within an integrated value network. Whereas monetary costs can be easily accounted for in inter-company transactions, ecological and social costs are not represented in the same way. Input factors bought in market transactions from external suppliers are typically not connected with the social and ecological costs their production has caused because these costs get externalized to third parties. From an economic perspective, cost externalities are at the core of the sustainability problem and the reason why a profit-based management strategy does not necessarily lead to sustainable results. With regard to controlling and company decision making, the imperfect representation of ecological and social costs may lead to distortions, especially in sourcing and make-or-buy decisions.

This chapter analyses this particular problem from a controlling perspective by differentiating the multidimensional and environmental cost information according to its causes and its relation to cost objects. On this basis it points out how incomplete information concerning externalized costs leads to decision-making problems, not only downstream but also upstream within a value network. The analysis derives key requirements for an improved accounting scheme. Apart from a proper scope, it finds that strategic (in-)transparencies are key features in ensuring that improved sustainability accounting produces better incentives for cost effectiveness with regard to ecological and social costs, without hampering competition and the economic incentives within value chains.

On the basis of the requirements identified, the chapter examines existing approaches in lifecycle analysis in order to ascertain whether they are suitable as a basis for enhanced sustainability accounting. The existing approaches have been developed to serve the information needs of third parties and not for management information systems. However, it becomes apparent that particular approaches may serve as a basis for developing a management information system for managing sustainability goals within a value chain.

Sustainability controlling as a condition for sustainable management

Although the terms sustainability and sustainable have enjoyed a remarkable career in the language of management and in political discourse since the late 1990s, corporate management on the basis of long-term and non-monetary goals is an important task that is by no means new (Burritt and Schaltegger, 2010; Freedman and Jaggi, 2010). The concept of sustainability originates from an economic and decidedly business-related issue raised by Hans Carl von Carlowitz, mining administrator in the state of Saxony, in his 1713 manuscript *Sylvicultura oeconomica*. He points out that the best long-term results in forest management can be achieved if only as much wood is felled each year as can be regrown through systematic reforestation. With this approach he established the systematic management of forests. Furthermore, the historical example illustrates the close connection between economic, ecological and social aspects. The management strategy described by Hans Carl von Carlowitz ensures the long-term preservation of the forest as a resource, of the socio-economic basis of those employed in forestry and at the following value creation stages (mainly metallurgy), while at the same time representing the long-term profit maximum from the point of view of the aristocratic forest owner.

In an abstract sense, the term sustainability is understood as the management of resources in such a way that the life opportunities of future generations are not unduly restricted. Under the postulate of sustainability the Brundtland Commission (1987) understood not only the need to take account of the interests of future generations (intergenerational justice) but also the need for a global balancing of interests among those living today (intragenerational justice). To flesh out the concept of sustainability even further, a differentiation is usually made on the basis of the three dimensions of sustainability called the triple bottom line (see Henriques and Richardson, 2004 for a comprehensive discussion of the concept; Shnayder *et al*, 2015 for a critique):

- economic sustainability;
- ecological sustainability;
- social sustainability.

The three perspectives are by no means alien to the theory of the firm. While the emphasis on the economic dimension is consistent with the market-based view of the firm (Porter, 1985) and places the focus on the requirements made of product and capital markets, ecological and social goals refer to the resource-based view (Wernerfelt, 1984; Barney *et al*, 2001), which places greater emphasis on suppliers, input materials, employees, etc.

From the point of view of economic theory, the sustainability problem of current management practices, that is the dominance of the economic perspective and the overlooking of ecological and social damage suffered by third parties, can be described as an external effect. In his 1960 essay 'The problem of social cost', Ronald Coase described how imperfections in the market system lead to an inefficient, that is collectively undesirable, level of economic activity. The historical example of a railway company he discusses, which by emitting sparks and hot ash causes damage in the fields of farmers, represents a case of unsustainable activity. The railway line causes environmental damage that is not inflicted on the railway line itself, but on third parties, which is why the railway line has no incentive to avoid it in the absence of appropriate regulation (for example by making changes to the construction of locomotives). Coase advocates a solution to the problem through negotiations, which presupposes clearly defined property rights. The damage issue is solved by including the costs previously externalized to the detriment of others in one's own considerations, that is, by internalizing them.

From a business management point of view, this means that damage to the ecological and social environment should be taken into account in decisions. Sustainable management, that is to say taking account of all three perspectives, results in a multidimensional goal function for management. In addition to financial goals, ecological and social goals also have to be pursued, which can lead to many possible complexities, conflicting aims, problems in the balancing of different positions and contradictions. Decision making becomes more complex.

If controlling is understood as ensuring rationality in corporate management (Weber and Schäffer, 2016; Becker and Ulrich, 2016), then it becomes clear that a stronger focus on sustainability goals does not lessen the need for support in decision making, but, rather, increases it. The addition of ecological and social concerns to the entrepreneurial goal function may relativize the dominance of financial ratios, but by no means the need for rational and inter-subjectively comprehensible decision making. Rather, the balancing of economic goals and other goals requires that the latter are consciously and systematically integrated into corporate management and rendered measurable. This is not a matter of documentation after the fact, but of adopting a forward-looking perspective – a challenge that many current practices in sustainability reporting with its focus on past events do not fulfil (Bennett *et al*, 2013; Taticchi *et al*, 2015; Tillman, 2000). Just as it is not possible to manage a company without defining and controlling for financial targets, it does not seem practicable to dispense with management accounting with regard to social and ecological goals (Vollmar, 2016).

So if sustainability goals are to be taken into account in the management of a company, this means that they must be represented in the management information system (Adams, 2002; Adams and Frost, 2008). There is not only a need for corresponding expectations towards management, but also for effective control possibilities (Thoradeniya *et al*, 2015). Otherwise sustainability goals would remain in the sphere of marketing and public relations, and would therefore be ultimately ineffective.

Relationship to existing management information systems

In order for sustainability goals to be taken into account in decision making, economic, ecological and social indicators have to be linked to the objects of the decisions. This is about attributing economic, ecological or social effects to processes or products. At the same time, sustainability controlling can draw upon pre-existing structures in cost accounting and can adapt and enhance them with regard to the specific characteristics of sustainability dimensions (Gleich *et al*, 2012). The common information systems in companies are traditionally subdivided into cost type accounting, cost centre accounting and cost unit accounting. The first answers the question about the type of cost where an (economic) consumption of resources has occurred. The second type of accounting aggregates this consumption of resources and attributes it to a stage of value creation, while the third type of accounting attributes the consumption of resources to the products of the value creation process (Schweitzer *et al*, 2016).

If the aim of sustainability controlling is to also take account of externalized costs and benefits in business management decisions (van den Bergh, 2010, 2012; Bithas, 2011; Eidelwein *et al*, 2018), this requires relevant information to be available in quantified form and to enter the information systems of management accounting. Externalized costs and services are to be re-internalized with the aid of suitable methods, so that they can be utilized as a basis for decisions. The cost accounting systems common in corporate practice are therefore incomplete in that they only measure the part of the operational, goal-related consumption of resources that affects company assets, either directly (through cash outflows) or indirectly (via accruals). The utilization and consumption of production resources in the possession of third parties, which is also operational (that is to say, is caused by business operations) and goal-related, is not considered in management accounting where such consumption is passed on through externalization. From this perspective, the expansion of cost accounting, through the reintegration of the externalized consumption of resources, in the direction of sustainability-based cost controlling does not so much represent a complete paradigm shift and rupture, but rather the systematic enhancement of the established notions (Günther and Steinke, 2016).

Such a holistic information base made up of economic cost components (ie cost components internalized in the production process) and social and environmental cost items (ie externalized cost components) can form the basis for more efficient coordination decisions which are therefore better from a macroeconomic point of view. Transparency with regard to social and environmental cost components is a necessary requirement so that they can be systematically controlled and reduced and thus become the subject of strategic business decisions. The collection and addition of externalized cost components would provide such environmental cost management with an information basis, which, with regard to the efficiency goal, would not only have to include the costs of one's own value creation stage, but also those of the upstream and downstream stages.

The goal relationships between purely economic cost and revenue accounting and the management of externalized costs can also assume various forms, depending on the situation (Morrison-Saunders and Pope, 2013; Hahn *et al*, 2010). Both goal congruence and goal indifference or goal conflict are possible. Although the first case, where environmental and social improvements go hand-in-hand with the increasing achievement of economic goals, repeatedly receives praise in the literature, it is nevertheless ultimately irrelevant for the conceptualization of sustainability controlling: in the case of goal congruence, the separate controlling of environmental and social goals cannot lead to their better achievement (for the role of goal systems in accounting see Küpper *et al*, 2013). Investments made in additional controlling in itself would therefore have no effect and would, in the final analysis, worsen the degree to which goals are achieved. In this case, only the reporting of environmental and social goals to stakeholders comes into consideration. The matter is different in the case of goal indifference or goal conflict. Here environmental and social controlling can produce added value with regard to better coordination decisions, such as when several alternatives involving different ecological or social damage or benefits are available, but where the economic costs are identical or similar. Particularly in the case of conflict, environmental controlling makes for better decision making as it highlights the ecological and social costs of achieving economic goals, even if these costs can ultimately be passed on to others through externalization. With the aid of such controlling, a company that sets itself social and ecological goals and cements them in its business strategy, for instance, will be in a position to make conscious and informed decisions in this respect.

The problematic nature of cross-company value networks

Information problem in the case of market transactions

An environmental goal function and the existence of sustainability controlling to achieve this goal, however, always leads to problems when decisions are to be taken at or across corporate boundaries. While sustainability goals in internal coordination, that is within the framework of internal, hierarchically structured transaction relations, can be pursued with the aid of multidimensional steering tools, such as a balanced scorecard (Figge *et al*, 2002), this is generally problematic in the case of market transactions with third parties (Balkau and Sonnemann, 2010). Internal coordination allows decisions to be taken on the basis of multidimensional goal functions; the collection and analysis of the information needed for this purpose can be organized within the company. The matter is different in the case of market transactions between two independent companies along the value chain. Input factors are evaluated on the basis of their purchasing price, which includes all economic costs contained in the upstream stages (if not distorted by subsidies). Social and ecological costs, however, are only contained in procurement prices to the extent that they are internalized by means of suitable politico-economic tools (such as the carbon dioxide certificate system). This is not the case in practice, however, apart from a few exceptions. Otherwise the separate pursuit of sustainability goals would also be superfluous as they would automatically result from the profit-maximizing behaviour of those involved, in the case of the full internalization of all social and environmental costs (case of goal congruence, see above).

In a company with a sustainability-based goal function the following problem would therefore arise: while internal processes would be assessed holistically with regard to both their economic and their social and ecological costs, input factors would only enter into the calculation with their economic weights. Their social and ecological cost structure would remain unknown. Sustainable procurement is usually limited to the auditing of production processes, so that the basically multidimensional measurements of burden are reduced to the binary information of whether they are above or below a more or less arbitrary reference value. This loss of information may result in poor decisions and rationality deficits, which will be discussed in detail below. At first, the focus is on more general characteristics of cost information.

Within the value network, the individual stages are similar to cost centres in a company. The problems of allocation can therefore be described in analogy to the structure of cost accounting in a company (for the structures of accounting see Schweitzer *et al*, 2016): an important distinction is whether or not the social and environmental burdens arise with the production of a certain unit of output. If the externalized burdens have the character of overheads, it follows that their allocation to cost units is only possible with the aid of more or less arbitrary assumptions. This inevitably gives rise to the diverse coordination and incentive problems of cost accounting, and also of the sustainability controlling of non-monetary burdens. Since more than three-quarters of the financial costs in modern industrial companies are overheads and cannot therefore be directly related to output, this casts heavy doubt on the relevance of cost accounting for decision making (see for the general problem Miller and Vollmann, 1985; Johnson and Kaplan, 1987; Chan and Suk-Yee Lee, 2003; Terzioglu, 2012; for consequences in supply chains Seuring, 2002). Whether a similar finding also applies to the ecological and social dimensions of resource consumption still needs to be researched empirically. However, it seems plausible that a similar picture would tend to emerge here.

Upstream stages

As explained in the previous paragraph, in cross-company value chains the input factors in accounting are always valued only at economic acquisition costs, while social and ecological externalities from the upstream stages are not taken into consideration. However, in view of the rationality principle, as an economic and fundamental value judgement, this seems problematical in several respects.

First of all, when procurement decisions are taken the ecological and social consumption of resources at the upstream stages is not taken into account when concentrating exclusively on monetary costs. This may entail decisions that are inefficient in terms of sustainability as they are based only on part of the relevant costs. They achieve a level of economic activity that makes microeconomic sense, but is not rational from a macroeconomic point of view as it causes excessive environmental damage. However, this is a classical external effect that is not new from a conceptual point of view (see Coase, 1960).

The matter is similar in the case of make-or-buy decisions, ie when the internal performance of a service is compared with the outsourcing of production stages or processes. In the calculation of a decision-making logic that restricts itself only to economic costs, the costs of the internal provision of a service are compared with the costs of its external purchase. This approach becomes problematic if social and environmental criteria are also used in reaching a decision. A sustainability-based company collects appropriate indicators within the framework of sustainability controlling that, however, can only relate to internal processes. For the alternative of purchasing the service externally, such information is typically not available or not available to the same degree. Consequently, the internal alternative seems too expensive as regards the consumption of resources.

This disincentive in favour of outsourcing, resulting from the inconsistencies of controlling, is intensified by the fact that corporate social responsibility reporting to the company's stakeholders is usually limited to one's own damage creation, while this is not disclosed for supplier partners as they are not part of the company. The systematic outsourcing of those particular parts of the value chain that cause intensive damage consequently improves the environmental and social indicators of one's own company, without actually bringing about a reduction in the consumption of resources.

Therefore information concerning damage creation at the company level without a detailed analysis of value creation depth cannot be interpreted meaningfully. This applies both with regard to a comparison of two companies at the same value creation stage and to the comparison of different periods for one company (intertemporal comparison), which can only show reliable results on the rather unrealistic assumption of an unaltered value creation configuration.

These considerations make it clear that the existing systems of sustainability controlling with regard to value networks are not particularly suitable. Rather, what is needed is an integrated view of the various dimensions of the consumption of ecological and social resources throughout different stages. In the notions of cost accounting, the status quo represents a form of cost centre accounting (being ascertained where environmental damage occurs in the value network) which in itself does not provide sufficient data for the calculation of products and services (as the output of the value network). What is needed is a cost-bearing unit-based view in order to adequately describe the environmental footprints of the products and services. The precondition for such a perspective is that the burdens of a company's input are also evaluated with regard to ecological and social indicators and that this additional information is passed on by the various upstream stages.

Downstream stages

The considerations in the previous section make it clear that the information needed for rational decision making concerning damage creation in the upstream stages has to be passed on to the downstream process stages, just like economic cost information, so that it can be utilized for decision processes at these stages. However, when a dynamic approach is adopted, which means assuming that products and processes change over time, such information is needed not only downstream, but upstream as well.

Assuming that a company can reduce the emission of pollutants at the downstream stages by changing its product, such as through simplified recycling or disposal, this innovation may now come up against higher financial costs or non-monetary expenses at one's own value creation stage. Then a meaningful balancing of options is only possible if information is available for both one's own expenses and for the savings to be made later on. As far as the economic costs are concerned, market processes guarantee corresponding coordination efficiency. If the product can be disposed of at lower cost, higher production costs would be enforceable even with the aid of higher prices if the savings made on disposal outweigh the higher production costs. In the sphere of environmental and social burdens, market coordination does not guarantee this balancing. Why should a company, for instance, emit more carbon dioxide itself (and thus worsen its environmental footprint) if this is counterbalanced by greater savings of emissions elsewhere in the value network?

Approaches in the recycling economy, such as the cradle-to-cradle method, call for the use and recycling of a product to be considered even at the time of its creation or construction, thus proving the necessity of damage creation transparency in both directions of the value chain (Bush *et al*, 2015), which currently, however, is still characterized by manifold information gaps (Boström *et al*, 2015).

Requirements for an integral evaluation system

From accounting to controlling

Unlike an external accounting system, whose primary function is to document business activities and inform stakeholders, controlling has a task that is more closely geared towards the needs of management. As a management information system, the internal accounting system serves to support the central tasks of management, namely 'coordination of enterprise and environment' (Macharzina and Wolf, 2018), through suitable information. The main task of controlling is coordination, which means the alignment of individual decisions towards a common goal (Horváth *et al*, 2015). Moreover, in the conceptualization of Weber and Schäffer (2016) controlling also has the task of ensuring the rationality of corporate management.

Thus, controlling as a task can be located in the overlap between the tasks of managers and controllers (Horváth *et al*, 2015; Becker and Ulrich, 2016). While the manager decides and bears responsibility for the result of decisions, the controller is responsible for transparency. The controller ensures the information basis for decisions and bears responsibility for such decisions being taken rationally. Controlling therefore represents an integrative management support function, requiring a different information basis from external reporting, which primarily focuses on accountability and documentation. In analogy to the systems of cost accounting, criteria will be developed in the following section that must be satisfied by environmental and social information so that it can be used for effective coordination in value networks.

Vertical coverage

Initially, the fundamental question is that of vertical coverage, ie to what depth information from the point of view of the individual company must be available upstream and downstream. The decision-based approach of controlling initially suggests an extension to direct customers and direct suppliers as, typically, it is only with these parties that a company has contractual relationships calling for decisions to be taken. However, in view of the theory of external effects explained at the beginning, this assumption must be called into question with regard to social and ecological criteria. If a company externalizes some of the costs caused by the consumption of resources to the detriment of third parties, this damage creation will not be reflected in transactions with its customers. However, a company lower down the value chain that acts sustainably will want to take account of this external effect in its own procurement decisions. The same approach is also conceivable in the opposite direction with regard to a company's own customers and the uses of the product. Thus it follows that, from an ideal point of view, rational decision making in relation to sustainability aspects is only possible if ecological and social damage creation at all previous and subsequent stages is known. Even if this can justifiably be criticized as a nirvana approach, it nevertheless follows that as much vertical coverage as possible is desirable.

Furthermore, the need for comprehensive documentation of instances of damage creation for sustainability controlling in integrated value chains highlights the necessity of having a standardized information base suitable for different companies and fields of application. Due to the volume of data required, the capture of damage creation data seems prohibitively expensive for individual ad hoc decisions. This is also confirmed by the criticism of many approaches adopted in the lifecycle assessment of environmental burdens.

Breadth of coverage

As regards horizontal coverage, it should be ensured that all relevant external effects, insofar as they are quantifiable, can be represented in the information system. In this sense, sustainability controlling needs to go beyond the requirement of reporting, which is often focused on particular instances of damage creation, such as carbon dioxide or the consumption of water (Gaussin *et al*, 2013 criticize the too narrow focus of lifecycle analysis on carbon footprinting). This is necessary simply because, otherwise, there would be new disincentives to substitute ecological resources whose consumption is measured in the system by those whose consumption is not represented.

Because the effort of collecting data and the complexity of the system increase with each additional dimension that is to be captured in the context of controlling, this is another reason for selecting an approach that is initially limited to the most important dimensions. This corresponds to the well-known principle of materiality in accounting. It may be conceivable, for instance, to focus on greenhouse gases (carbon dioxide, methane, etc), important emissions of pollutants (lead, mercury, etc), volumes of waste and the consumption of water. This question is much more difficult when it comes to social indicators. First of all, sustainable activity in this area is frequently not quantifiable; second, the question of social desirability or undesirability presents itself very differently in many cases (some examples being the participation of women in the labour market or the treatment of social minorities) and is not globally definable across cultural borders.

Moreover, the approach described always assumes linearity in damage creation, which is often not likely to be the case in reality. Very often, toxic substances only become harmful from a certain threshold value, and also in the case of waste water the places where it occurs are probably a major determinant of its harmfulness. The externalization of ecological and social costs usually has a local impact, while viewing them as a whole across the entire value chain suggests the opposite. It is only greenhouse gas emissions that are independent of place and linear, and so they can be regarded in the aggregate, in a similar way to economic costs.

Individual offsetting

A further problem arises when multidimensional instances of damage creation are aggregated in the context of operational decision making and are finally to form a single indicator or score. As a first step, the instances of damage creation in the various dimensions have to be added up. This produces a damage creation vector Vn with m dimensions, m being the number of damaging events captured (breadth) and n being the number of value creation stages taken into account (depth). Here it is to be reminded that this procedure assumes a linearity of damaging events, which is not necessarily so empirically. The implied assumption fails to take account of a possible subadditivity or hyperadditivity of damaging events.

In order to arrive at a one-dimensional result, this vector must now be multiplied by an evaluation vector, also with m dimensions. This evaluation vector expresses the relative ratios of the individual damage dimensions to each other. It must be assumed that this evaluation of the ecological and social burdens is based on subjective values and cannot be generalized.

This dual-level approach is supposed to ensure that the documentation of damage potential and of its evaluation can be logically separated from one another. In this way, the controlling system itself remains free of value judgements and open for the different preferences of its users. Consequently, the companies participating in the value network do not need to agree in advance on common evaluation benchmarks. In this way, the information gathered can be evaluated and processed further in different ways for different contexts.

Fixed and variable elements

As a management information system, sustainability controlling in integrated value chains is to serve as a basis for decisions. Unlike reporting systems aimed at external addressees, its benefit lies not in the documentation of past events, but, rather, in the shaping of future events. Consequently, a major quality issue is the relevance for decision making of the information contained. In each decision-making situation it must be clearly evident which environmental and social burdens could be influenced by the decision to be taken.

The following example illustrates the problem this involves. A company would like to make a procurement decision and thus compares various alternatives from the point of view of their ecological footprint, in accordance with the addition and evaluation logic that has been described. The result suggests that the choice of alternative A involves a certain amount of emissions that would be absent in the case of a decision taken against A. The total damage creation would be implicitly treated as variable costs. This assumption seems highly problematic in view of the reality faced in business. While it seems possible and realistic to differentiate according to fixed and variable elements in one's own company, this distinction would be lost when adding them up along the value chain.

This problem is known from cost accounting systems in other contexts. Hence, transfer prices, for instance, which are used to coordinate transactions within a corporate structure, also suggest that costs are variable, from the point of view of the procuring company, but such variability does not in fact exist if the group is regarded as a whole (Weber and Schäffer, 2016; Schweitzer *et al*, 2016). This phenomenon can be described as a contamination of cost structures. The problem can be solved by always quoting the proportion of fixed costs contained or passed on in each transfer price. In this way, it can always be ascertained which part of the costs can be influenced and which part cannot, and also at subsequent points in the value creation process.

A similar procedure also seems necessary for sustainability controlling in integrated value chains as otherwise, in a similar way to the transfer price problem in a corporate structure, false implications would be generated concerning the possibility of influencing the ecological and social indicators. Each indicator must always be shown on every level as having a fixed and a variable part. This requirement arises because controlling focuses on decision making, unlike the documentation function of reporting approaches.

The problem of (in)transparency

For an informed observer, comprehensive information concerning the harmful substances and environmental pollution released at a particular value creation stage allows conclusions to be drawn concerning the production process selected. Together with further information in the public domain, such as information gleaned from annual financial statements or reports in the media, it might also be possible to identify individual companies in this way. This presents no problem in relation to first-level suppliers and customers, as they are the direct business partners of the observing company. The connection between depth of coverage and informational content, however, makes it possible to identify suppliers and customers of the second level and higher.

This can be problematic from the point of view of competition and it induces companies to opt out of integrated sustainability controlling (Egels-Zandén *et al*, 2015; Mol, 2015). Thus, a trading or manufacturing company would disclose its suppliers to its customers, which is likely to be disadvantageous in price negotiations, for instance. From the point of view of the individual company, these disadvantages could quickly outweigh the benefits that the company itself can gain for itself by participating in a corresponding information network. Therefore, there is a need for targeted mechanisms to manage the issue of intransparency and with which it can be ensured that only as much information as is necessary is made available in each case.

Consequently, it would be conceivable for enquiring companies to be informed about environmental burdens at higher or subsequent stages in the value chain not individually, stage by stage, but only as an aggregate, however differentiated according to fixed and variable elements. This aggregate could then be weighted with the aid of the company's own evaluation vector and play a role in decision making.

The need for intransparency on the one hand and for valid and verifiable data volumes on the other produces a tension that is not so easily resolved. Rather, it should be examined which structures and systems of data storage can guarantee the integrity of the stored contents while at the same time allowing calculated intransparency. Whether blockchain technology can be utilized in this field of application is an open question that should be researched. Conceptual studies already exist regarding the application possibilities and limits of this technology in classical financial accounting and can serve as a basis here (eg Dai and Vasarhelyi, 2017; Fanning and Centers, 2016; Kokina *et al*, 2017; Scott *et al*, 2017).

Suitability of existing approaches in lifecycle assessments

Adaptation and redefinition

The aim of including environmental and social burdens in controlling decisions in value chains calls for an information system that meets the requirements outlined above. The construction of a completely new system of this type does not seem particularly practicable for two reasons. First of all, the volume of investment needed to assemble such a large information base is prohibitively high, especially in view of the fact that the benefit of the system would not become apparent until a sufficient breadth and depth of coverage had been achieved. Second, the academic debate concerning lifecycle assessments and lifecycle analyses abounds with pre-existing theoretical concepts (for an overview see Guinée *et al*, 2011), while an integrated perspective for business practice tends to be missing.

For these reasons the following sections will evaluate pre-existing concepts from the lifecycle assessment with regard to their usefulness and development potential for controlling purposes in integrated value chains. The approach of building up on existing data and preparing and purposefully adapting it for use in operational decision-making situations is by no means alien to controlling. Financial controlling in companies is also usually based on bookkeeping data that is recoded into cost and revenue indicators for purposes of management control. Common controlling concepts, such as value-based management, have emerged as further developments of external accounting. Here, too, the range of reporting tools developed with regard to external parties was extended in order to support decision making (Chen and Dodd, 1997; Grant, 2003).

However, what all approaches discussed below have in common is that they fail to differentiate between fixed and variable emission components. This is in keeping with their purpose, which is to serve as information tools for external parties, but it limits the extent to which the data can be used for management decisions. Furthermore, they lack the element of calculated intransparency for different user groups, which can also be explained by the fact that the addressees in mind are the general public. Consequently, all reporting methods have to be supplemented in the light of these two criteria in order to render them useful for internal decisions.

One-dimensional approaches: Carbon footprint and virtual water

With the carbon footprint and the measurement of water consumption we already have two one-dimensional concepts that have also found manifold application in value chains. The carbon footprint is an indicator for the volume of greenhouse gases emitted through economic activity. Its use is directly connected with climate protection goals, such as the limitation of global warming to 2 degrees centigrade. The concept of the carbon footprint was developed by Wackernagel and Rees (Rees *et al*, 1996), and since then has found manifold application, especially with regard to a product's complete lifecycle. So, starting with the manufacture of preliminary products and raw materials and ending with disposal, it includes all emissions associated with the reference product. The concept's vertical depth of coverage therefore meets all requirements in order to be used for controlling purposes. In addition to carbon dioxide, its horizontal coverage also includes other greenhouse gases that are converted into carbon dioxide in accordance with predefined equivalence numbers. This means that this approach is limited to greenhouse gases and is therefore too narrow, on the one hand, while allowing no company-specific weighting on the other. However, this would be necessary at the latest when the concept is broadened to include other indicators that have nothing to do with climate protection.

The consumption of virtual water is calculated in a very similar way. In terms of its horizontal coverage, the method is restricted to the use of water and originates from Allan (1998). In terms of its vertical coverage, all water consumed during production, including the upstream process stages, is taken into account but not usually during the use and disposal of a product. Due to the one-dimensionality of the concept, there is no evaluation problem; the breadth and depth of coverage indicate that the concept would be of use in a controlling context. A weakness of this approach, however, is in the assumption of linearity discussed above. First, the problem of high water consumption, in particular, differs from region to region and depends on the scarcity of water; and second, water contamination is mainly due to harmful substances discharged into the water and not to the volume of service water in which they are more or less diluted. In general, it can be said that the carbon footprint and virtual water in themselves do not provide a sufficient basis for sustainability controlling in value chains, but they are nevertheless two important dimensions of the same.

Eco-indicator 99

The Eco-indicator was developed for the Dutch Ministry of Housing, Spatial Planning and the Environment. It is intended to represent environmental damage throughout a product's entire lifecycle (see Goedkoop and Spriensma, 2001; Vogtländer *et al*, 2001). It was specifically created for use in product management (integrated product policy, IPP), and thus for management decisions. Vertically, the indicator covers a product's entire lifecycle and consequently includes its use and disposal.

Horizontally, the indicator describes three categories of damage: the category 'human health' shows the impact on the health of present and future generations on the basis of disability adjusted life years and therefore includes years lost due to premature death as well as years impaired by illness. The category 'ecosystem quality' is supposed to indicate how heavily biodiversity is impaired and covers many influencing factors (toxins, land usage and so on). The category 'resource reserves' refers to the consumption of natural resources and fossil fuels. The breadth of coverage can therefore be easily linked with the sustainability concept of the triple bottom line as the impacts on human beings, the environment and economic resources are considered to the same degree.

The Eco-indicator compresses the damage categories with their varying dimensions with the aid of weighting factors to form an aggregate measure that lacks dimensions. This is done on the basis of expert estimates, presuming the ecological conditions prevalent in Europe. An individual evaluation by the company applying it is not therefore possible and it is probably doubtful whether it can be used outside Europe. The fact that the approach lacks international proliferation would suggest that it is unsuitable for such use.

The CML method

The CML method for carrying out lifecycle assessments was developed at the Centrum voor Milieukunde (CML), Leiden University, by Heijungs *et al* (1992), and it has been repeatedly revised since then (for an overview see Guinée *et al*, 2011). The aim is to gain a quantitative picture of all direct material and energetic interactions between the natural environment and the product system. The vertical depth of coverage covers a product's entire lifecycle, including application and disposal, and can therefore be regarded as sufficient. In horizontal terms the CML method comprises nine damage categories: the exhaustion of abiotic resources, the greenhouse effect, the depletion of the ozone layer, human toxicity, aquatic ecotoxicity, terrestrial ecotoxicity, the formation of photooxidants, the acidification potential and the nutrification potential. The breadth of coverage thus includes indicators of all three dimensions of sustainability.

As regards the offsetting of the indicators with their different dimensions, the CML method suggests a two-stage approach. Within the damage categories, the various harmful substances are aggregated with the aid of predetermined equivalence numbers based on the assessment of experts. In principle, the weighting of the nine damage categories against each other can be freely selected in the second step. Here the literature suggests focusing on threshold values (as proposed by Schaltegger and Sturm, 1994), the determining of the weighting factors by a panel of experts or taking political targets as a basis. The suggestion of engaging a panel of experts seems to make sense with regard to strategic entrepreneurial considerations, as this offers scope for the integration of company-individual weighting and sustainability goals.

Critical volumes

The method of using critical volumes to determine and compare ecological damage creation originates from an approach taken by the Swiss Federal Office for the Environment (FOEN) (Günther, 2008; Hofstetter and Braunschweig, 1994). This approach does not take account of the social dimension of sustainability and subdivides ecology into three areas: air, water and the soil. Emission volumes of various harmful substances are converted into correspondingly contaminated volumes of air, water and soil with the aid of statutory threshold values which, taken by themselves, can be added up. The result does not indicate the volume actually contaminated for each absorption medium (possibly going beyond the threshold value or also by various harmful substances simultaneously), but only the theoretical critical volumes where each medium is only contaminated with a single harmful substance, concentrated at the threshold level.

In terms of vertical coverage, the critical volume method meets the requirements outlined at the beginning as it can be applied across the entire value chain. The breadth of coverage is limited to the ecological sustainability dimension and here merely captures harmful emissions in a narrower sense, but not emissions of carbon dioxide, because it is not a toxic substance. The method also seems problematic with regard to the possibility of individually offsetting instances of damage creation because threshold values vary from region to region and cannot ultimately deliver a relative comparison of the harmfulness of individual substances.

Method of the Federal Environment Agency

The method used by the German Environment Agency (UBA) for lifecycle assessments is an approach used primarily in Germany. It is used for making lifecycle assessments for products, processes and services or for entire companies (Schmitz and Paulini, 1999). The vertical coverage of the method is variable (cradle to gate) and can be extended step by step. In horizontal terms, the approach is suitable for all categories of environmental damage.

Within each category to be defined (such as the greenhouse effect) different impact indicators are measured which are standardized and added up in the various categories on the basis of equivalence numbers. In this way, a one-dimensional ratio is achieved in each category, the impact indicator.

For the process or the product under observation, this generates a resultant vector containing the multi-dimensional indicator results. The amalgamation of the individual dimensions in an abstract resultant value is not generally intended, but approaches exist for the relative comparison of various alternatives on the basis of relative additional burdens in the individual dimensions. Furthermore, the various dimensions are given different qualitative priorities.

The basic openness of the process with regard to the evaluation and offsetting of multidimensional burdens appears as an advantage from the point of view of its use for controlling purposes, but it increases complexity when used on company level. A positive feature to be emphasized is also the procedure that, in comparison with other methods, is more strongly geared towards its relevance for decision making instead of having a documentation purpose. The evaluation methods are designed for questions concerning the selection of products or processes. However, they too fail to take account of the problem of the relevance for decision making of certain instances of damage creation, as there is no differentiation between components that can be influenced (variable) and those that cannot be influenced (fixed).

Method of the European Commission Joint Research Centre (EU-JRC)

The European Commission operates a European Platform on Life Cycle Assessment as a Joint Research Centre. With its International Reference Life Cycle Data System, this institution provides a data basis for the performance of lifecycle assessments and, in the context of the Single Market for Green Products Initiative, is driving forward the standardization of methods for the calculation of the ecological footprint of products and companies (European Commission, 2019). The approach adopted by the EU-JRC is multidimensional and, in addition to numerous dimensions of ecological damage, also takes account of many social aspects (such as toxicity for humans) and economic categories (such as the consumption of fossil resources), albeit that the environmental indicators dominate (European Commission, 2010). Consequently, its horizontal breadth of coverage goes slightly beyond the ecological dimension, but without adopting a genuinely holistic perspective. As regards the depth of coverage, the approach is broadly defined, that is to say it generally includes all stages of the value chain.

The weighting and aggregation of the damage categories with their multi-dimensional definition receives detailed attention in the approach of EU-JRC. Here the methodology not only allows different evaluation approaches, but also supports their application by providing appropriate data. In addition to normative approaches based on threshold values, survey-based approaches with the aid of stakeholder or expert opinions, evaluations concerning monetary equivalents (such as willingness to pay, damage costs, etc) and combined metamodels are also possible (Sala *et al*, 2018). In this respect, the method of the EU-JRC offers the broadest basis for taking account of individual ethical preferences when used in a corporate context.

Conclusion and research programme

These considerations have made it clear that responsible behaviour with regard to environmental and social goals requires an effective system of sustainability controlling in a company. While many relevant methods and approaches are already established for this purpose, these run up against their conceptual limits when taking a holistic view of value networks. In the chapter it has been argued that this is an inevitable consequence of market coordination because in markets the price – and therefore an exclusively economic indicator – serves as a coordination tool, in contrast to hierarchically structured, internal coordination alternatives. Consequently, an integrated value chain whose individual links are connected through market transactions inevitably fails to establish consistent environmental and social goals, unless this shortcoming is compensated for by controlling system across the entire value chain.

The chapter has described specific requirements and application conditions under which sustainability controlling for integrated value chains can meaningfully add environmental and social dimensions to the economic costs. As necessary features it has identified horizontal and vertical coverage, the possibility of individual evaluation systems, differentiation according to fixed and variable impact components with regard to concrete decision-making situations and also the possibility of strategic (in)transparency.

The chapter then went on to discuss to what extent pre-existing approaches and methodologies used in lifecycle assessments can be utilized for the purposes of a management information system in value chains. This approach not only seems advisable in view of the plethora of pre-existing methods and the huge practical effort of collecting data, but in some ways reflects a basic pattern in the development of controlling. Historically, the decision-oriented systems of operational cost accounting were also developed by building up on pre-existing systems in bookkeeping and external accounting, which had proved to be of limited suitability for decision making. Of the approaches discussed, the CML method and the EU-JRC model look the most promising. What both approaches have in common is a broad coverage and openness for subjective value benchmarks. However, what speaks against their use in entrepreneurial decision-making situations is that, first, the approaches fail to distinguish between fixed and variable damage creation and, second, they do not provide for calculated intransparency. Both of these shortcomings follow from the fact that these approaches were designed as accounting and documentation tools, for which the two distinctions are not relevant. This, again, seems to be a common pattern in the history of managerial accounting.

Consequently, future research projects should consider how far the CML method or the EU-JCR model could be developed into a controlling tool. On the basis of case studies and experimental fields of application it should be examined to what extent the approach outlined here, when used under real business conditions, can generate useful information that can be of assistance in controlling a value network with regard to sustainability goals. The need for such an information system is obvious when considering the growing ecological and social burdens and the increasing economic interdependence of worldwide supply chains.

References

Adams, CA (2002) Internal organisational factors influencing corporate social and ethical reporting, *Accounting, Auditing and Accountability Journal*, **15** (2), pp 223–50

Adams, CA and Frost, GR (2008) Integrating sustainability reporting into management practices, *Accounting Forum*, **32** (4), pp 288–302

Allan, JA (1998) Virtual water: A strategic resource, *Ground Water*, **36** (4), pp 545–47

Balkau, F and Sonnemann, G (2010) Managing sustainability performance through the value-chain, *Corporate Governance: The international journal of business in society*, **10** (1), pp 46–58

Barney, J, Wright, M and Ketchen, DJ (2001) The resource-based view of the firm: Ten years after 1991, *Journal of Management*, **27** (6), pp 625–41

Becker, W and Ulrich, P (eds) (2016) *Handbuch Controlling*, Springer, Wiesbaden

Bennett, M, Schaltegger, S and Zvezdov, D (2013) *Exploring Corporate Practices in Management Accounting for Sustainability*, Institute for Chartered Accountants of England and Wales (ICAEW), London

Bithas, K (2011) Sustainability and externalities: Is the internalization of externalities a sufficient condition for sustainability? *Ecological Economics*, **70** (10), pp 1703–06

Boström, M, Jönsson, AM, Lockie, S, Mol, APJ and Oosterveer, P (2015) Sustainable and responsible supply chain governance: Challenges and opportunities, *Journal of Cleaner Production*, **107**, pp 1–7

Brundtland, GH (1987) Our common future: Call for action, *Environmental Conservation*, **14** (4), pp 291–94

Burritt, RL and Schaltegger, S (2010) Sustainability accounting and reporting: Fad or trend?, *Accounting, Auditing and Accountability Journal*, **23** (7), pp 829–46

Bush, SR, Oosterveer, P, Bailey, M and Mol, APJ (2015) Sustainability governance of chains and networks: A review and future outlook, *Journal of Cleaner Production*, **107**, pp 8–19

Chan, SY and Suk-Yee Lee, D (2003) An empirical investigation of symptoms of obsolete costing systems and overhead cost structure, *Managerial Auditing Journal*, **18** (2), pp 81–89

Chen, S and Dodd, JL (1997) Economic Value Added (EVA™): An empirical examination of a new corporate performance measure, *Journal of Managerial Issues*, **9** (3), p 318

Coase, RH (1960) The problem of social cost, *The Journal of Law and Economics*, **3**, pp 1–44

Dai, J and Vasarhelyi, MA (2017) Toward blockchain-based accounting and assurance, *Journal of Information Systems*, **31** (3), pp 5–21

Egels-Zandén, N, Hulthén, K and Wulff, G (2015) Trade-offs in supply chain transparency: The case of Nudie Jeans Co, *Journal of Cleaner Production*, **107**, pp 95–104

Eidelwein, F, Collatto, DC, Rodrigues, LH, Lacerda, DP and Piran, FS (2018) Internalization of environmental externalities: Development of a method for elaborating the statement of economic and environmental results, *Journal of Cleaner Production*, **170**, pp 1316–27

European Commission (2010) *International Reference Life Cycle Data System (ILCD) Handbook: General guide for life cycle assessment – provisions and action steps, EUR – Scientific and Technical Research Reports*, Publications Office of the European Union, Luxembourg

European Commission (2019) [accessed 23 September 2020] Single market for green products: The Product Environmental Footprint Pilots [Online] https://ec.europa.eu/environment/eussd/smgp/ef_pilots.htm (archived at https://perma.cc/AC3S-ZBST)

Fanning, K and Centers, DP (2016) Blockchain and its coming impact on financial services, *Journal of Corporate Accounting and Finance*, **27** (5), pp 53–57

Figge, F, Hahn, T, Schaltegger, S and Wagner, M (2002) The Sustainability Balanced Scorecard: Linking sustainability management to business strategy, *Business Strategy and the Environment*, **11** (5), pp 269–84

Freedman, M and Jaggi, B (eds) (2010) *Sustainability, Environmental Performance and Disclosures: Advances in environmental accounting and management*, vol 4, Emerald, Bingley

Gaussin, M, Hu, G, Abolghasem, S, Basu, S, Shankar, MR and Bidanda, B (2013) Assessing the environmental footprint of manufactured products: A survey of current literature, *International Journal of Production Economics*, **146** (2), pp 515–23

Gleich, R, Bartels, P and Breisig, V (Eds) (2012) *Nachhaltigkeitscontrolling: Konzepte, Instrumente und Fallbeispiele zur Umsetzung*, Haufe, Freiburg, München

Goedkoop, MJ and Spriensma, R (2001) *The Eco-Indicator 99: A damage oriented method for life cycle impact assessment – Methodology report*, 3rd edn, Pre Consultants, Amersfoort

Grant, JL (2003) *Foundations of Economic Value Added*, 2nd edn, Wiley, New Hope

Guinée, JB, Heijungs, R, Huppes, G, Zamagni, A, Masoni, P, Buonamici, R, Ekvall, T and Rydberg, T (2011) Life cycle assessment: Past, present, and future, *Environmental Science and Technology*, **45** (1), pp 90–96

Günther, E (2008) *Ökologieorientiertes Management*, Lucius & Lucius, Stuttgart

Günther, E and Steinke, K-H (2016) *CSR und Controlling: Unternehmerische Verantwortung als Gestaltungsaufgabe des Controlling, Management-Reihe Corporate Social Responsibility*, Springer Gabler, Berlin, Heidelberg

Hahn, T, Figge, F, Pinkse, J and Preuss, L (2010) Trade-offs in corporate sustainability: You can't have your cake and eat it, *Business Strategy and the Environment*, **19** (4), pp 217–29

Heijungs, R, Guinée, JB, Huppes, G, Lankreijer, RM, Udo de Haes, HA, Wegener Sleeswijk, A, Ansems, AMM, Eggels, PG, van Duin, R and Goede, HP de (1992) *Environmental Life Cycle Assessment of Products: Guide and backgrounds*, CML, Leiden

Henriques, A and Richardson, J (eds) (2004) *The Triple Bottom Line: Does it all add up?* Routledge, London

Hofstetter, P and Braunschweig, A (1994) Bewertungsmethoden in Ökobilanzen – ein Überblick, *GAIA – Ecological Perspectives for Science and Society*, **3** (4), pp 227–36

Horváth, P, Gleich, R and Seiter, M (2015) *Controlling*, 13th edn, Franz Vahlen, München

Johnson, TH and Kaplan, RS (1987) *Relevance Lost: The rise and fall of management accounting*, Harvard Business School Press, Cambridge

Kokina, J, Mancha, R and Pachamanova, D (2017) Blockchain: Emergent industry adoption and implications for accounting, *Journal of Emerging Technologies in Accounting*, **14** (2), pp 91–100

Küpper, H-U, Friedl, G, Hofmann, C, Hofmann, Y and Pedell, B (2013) *Controlling: Konzeption, Aufgaben, Instrumente*, 6th edn, Schäffer-Poeschel Verlag, Stuttgart

Macharzina, K and Wolf, J (2018) *Unternehmensführung: Das internationale Managementwissen: Konzepte – Methoden – Praxis*, 10th edn, Springer Gabler, Wiesbaden

Miller, JG and Vollmann, TE (1985) The hidden factory, *Havard Business Review*, **63** (5), pp 142–50

Mol, APJ (2015) Transparency and value chain sustainability, *Journal of Cleaner Production*, **107**, pp 154–61

Morrison-Saunders, A and Pope, J (2013) Conceptualising and managing trade-offs in sustainability assessment, *Environmental Impact Assessment Review*, **38**, pp 54–63

Porter, ME (1985) *Competitive Advantage: Creating and sustaining superior performance*, The Free Press, New York

Rees, W, Wackernagel, M and Testemale, P (1996) *Our Ecological Footprint: Reducing human impact on the earth*, New Society Publishers, Gabriola Island

Sala, S, Cerutti, AK and Pant, R (2018) *Development of a Weighting Approach for the Environmental Footprint*, Publications Office of the European Union, Luxembourg

Schaltegger, S and Sturm, A (1994) *Ökologieorientierte Entscheidungen in Unternehmen: Ökologisches Rechnungswesen statt Ökobilanzierung: Notwendigkeit, Kriterien, Konzepte*, Zugl: Basel, Univ, Diss S Schaltegger, A Sturm, 1992, *Schriftenreihe des Instituts für Betriebswirtschaft, Wirtschaftswissenschaftliches Zentrum der Universität Basel*, vol 27, 2nd edn, Haupt, Bern

Schmitz, S and Paulini, I (1999) *Bewertung in Ökobilanzen: Methode des Umweltbundesamtes zur Normierung von Wirkungsindikatoren, Ordnung (Rangbildung) von Wirkungskategorien und zur Auswertung nach ISO 14042 und 14043; Version99*, Umweltbundesamt, Berlin

Schweitzer, M, Küpper, H-U, Friedl, G, Hofmann, C and Pedell, B (2016) *Systeme der Kosten- und Erlösrechnung, Vahlens Handbücher*, 11th edn, Vahlen, München

Scott, B, Loonam, J and Kumar, V (2017) Exploring the rise of blockchain technology: Towards distributed collaborative organizations, *Strategic Change*, **26** (5), pp 423–28

Seuring, S (2002) Supply chain costing: A conceptual framework, in *Cost Management in Supply Chains*, ed S Seuring and M Goldbach, Physica-Verlag, Heidelberg

Shnayder, L, van Rijnsoever, FJ and Hekkert, MP (2015) Putting your money where your mouth is: Why sustainability reporting based on the triple bottom line can be misleading, *PloS one*, **10** (3), e0119036

Taticchi, P, Garengo, P, Nudurupati, SS, Tonelli, F and Pasqualino, R (2015) A review of decision-support tools and performance measurement and sustainable supply chain management, *International Journal of Production Research*, **53** (21), pp 6473–94

Terzioglu, B (2012) Intricacies of overhead cost allocations and distortion in costing: A synthesis of the literature, *Asia-Pacific Management Accounting Journal*, **7** (1), pp 115–39

Thoradeniya, P, Lee, J, Tan, R and Ferreira, A (2015) Sustainability reporting and the theory of planned behaviour, *Accounting, Auditing and Accountability Journal*, **28** (7), pp 1099–137

Tillman, A-M (2000) Significance of decision-making for LCA methodology, *Environmental Impact Assessment Review*, **20** (1), pp 113–23

van den Bergh, JCJM (2010) Externality or sustainability economics? *Ecological Economics*, **69** (11), pp 2047–52

van den Bergh, JCJM (2012) What is wrong with externality? *Ecological Economics*, **74**, pp 1–2

Vogtländer, JG, Brezet, HC and Hendriks, CF (2001) The virtual eco-costs 99: A single LCA-based indicator for sustainability and the eco-costs-value ratio (EVR) model for economic allocation, *The International Journal of Life Cycle Assessment*, **6** (3), pp 157–66

Vollmar, BH (2016) Controlling und Nachhaltigkeit, in *Handbuch Controlling*, ed W Becker and P Ulrich, vol 11, Springer, Wiesbaden, pp 797–833

von Carlowitz, HC (1713) *Sylvicultura Oeconomica, oder haußwirthliche Nachricht und naturmässige Anweisung zur wilden Baumzucht*, Johann Friedrich Braun, Leipzig

Weber, J and Schäffer, U (2016) *Einführung in das Controlling*, 15th edn, Schäffer-Poeschel, Stuttgart

Wernerfelt, B (1984) A resource-based view of the firm, *Strategic Management Journal*, **5** (2), pp 171–80

Measuring diversity among competing supply-value chains 07

KRISTAN A SCHNEIDER

Abstract

Porter's value chain, introduced in the 1980s, emerged as a powerful analysis tool for strategic planning that soon acted as a catalyst facilitating international investment and trade. Rather than merely considering added values, it engaged in identifying added values of particularly profitable specific activities. While comparison of two alternative supply chains (of eg competing businesses) is quite straightforward, identifying profitable business models within the plethora of competing supply chains is much more complex. In this chapter, a quantitative approach to compare value chains is proposed. Namely, a continuum of statistical indices describing the diversity among supply chains within and across various strata (eg, different company structures, or company size) has the potential to support strategic planning by identifying, eg, profitable business activities or activities compatible with corporate social responsibility (CSR). More precisely, the indices define diversity curves for supply-value chains within Porter's framework. Visual inspection of diversity curves allows successful business models to be determined. This particularly includes alternative approaches that yield higher value for buyers by, eg, encouraging CSR. The focus of this work is the precise mathematical formulation and properties of diversity curves, which contain various indices used across scientific disciplines including econometrics, political sciences, ecology, or genetics as special instances. The approach is illustrated by hypothetical examples. The concept of measuring diversity is in general not restricted to value chain analysis.

Introduction

A business's leverage over its competitors is known as competitive advantage. Ultimately, a firm is only profitable if its total revenue exceeds the costs of creating products. Hence, the goal of any generic strategy must be the creation of values for buyers in excess of production costs (cf Porter, 1996). However, competitive advantage is not just increased by providing equivalent value for lower costs, but also by providing better value for equivalent costs (eg, Urbig, 2003). Indeed, firms are often willing to raise their costs to command premium prices via differentiation (Porter, 1985). For instance, in the production of fair-trade products higher commodity prices are accepted to charge premium prices (Nicholls and Opal, 2005). Michael Porter advocated that competitive advantage cannot be understood by looking at a firm as a whole, because it stems from many discrete activities performed by that firm. This reasoning led to the concept of the value chain, first defined in Porter (1985) (cf Porter, 1996).

Since its introduction, the concept of value chains – with several generalizations and extensions – has flourished as a powerful tool for strategic planning. Importantly, the value-chain concept has been extended beyond the level of individual firms. Particularly, the concept of global value chains, describing activities involved in the production of goods and services, which are coordinated across countries, was emphasized in the 1990s and facilitated international investment and trade. The analysis of global value chains to facilitate sustainable enterprise development in the context of CSR is of particular importance and became the mainstream practice of international business. Rather than just looking at the difference between revenue and costs, the value chain aims to display the total value projected to value activities and margin. Porter (1985) emphasized a firm's activity in a business unit as the relevant level of constructing a value chain, by arguing that industry- or sector-wide approaches are too broad and might obscure important sources of competitive advantage. However, on a sector- or industry-wide level, competing value chains can be contrasted to discover the potential to increase competitive advantage – either by increasing operational effectiveness or by strategic positioning (cf Porter, 1996).

Naturally, the concept of value chains has a prominent role in the field of strategic management. While analyses of value chains tend to be qualitative, complementing quantitative tools to sustain decision support and strategic management decisions are desirable to facilitate optimization with regard to reducing costs, increasing value for buyers, or ecological sustainability. Here, a method to quantify individual values chains and contrast competing ones is emphasized. The method is based on diversity measures or indices used across many scientific disciplines. More precisely, our approach adopts the concept of species diversity introduced by Whittaker (1960) in the field of species ecology.

The idea underlying the diversity measures introduced by Whittaker (1960) is to consider the total species diversity within a landscape (termed γ-diversity) as being determined by the mean diversity in smaller habitats (α-diversity) and a residual component (β-diversity), interpreted as the amount of differentiation between habitats. Several competing diversity measures exist in the literature (cf Jost, 2006, for a comprehensive review), which were all criticized due to their shortcomings (cf Jost, 2007, 2008). Importantly, these shortcomings are compensated for in the approach advocated here.

The basic concepts supporting diversity measures have been circulating for several decades and were transferred to or originated independently in other disciplines including genetics, econometrics, sociology and political sciences. In essence, diversity measures are summary statistics that attempt to capture the characteristics of distributions over discrete entities. The Simpson index (Simpson, 1949) was introduced to describe biodiversity by measuring the relative abundance of distinct species in a community. In genetics this statistic is known as heterozygosity and corresponds to the probability of observing heterozygous individuals in a population under the assumption of random mating (cf Hartl and Clark, 1997). In social sciences, the inverse Simpson index was introduced as the effective number of political parties by Laakso and Taagepera (1979). The Herfindahl-Hirschman index (Hirschman, 1964) is a related measure for the amount of competition between firms within an industry. The Shannon entropy is another popular measure, originally derived in the context of information theory (Shannon, 1948). It is closely related to the Theil index (Theil, 1965), a popular index for economic inequality (cf Shorrocks, 1984), which was applied in social sciences to measure segregation (Hutchens 2004). The reason for the relatedness of all these statistics is described in Hill (1973), where a continuum of diversity measures is established that contains popular measures as special instances.

Here, the definition of Hill (1973) is combined with the approach of Whittaker (1960) to partition diversity into three components and applied to value chains within the framework of Porter's model. Namely, by regarding value chains as a discrete distribution of discrete activities, they appropriately fit in the scope of diversity measures, facilitating a quantitative approach for value chain analysis. The essence of the methodology introduced here is to consider diversity not as point measures but as a continuum of measures, according to Hill (1973).

This chapter does not attempt to provide a comprehensive framework or guidelines for comparisons between value chains. It seeks to introduce a generic quantitative framework and attempts to stimulate future fundamental research in value chain analysis. The work exemplifies how Porter's model can be employed to quantify and compare value chains. A graphical approach based on quantitative measures is proposed with the potential to complement value chain analysis. Although the description in the chapter focuses on the cost distribution of comparable value chains as an example, the approach per se can be adapted to more general situations or different foci of value chain analysis.

The next section shows how the concept of diversity measures is adapted for a single value chain. The concept is then extended to compare value chains. The correct interpretation of results is exemplified. While the description is based on hypothetical examples with a simple interpretation, the methodology is not restricted to such simple applications. The discussion is devoted to alternative interpretations and applications.

Diversity curves within Porter's model

The backbone of Porter's model is to consider a process of manufacturing goods or creating services as an organizational system, constituting of subsystems, each with inputs, transformation processes, and outputs. The generic model divides activities into primary and secondary activities (see Figure 7.1).

Porter's framework provides a means to project the costs of manufacturing a product (physical or virtual) on a set of pre-specified primary and secondary activities. (In the examples, the margin, which can easily be included, is not considered.) For this purpose, let C be the total costs needed to manufacture a product. Let p_i be the proportion of the total costs needed for activity i. By default, these activities are the five primary activities (i) inbound logistics, (ii) operations, (iii) outbound logistics, (iv) marketing and

Figure 7.1 Illustration of Porter's value chain model

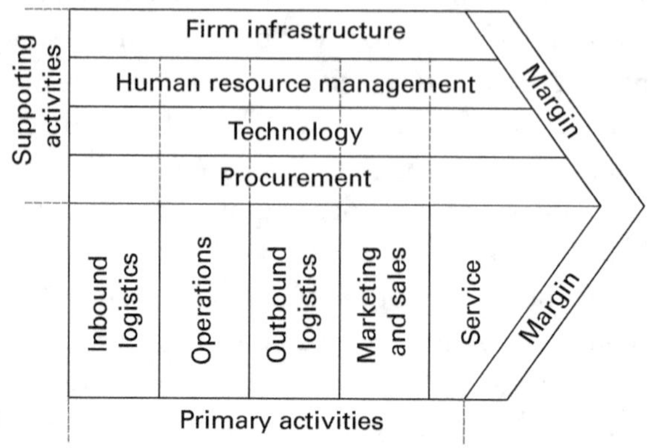

sales, and (v) service as well as the secondary activities (vi) firm infrastructure, (vii) human resource management, (viii) technology, and (ix) procurement, amounting to nine core activities (cf Figure 7.1). Notably, additional activities can be introduced at a finer level of granularity if appropriate and not all activities need to be considered. Indeed, in some cases it might be appropriate to single out certain primary or secondary activities. As the number of considered activities depends on the concrete application, it is generically denoted by n. Thus, Cp_i are the costs of activity i. In mathematical terms the proportions p_i composes a discrete probability distribution, satisfying $\sum_{i=1}^{n} p_i = 1$. Jointly, the vector of proportions is denoted by $\boldsymbol{p} = (p_1, \ldots, p_n)$. The frequency distribution $\boldsymbol{p}$ quantifies how predefined activities in the production process amount to the total manufacturing costs.

Clearly, in practice it is the specific internal accounting scheme that attributes the accruing costs to the proper activities. Consequently, it will be crucial to decide on a well-defined accounting scheme when quantitatively comparing different value chains. With such an accounting scheme in place, the distribution of costs over the set of activities can be employed as a means to compare value chains. While such an endeavour is straightforward for two value chains with a limited number of activities, it becomes less obvious when comparing several value chains, changes in a particular value chain on temporal and spatial scales, or value chains with a complex fine grid of activities. Naturally, the distribution of costs over the particular activities is not uniform but skewed. To quantify differences in value chains, an approach is pursued to compare the skewness in distributions. The key definition is that of diversity curves, which are defined below and follow Hill (1973).

To measure the skewness of the cost distribution over the activities in a value chain weighted Hölder means are adapted. The weighted Hölder mean with parameter q of the cost proportions, $p_1, \ldots, p_n$ weighted by themselves, is defined by

$$M_{q-1}(\boldsymbol{p};\boldsymbol{p}) = \left(\sum_{k=1}^{n} p_k (p_k)^{q-1}\right)^{\frac{1}{q-1}} = \left(\sum_{k=1}^{n} p_k^{\,q}\right)^{\frac{1}{q-1}}. \tag{1a}$$

Depending on the choice of the parameter q, the above becomes the weighted arithmetic mean ($q = 2$), geometric mean ($q = 1$), or harmonic mean ($q = 0$). The parameter q can be considered a quantity penalizing 'minor' activities, ie, activities that contribute only little to the total costs. The larger q, the stronger is the penalization. The proper weighting of the activities is crucial. Namely, activities are not considered to be equally important. Rather, the importance of each activity is the proportion of costs it causes.

Notably, in the special case $q = 1$, the above definition needs to be replaced by

$$M_0(\boldsymbol{p};\boldsymbol{p}) = \prod_{k=1}^{n} p_k^{\,p_k} = \mathrm{Exp}\left(\sum_{k=1}^{n} p_k \log p_k\right), \text{ where } 0^0 = 0 \cdot \log 0 := 1. \tag{1b}$$

This corresponds to the limits $q \rightarrow 1$ in (1a), as this equation is not defined for $q = 1$. Also for $q = 0$ the above expression needs to be considered with caution. Namely, in the case $p_k = 0$ for some k, the above needs to be replaced by

$$M_{-1}(\boldsymbol{p};\boldsymbol{p}) = \frac{1}{\sum_{\substack{1 \le k \le n:\\ p_k \neq 0}} 1}, \tag{1c}$$

where the denominator is the number of activities in which costs occur. Although accounting for activities that do not cause costs seems unrealistic when working only with the nine core activities in Porter's generic model, it is nevertheless important to include such activities in general, not only when comparing value chains that do not fully overlap with regard to the involved activities, but also when analysing single value chains at a finer level of granularity. For instance, assume marketing activities contain sub-activities including online, social media, TV, and radio advertisements. TV advertisements would not cause costs if a product is not advertised on TV.

While in the cases $q > 0$ cost-free activities can be easily included, and definition (1c) also permits it for $q = 0$, when choosing $q < 0$, the Hölder means are not properly defined as soon as $p_k = 0$. Therefore, $q \geq 0$ is imposed in the following.

The Hölder means $M_{q-1}(\boldsymbol{p};\boldsymbol{p})$ ascertain the evenness of the distribution $\boldsymbol{p}$, with the minimum value $\frac{1}{n}$ being attained if all activities have the same costs, ie, $p_k = \frac{1}{n}$ for all k, and the maximum value being 1, which is attained if the total costs are concentrated on a single activity, ie, $p_k = 1$, for one k. Since the choice of q mediates how activities with low costs are penalized, rather than considering just a particular choice of q, it is more informative to consider the Hölder means as a function of the parameter q for a fixed distribution of costs $\boldsymbol{p}$.

A value chain that distributes costs more evenly across activities can be considered more diverse or more even. It is hence more natural to consider inverse Hölder means to quantify a value chain's diversity. Hence, let

$$D^{(q)}(\boldsymbol{p};\boldsymbol{p}) = \left(\sum_{k=1}^{n} p_k{}^{q}\right)^{-\frac{1}{q-1}} \tag{2a}$$

be regarded as a function of $q \geq 0$ and be called the value chain's diversity curve or diversity profile. In the case $q = 1$ the above definition needs to be replaced by

$$D^{(1)}(\boldsymbol{p};\boldsymbol{p}) = \operatorname{Exp}\left(-\sum_{k=1}^{n} p_k \log p_k\right), \text{ where } 0^0 = 0 \cdot \log 0 := 1, \tag{2b}$$

whereas for $q = 0$ the definition becomes

$$D^{(0)}(\boldsymbol{p};\boldsymbol{p}) = \sum_{\substack{1 \leq k \leq n: \\ p_k \neq 0}} 1 . \tag{2c}$$

Notably, the definitions of diversity curves have been proposed as diversity measures in ecology and are called Hill numbers (cf. Hill, 1973; Jost, 2006). For particular choices of q, the diversity curves coincide with indices commonly employed as diversity measures across disciplines. In particular, the inverse Simpson index, which was introduced as the effective number of political parties in Laakso and Taagepera (1979), coincides with the diversity curves at $q = 2$. This is exactly the reciprocal Herfindahl-Hirschman index (Hirschman, 1964), an indicator for the amount of competition between firms within an industry. This economic concept was also applied to competition law and antitrust as well as to technology management (cf Liston-Heyes and Pilkington, 2004). Furthermore, it is related to the Simpson index (Simpson, 1949), a measure of diversity in ecology, which is also known as heterozygosity in genetics (cf Hartl and Clark, 1997). For $q = 1$ the expression $D^{(1)}(\boldsymbol{p}; \boldsymbol{p})$ coincides with the exponential Shannon entropy (Shannon, 1948), originating from information theory. The Theil index (Theil, 1965) is a simple transformation of the Shannon index, primarily used to measure economic inequality. Moreover, a popular measure in conservation ecology, species richness (cf Colwell, 2009), is recovered for $q = 0$. Furthermore, in the limit $q \to \infty$ the diversity curve approaches the value $\frac{1}{\max\{p_1, \ldots, p_n\}}$, which is the Berger-Parker index (Berger and Parker, 1970). The fact that such a variety of statistics is subsumed as special cases of the diversity curves already suggests that the latter produce a richer and more comprehensive picture of the underlying cost distributions.

Before extending the concept of diversity curves to appropriate comparisons of value chains, definition (2) is illustrated by hypothetical examples in Table 7.1.

Example 1

Consider the value chains summarized in Table 7.1. The values are chosen to demonstrate the behaviour of diversity curves rather than to reflect realistic value chains. Figure 7.2 displays the corresponding diversity curves according to definition (2).

Comparisons between the diversity curves are informative on how costs distribute over activities. Consider only the first four value chains of Table 7.1 (Figure 7.2a). The values at $q = 0$, 1, and 2 coincide with each value chain's species richness, exponential Shannon entropy, and Hirschman index. At $q = 0$ all curves equal 9, indicating that each of the nine primary and secondary activities within Porter's model cause costs, ie, $p_k > 0$. As q increases to infinity, each curve approaches its asymptotic value, which is the inverse proportion of the dominant activity (Berger-Parker index), ie, $\frac{1}{\max\{p_1, \ldots, p_n\}}$, indicated by the horizontal lines.

The first value chain's diversity curve declines faster than that of the second. This is attributed to the higher skewness of the first value chain, due to the dominant activity (in this case operations) amounting to 30 per cent of the costs in comparison to 25 per cent for the second value chain – these values determine the curves' asymptotic values (dashed horizontal lines). The slope of the diversity curves and the speed at which they approach their asymptotic values is similar, reflecting an overall similarity in the underlying value chains.

The third value chain is even less skewed than the second and its diversity curve approaches its asymptotic value slightly slower. The reason is that

Table 7.1 Percentages of costs for eight hypothetical value chains attributed to the primary and secondary activities of Porter's model (Figure 7.1). The costs in the first four value chains are similarly distributed over the activities, however the percentage of costs spend on marketing and sales is noticeably smaller in the fourth value chain compared to the others. Also listed are the equally-weighted averages of value chains 1 and 8, 1–4, and 4–7, respectively

	Value chain								Average value chain		
Activity	**1**	**2**	**3**	**4**	**5**	**6**	**7**	**8**	**1, 8**	**1–4**	**4–7**
Inbound logistics	15.0	14.5	14.0	16.0	5.0	1.0	1.0	5.0	10.0	14.875	5.75
Operations	30.0	25.0	21.0	33.3	33.3	33.3	33.3	5.0	17.5	27.325	33.30
Outbound logistics	4.0	4.5	5.0	4.5	2.5	2.5	2.5	15.0	9.5	4.500	3.00
Marketing and sales	15.0	18.6	23.0	5.6	5.4	5.4	5.4	5.0	10.0	15.550	5.45
Service	5.0	5.0	4.3	5.6	5.6	2.6	2.6	15.0	10.0	4.975	4.10
Firm infrastructure	5.0	4.9	4.6	5.6	5.6	2.6	2.6	30.0	17.5	5.025	4.10
HR management	15.0	16.9	18.0	16.8	30.0	33.0	33.0	4.0	9.5	16.675	28.20
Technology	6.0	5.8	6.0	6.8	6.8	17.8	19.6	15.0	10.5	6.150	12.75
Procurement	5.0	4.8	4.1	5.8	5.8	1.8	0.0	6.0	5.5	4.925	3.35

Figure 7.2 Diversity curves of value chains in Table 7.1. The vertical lines mark the values and q = 0, 1 and 2. The horizontal dashed lines indicate the asymptotic values of the diversity curves

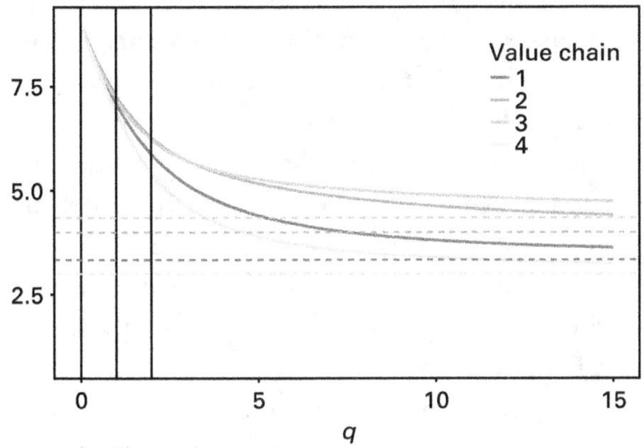

(a) Diversity curves for value chains 1–4

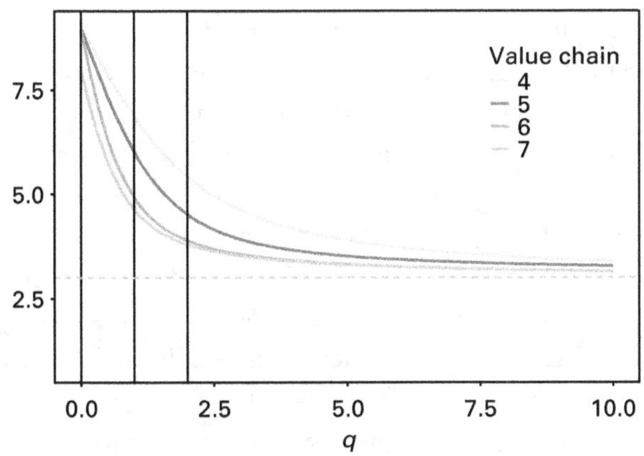

(b) Diversity curves for value chains 4–7

some activities have rather large proportions. Particularly, the proportion of costs spent on operations (21 per cent), marketing and sales (23 per cent), and human resource management (18 per cent) are rather similar. However, in comparison to the second value chain, the diversity curve initially declines faster, because some activities cause rather small proportions of the total costs (4.1 per cent and 4.3 per cent for procurement and service, respectively). Together this results in an intersection of the two curves.

The fourth value chain has the most skewed cost distribution, with a dominant frequency of 33.3 per cent, resulting in the lowest asymptotic value. However, it does not decline too fast initially as the minor activities (outbound logistics) amounts to 4.5 per cent, which is a larger percentage than for the first three value chains, which additionally tend to have more activities contributing little to the total costs.

To further emphasize the behaviour of diversity curves, consider those of value chains four to eight. All value chains have the same dominant activity, resulting in the same asymptotic value. However, the diversity curve of value chain 5 approaches this value faster than that of value chain 4, because value chain 5 has a rather skewed cost distribution with many activities amounting to very small proportions of costs. A consequence is the rapid initial decrease of the diversity curve. This is even more pronounced for value chain 6, whose diversity curve decreases initially so fast that the asymptotic value is reached even faster.

Value chain 7 illustrates the unrealistic case that one activity does not cause costs. This is immediately seen from the diversity curve at $q = 0$.

Finally, consider supply chain 8. It has the same proportions as the first supply chain, but the values are permuted. Hence, these are very different value chains, but their diversity curves coincide. □

The interpretation of diversity curves becomes clear from the above example. The asymptotic value yields the inverse proportion of the dominant activity. The more activities contributing very little to the costs, the faster the initial decline of the diversity curve. The curve's value at $q = 0$ yields the number of activities that cause costs in the supply chain.

Notably, the example also showed that totally different supply chains can have similar diversity curves, if the costs are split into similar proportions, which are associated with different activities. Additionally, the total costs of supply chains will in general differ, so that a comparison of the diversity curves is insufficient. A proper approach for comparisons of supply chains is introduced next.

Diversity within several value chains

Consider L value chains. These are not necessarily value chains corresponding to different companies or products, but could be the 'same' value chain at L different time points, or across L different production sites. Such analyses are relevant if firms want to analyse the changes in profitability of production, or identify strategic locations for cheaper production. Let the cost of value chain l be denoted by C_l, and the proportion of costs caused by activity k by $p_{k,l}$

(satisfying $\sum_{k=1}^{n} p_{k,l} = 1$). Collectively, these are denoted by $\boldsymbol{p}_l$ and correspond to a conditional frequency distribution. The vector of conditional frequency distributions is denoted by $\boldsymbol{P} = (\boldsymbol{p}_1, \dots, \boldsymbol{p}_L)$.

When aiming to compare the L value chains, their relative importance should be taken into account. Let the respective weights be denoted by $\boldsymbol{\alpha} = (\alpha_1, \dots, \alpha_L)$ with $\sum_{l=1}^{L} \alpha_l = 1$. Clearly, $\boldsymbol{\alpha}$ is again a probability distribution. For instance, the relative costs in comparison to each other can be employed to weight the value chains, ie, $\alpha_l = \frac{C_l}{\sum_{j=1}^{L} C_j}$. If the costs are irrelevant for a certain comparison and the value chains can be regarded as equally important, equal weights can be assigned to the value chains, i.e., $\alpha_l = \frac{1}{L}$.

The average percentage of costs spent on activity k among the L value chains is

$$p_k = \sum_{l=1}^{L} p_{k,l}\alpha_l. \tag{3}$$

The distribution p_k specifies the percentages of costs invested in the activities by an average or aggregated value chain.

The total diversity curve (TDC) or γ-diversity curve is then defined as the diversity curve (2) using the average distribution (3), ie,

$$D_\gamma^{(q)}(\boldsymbol{P};\boldsymbol{\alpha}) := D_\gamma^{(q)}(\boldsymbol{P}) =: \begin{cases} \left(\sum_{k=1}^{n}\left(\sum_{l=1}^{L} p_{k,l}\alpha_l\right)^q\right)^{\frac{1}{1-q}} & \text{for } q \neq 0, 1; \\ \operatorname{Exp}\left(-\sum_{k=1}^{n}\left(\sum_{l=1}^{L} p_{k,l}\alpha_l\right)\log\sum_{l=1}^{L} p_{k,l}\alpha_l\right) & \text{for } q = 1; \\ \sum_{\substack{1\leq k\leq n:\\ \exists l: p_{k,l}\neq 0}} 1 \text{ for } q = 0. \end{cases} \tag{4}$$

This diversity curve is informative about the skewness of the distribution of an average value chain.

In comparison, according to (2) the diversity curve of supply chain l is

$$D^{(q)}(\boldsymbol{p}_l) := D_{\gamma}^{(q)}(\boldsymbol{p}_l) =: \begin{cases} \left(\sum_{k=1}^{n} p_{k,l}{}^{q}\right)^{\frac{1}{1-q}} \text{ for } q \neq 0, 1; \\ \operatorname{Exp}\left(-\sum_{k=1}^{n} p_{k,l} \log p_{k,l}\right) \text{for } q = 1; \\ \sum_{\substack{1 \leq k \leq n: \\ p_{k,l} \neq 0}} 1 \text{ for } q = 0. \end{cases} \tag{5}$$

The maximum value of the total diversity curve is reached if each activity causes on average the same costs, ie, $p_k = \frac{1}{n}$. In other words, the average costs distribute uniformly over the activities. This does not imply that the activities of each value chain distribute evenly, ie, $p_{k,l} = \frac{1}{n}$ does not necessarily need to hold. Indeed, if the single value chains have skewed distributions with different dominating activities, their average can have a perfectly uniform distribution. The minimum value 1 is attained in the unrealistic case $p_k = 1$ for one k, ie, if all value chains concentrate their costs on the same single activity. If the penalization parameter q tends to infinity the TDC approaches the Berger-Parker index, $\frac{1}{\max\{p_1, \dots, p_n\}}$.

Rather than considering the diversity curve of an average of value chains, an average diversity curve (ADC) can be considered. The information curve (2) is an inverse weighted Hölder mean regarded as a function of the exponent q. To be consistent, it is reasonable to consider also a Hölder mean of diversity curves. Namely, a weighted Hölder mean of the Hölder means

$$M_{q-1}(\boldsymbol{p}_l; \boldsymbol{p}_l) = \left(\sum_{k=1}^{n} p_{k,l}{}^{q}\right)^{\frac{1}{q-1}} \tag{6}$$

can be considered. A natural assumption is to use the values α_l as weights. This gives

$$M_{q-1}\left(M_{q-1}(\boldsymbol{p}_1; \boldsymbol{p}_1), \dots, M_{q-1}(\boldsymbol{p}_n; \boldsymbol{p}_n); \alpha\right) = \left(\sum_{k=1}^{n} \alpha_l \left(M_{q-1}(\boldsymbol{p}_l; \boldsymbol{p}_l)\right)^{q}\right)^{\frac{1}{q-1}}.$$

Taking the inverse of this expression yields the average diversity curve or α-diversity curve of the value chains as

$$D_{\alpha}^{(q)}(\boldsymbol{P}; \alpha) := \left(\sum_{l=1}^{L} \alpha_l \sum_{k=1}^{n} p_{k,l}{}^{q}\right)^{\frac{1}{1-q}} = \left(\sum_{k=1}^{n} \sum_{l=1}^{L} \alpha_l p_{k,l}{}^{q}\right)^{\frac{1}{1-q}}, \tag{7a}$$

which satisfies again the convenient property that its maximum and minimum values are n and 1, respectively. The maximum value is attained if all supply chains are most diverse, ie, $p_{k,l} = \frac{1}{n}$. Unlike for the TDC, for the ADC every single value chain must have a uniform distribution. The ADC's minimum value of 1 is attained if all values chains are least diverse, which holds if the costs of each value chain are concentrated on a single activity, i.e., for each l an activity k exists satisfying $p_{k,l} = 1$. Importantly, unlike for the TDC, the costs do not have to be concentrated on the same activity for all value chains. Also, the ADC approaches an asymptotic value if q tends to infinity, namely the inverse of the maximum dominant activity among all value chains, $\frac{1}{\max\{p_{k,l}\}}$.

Again the special cases $q = 0$ and $q = 1$ need to be treated separately, namely

$$D_{\alpha}^{(1)}(\boldsymbol{P};\boldsymbol{\alpha}) = \operatorname{Exp}\left(-\sum_{l=1}^{L} \alpha_l \sum_{k=1}^{n} p_{k,l} \log p_{k,l}\right) \tag{7b}$$

and

$$D_{\alpha}^{(0)}(\boldsymbol{P};\boldsymbol{\alpha}) = \sum_{l=1}^{L} \alpha_l \sum_{\substack{1\le k\le n:\\ p_{k,l}\neq 0}} 1. \tag{7c}$$

While the TDC reflects the behaviour of an average value chain, the ADC reflects how the information curves of value chains behave on average. By using Jensen's inequality it can be shown that for each q the ADC can never exceed the TDC. The definition of TDC and ADC corresponds to an extension of γ- and α- diversity in Whittaker (1960) to the definition of Hill (1973). Contrasting the TDC and ADC provides a graphical, but quantitative, means to compare a set of value chains, as explained below.

Interpreting information curves

Comparing the ADC and TDC reveals more information than comparing individual information curves. This is illustrated in the next example, before turning to the general interpretation.

Example 2

Consider again the eight hypothetical value chains from Table 7.1. First, consider only value chains 1 and 8 with equal weights (Figure 7.3).

Figure 7.3 TDC, ADC and ration TDC/ADC for comparison of the value chains in Table 7.1. The vertical line marks the values q = 0, 1 and 2. The horizontal dashed lines indicate the asymptotic values of the respective curves

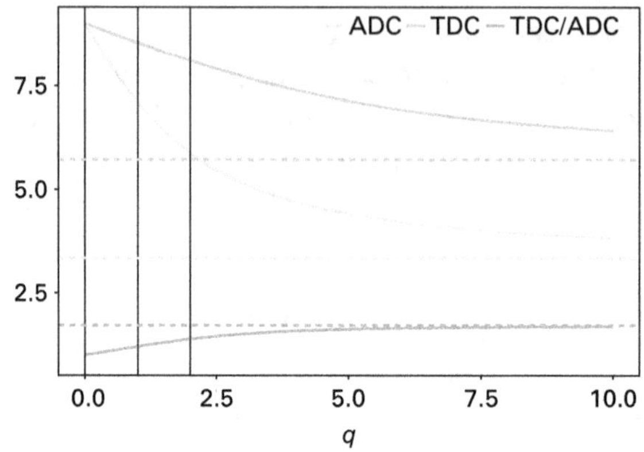

(a) Comparison of value chains 1 and 8

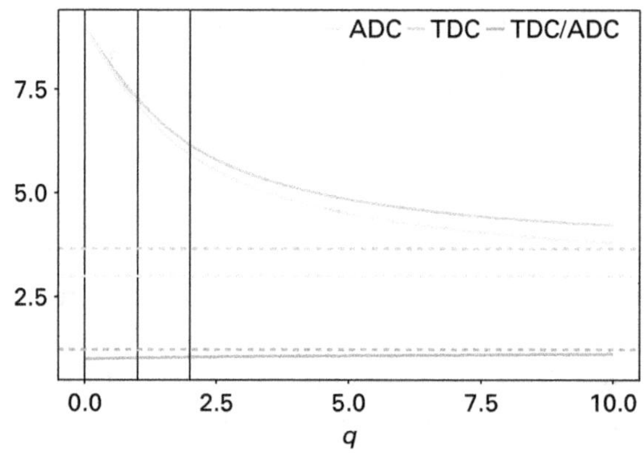

(b) Comparison of value chains 1–4

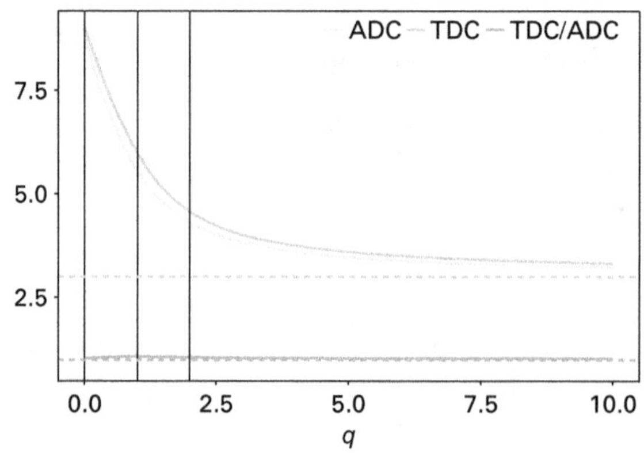

(c) Comparison of value chains 4–7

The cost distribution of value chain 8 is just a permutation of that of value chain 1. Hence, as noted before, the information curves are identical (although the value chains are different). Therefore, the ADC coincides with the individual information curves (regardless of the given weights). However, the TDC is much flatter than the ADC (cf Figure 7.3a). Thus, the average cost distribution is much more even that those of the individual supply chains (cf Table 7.1). This is necessarily a consequence of the individual supply chains having skewed distributions with complementary activities carrying large and small proportions of the costs, respectively.

Also the ratio of the TDC and ADC is informative. It reaches its asymptotic value much faster than both the TDC and ADC, indicating that both supply chains have common activities, which cause only small proportions of the costs. Therefore, the averaged chain shares some minor activities with both individual value chains that contribute similarly to the costs. Additionally, the ratio TDC/ADC lies below its asymptotic value, a consequence of the more even cost distribution of the averaged value chain in comparison to the individual ones.

Next, consider a comparison of the first four value chains from Table 7.1 (Figure 7.3b) again with equal weights. The TDC and ADC are similar. However, the cost distribution of the averaged value chain is more even. This indicates that some value chains concentrate their costs more on certain activities than others. Neither the TDC nor the ADC approaches their asymptotic value fast, reflecting the absence of activities carrying only negligible proportions of the costs. Notably, the TDC approaches its asymptotic value faster than the ADC, which is seen from the ratio TDC/ADC approaching its asymptotic value not too fast either. Namely, the averaged value chain distributes small amounts of costs to a larger number of activities than most of the individual chains (cf Table 7.1). This can occur only if more than one individual chain distributes a lower amount of costs to certain activities than the others.

When considering value chains 4–7 the TDC and ADC are similar. Value chain 7 does not attribute costs to procurement. Consequently, the ADC at $q = 0$ is less than the TDC. Both curves reach the same asymptotic value because the dominant activity in each value chain (operations) amounts to exactly the same percentage (33.3 per cent). The ratio TDC/ADC lies above its asymptotic value (in this case it equals 1), because the ADC approaches its asymptotic value faster than the TDC. The reason is that the individual value chains have a much more skewed cost distribution than their average (cf Table 7.1). □

As seen from the above example, a comparison of the TDC and the ADC is informative about how skewed the cost distributions of individual value chains are in comparison to that of an averaged one. Guided by this example, general rules how to interpret diversity curves can be deduced.

The value of the ADC in comparison to that of the TDC at $q = 0$ indicates whether all chains attribute costs to all activities. While this is less relevant when considering the core activities defined by Porter's model (cf Figure 7.1), it becomes important when considering a more elaborate and specific set of activities, where some are not relevant to all value chains under comparison.

The difference in the asymptotic values of the TDC and ADC reflects the proportion of costs of the activity that is on average dominant in comparison to the activity causing the highest cost proportion among all value chains. The TDC's and ADC's slopes represent the skewness of the average value chain in comparison to the average skewness of the individual chains. The faster they approach their asymptotic values, the more skewed the distributions, in the sense that few activities share approximately the same large proportion of costs, while many activities cause only small proportions of costs. The ratio TDC/ADC reveals whether the TDC or the ADC reaches their asymptotic value faster again reflecting the skewness of the cost distribution. Sharp declines around $q = 0$ reflect activities causing small percentages of costs. The number of activities with relatively small proportions of costs will determine how fast the asymptotic values are reached.

In summary, the TDC and ADC provide a practical means to compare the cost distributions of value chains. The examples provided had only an illustrative character, since a handful of value chains can also be easily compared directly. However, if a large number of value chains within an industry are analysed, comparisons are too complex. Here, the approach provides a simple graphical method that captures particular characteristics of the cost distributions.

Extensions and alternative applications

Discrepancies between the TDC and ADC reflect heterogeneity between a set of value chains. If only profitable value chains are compared, such heterogeneity reflects that competitive value is generated by different activities across the value chains. When each company operates at the productivity frontier, so that no or hardly any improvement in operational effectiveness is possible, diversity across profitable value chains should reflect strategic positioning being responsible for the value chains' competitive advantage

(Porter, 1996). A more detailed analysis of these differences can be adopted to identify possibilities for optimizing strategic positioning or diversification in order to increase margin. On a temporal scale, heterogeneity in diversity between the same value chains would correspond to a changing market. Identifying temporal changes might help a firm to deduce market trends that support strategic decision making to change, stop or facilitate production. Similarly, a comparison of the differences across different production sites can be employed to shift production towards the most profitable sites.

The method to quantify differences between several value chains by diversity curves is not restricted to the core activities of Porter's model as presented in the examples. As mentioned before, comparisons can be made at different levels of granularity, ie, a finer partition of activities within Porter's model can be chosen, and not all activities within Porter's model need to be considered. For instance, the analysis can be restricted only to marketing and sales, with more specific sets of activities. Such a set can be defined to reflect certain marketing activities across target groups of buyers, eg, online marketing activities targeted at low-budget *vs* high-budget buyers, which allow making inferences on the company's strategic positioning.

Notably, the analytical method is not just applicable to a comparison of individual value chains within an industry. Groups of value chains can be compared by considering group averages rather than individual value chains. Suppose some value chains are classified as particularly profitable, while others are in deficit. A comparison of the average value chain in deficit with the average profitable chain facilitates the detection of differences in the cost distribution, strategic positioning, and hence of potential for optimization. In addition, comparing the value chains within each group allows diversity to be mined between the value chains. If profitable value chains for comparable products are diverse, obviously the added value is created by different activities. This can be adapted to cut the costs of some activities in order to maximize the margin if the strategic positioning creating competitive advantage is not compromised. If a group of profitable value chains, representative for an industry, is very similar, there must be an apparent lack of diversification in the process of producing the good or service under consideration. Such a situation could reflect the potential to increase competitive advantage by alternative business strategies, eg, by creating higher value for buyers or by scaling up production. However, it could also reflect a highly optimized and saturated market that allows only for narrow margins.

Discussion

The concept of value-adding activities, either physical or virtual, contributing to manufacturing products introduced by Porter (1985) facilitates strategic management of firms in order to generate competitive advantage. While the concept is a generic model without precise accounting standards that could apply to a large variety of industries, value chain analysis is mainly qualitative and hence has a subjective character. Nevertheless, approaches have been proposed for quantitative analysis of value chains, eg, Bellù (2013). As profitability, which is naturally quantitative in a monetary sense, must be the ultimate goal of any firm, such quantitative approaches are consequently desirable. Particularly, quantitative approaches entail the advantage of providing clear means to monitor the profitability of value chains over time, across production sites, or to compare competing value chains within an industry. Assuming that the costs of value chains can be quantified within Porter's model, a quantitative method for comparison of value chains was proposed. For this purpose the concept of diversity measures according to Whittaker (1960), originating from ecology, were combined with the statistics introduced by Hill (1973). Notably, diversity measures do not originate from ecology but were introduced across many disciplines, typically as point measures, yielding only highly aggregated information, eg, Herfindahl-Hirschman index (Hirschman, 1964), Shannon entropy (Shannon, 1948), or Theil index (Theil, 1965) in social sciences and economy. While typically single summary statistics are used as diversity measures, here a continuum of such measures was proposed leading to diversity curves.

Diversity curves as introduced above capture the skewness of the cost distribution over the core activities of a value chain. It is proposed here that comparing the total diversity curve (TDC), which is the diversity curve of an averaged value chain, with the average diversity curve (ADC), which is an average over individual value chains' diversity curves, provides a means to detect and quantify differences between value chains. Rather than providing a comprehensive and concise mathematical and accounting framework, here the basic definitions are provided under the assumption that value chains can be quantified within Porter's model. The latter is subject to complementary quantitative analysis, eg, as suggested in Bellù (2013). The comparison emphasized here is based on hypothetical examples illustrating the behaviour of the TDC and ADC and how to interpret them. For this purpose only, a naive graphical approach was provided. Notably, it can be extended by fitting the diversity curves by parametric families of functions that summarize their behaviour by a few parameters, which yield informative summary statistics, capturing more information than individual point measures, and at the same time are appropriate quantities for quantitative decision support as sustained, eg, by hypothesis testing. However, such extensions are subject to future research.

To derive a diversity curve, it must be possible to project costs on the key activities defining a supply chain. This implicitly assumes clear-cut definitions and well-established, rigorous accounting standards, which is unrealistic in practice. In fact, some uncertainty in defining the cost distribution of a supply chain arises naturally. The current approach does not adequately address this issue. However, it can be included in general by defining confidence regions of the cost distribution, which will translate into confidence bands of diversity curves by, eg, bootstrap techniques (cf. Efron and Tibshirani, 1994). This involves a number of more technical arguments that are beyond the scope of this chapter.

The method per se is not restricted to Porter's model, or more generally to value chain analysis, and might focus on other aspects than costs. In the context of supply chain sustainability, the distribution of CO_2 emissions caused by the core activities of a value chain can be considered instead of costs. This corresponds to reinterpreting Porter's model as an emission-adding instead of value-adding organizational system of activities. Evidently, by such an approach, the potential to reduce CO_2 emissions can be explored. Reducing CO_2 emissions can also be part of strategic positioning to achieve premium buyer's value.

Another field of application of the proposed method is CSR. Because the goals of CSR are philanthropic, they are extremely subjective and difficult to quantify. Hence, the impact of CSR on a sustainable economy is by nature difficult to measure, although highly desirable (cf Crane *et al*, 2017). However, indices to quantify CSR have been proposed, eg, see Hopkins (2005) for a review of six different measures and El-Masry and Kamal (2013). Once CSR can be quantified, its impact can be measured by correlation with financial impact, as pursued in Cho *et al* (2019). By projecting the effect of CSR measures on a set of activities, the approach advocated here can be used to monitor and facilitate CSR.

By using Porter's framework as a reference point, different aspects of value chain analyses can be combined. Namely, regardless of whether a supply chain is considered with respect to added value, CSR or sustainability, it is summarized by a discrete probability distribution over a set of activities.

For the same value chain, these distributions are comparable by the methods proposed here. Diversity in this context helps to identify activities that exhibit discrepancies concerning different aspects. For instance, certain activities within inbound logistics might be cost efficient, but neither ecologically sustainable nor support good ethical practices. The proposed method is appropriate to detect such diametric aspects and can be further put forward to optimize the interplay of different activities within a supply chain.

Despite these possibilities, the proposed method relies on accounting standards that allow quantifiable aspects of a value chain to be projected on a clearly defined set of activities. This is only possible if proper accounting schemes can be defined within certain industries. That is beyond the scope of this chapter and should be subject to further research.

References

Bellù, LG (2013) *Value Chain Analysis for Policy Making: Methodological guidelines and country cases for a quantitative approach*, EASYPol, Food and Agriculture Organization of the United Nations, Series 129

Berger, WH and Parker, FL (1970) Diversity of planktonic foraminifera in deep-sea sediments, *Science*, **168** (3937), June, pp 1345–47

Cho, S, Chung, C and Young, J (2019) Study on the relationship between CSR and financial performance, *Sustainability*, **11**, January, p 343

Colwell, RK, (2009) Biodiversity: Concepts, patterns, and measurement, *The Princeton Guide to Ecology*, ed S Levin and S Carpenter, Princeton University Press, NJ, pp 257–63

Crane, A, Henriques, I, Husted, B and Matten, D (2017) Measuring corporate social responsibility and impact: Enhancing quantitative research design and methods in business and society research, *Business and Society*, **56**, July, pp 787–95

Efron, B and Tibshirani, RJ (1994) *An Introduction to the Bootstrap*, vol 57, CRC Press, Boca Raton

El-Masry, A and Kamal, N (2013) *Corporate Responsibility Index*, January, pp 528–34

Hartl, DL and Clark, AG (1997) *Principles of Population Genetics*, 3rd edn, 8vo xiii, 542 pp, Edition, Sinauer Sunderland, MA

Hill, MO (1973) [accessed 23 September 2020] Diversity and evenness: A unifying notation and its consequences, *Ecology*, **54** (2), pp 427–32 [Online] https://esajournals.onlinelibrary.wiley.com/doi/abs/10.2307/1934352 (archived at https://perma.cc/2LM6-EUCP)

Hirschman, AO (1964) The paternity of an index, *American Economic Review*, **54**, 761

Hopkins, M (2005) Measurement of corporate social responsibility, *International Journal of Management and Decision Making*, **6**, January

Hutchens, R (2004) [accessed 23 September 2020] One measure of segregation, *International Economic Review*, **45** (2), pp 555–78 [Online] http://www.jstor.org/stable/3663531 (archived athttps://perma.cc/UV5X-ET54)

Jost, L (2006) [accessed 23 September 2020] Entropy and diversity, *Oikos*, **113** (2), pp 363–75 [Online] https://onlinelibrary.wiley.com/doi/abs/10.1111/j.2006.0030-1299.14714.x (archived at https://perma.cc/H4B9-AC8M)

Jost, L (2007) [accessed 23 September 2020] Partitioning diversity into independent alpha and beta components, *Ecology*, **88** (10), pp 2427–39 [Online] https://esajournals.onlinelibrary.wiley.com/doi/abs/10.1890/06-1736.1 (archived at https://perma.cc/2S5V-LVL3)

Jost, L (2008) [accessed 23 September 2020] GST and its relatives do not measure differentiation, *Molecular Ecology*, **17** (18), pp 4015–26 [Online] https://onlinelibrary.wiley.com/doi/abs/10.1111/j.1365-294X.2008.03887.x (archived at https://perma.cc/YP6Q-Q876)

Laakso, M and Taagepera, R (1979) [accessed 23 September 2020] 'Effective' number of parties: A measure with application to West Europe, *Comparative Political Studies*, **12** (1), pp 3–27 [Online] https://doi.org/10.1177/001041407901200101 (archived at https://perma.cc/7LFV-NCAA)

Liston-Heyes, C and Pilkington, A (2004) [accessed 23 September 2020] Inventive concentration in the production of green technology: A comparative analysis of fuel cell patents, *Science and Public Policy*, **31** (1), February, pp 15–25 [Online] https://doi.org/10.3152/147154304781780190 (archived at https://perma.cc/8R47-7BPG)

Nicholls, A and Opal, C (2005) *Fair Trade: Market-driven ethical consumption*, SAGE Publications, London

Porter, M (1985) *Competitive Advantage: Creating and sustaining superior performance*, Free Press, New York

Porter, ME (1996) What is strategy? *Harvard Business Review*, **74** (6), pp 61–78

Shannon, CE (1948) A mathematical theory of communication, *The Bell System Technical Journal*, **27** (3), July, pp 379–423

Shorrocks, AF (1984) [accessed 23 September 2020] Inequality decomposition by population subgroups, *Econometrica*, **52** (6), pp 1369–85 [Online] http://www.jstor.org/stable/1913511 (archived at https://perma.cc/SP2T-HL44)

Simpson, EH (1949) Measurement of diversity, *Nature*, **163** (4148), p 688 [Online] https://doi.org/10.1038/163688a0 (archived at https://perma.cc/WD6C-DD4Z)

Theil, H (1965) [accessed 23 September 2020] The information approach to demand analysis, *Econometrica*, **33** (1), pp 67–87 [Online] http://www.jstor.org/stable/1911889 (archived at https://perma.cc/89NJ-K8XE)

Urbig, D (2003) The value chain's values: Interpretations and implications for firm and industry analysis, in *Proceedings of Perspectives in Business Informatics Research (BIR): Berlin 2003*, pp 1–15

Whittaker, RH (1960) [accessed 23 September 2020] Vegetation of the Siskiyou Mountains, Oregon and California, *Ecological Monographs*, 30 (3), pp 279–338 [Online] https://esajournals.onlinelibrary.wiley.com/doi/abs/10.2307/1943563 (archived at https://perma.cc/DXJ7-96JS)

Sustainable buyer behaviour in value chains 08

Determinants and marketing implications

GUIDO GRUNWALD AND VALÉRIE SWAEN

Introduction

In the western industrialized nations, private consumption vastly exceeds what is needed to satisfy existential needs. For example, household consumption alone is responsible for more than 70 per cent of global greenhouse gas emissions (Dubois *et al*, 2019). In addition to the environmental side effects of private consumption, the social consequences cannot be overlooked. For example, the production of consumer goods in some developing and emerging countries violates labour and human rights. The relevant scandals on this are well known and often show only the 'tip of the iceberg'.

Ultimately, the responsibility for such aberrations lies partly with the consumer who, at the end of a value chain, impacts the decisions of upstream suppliers, manufacturers and distributors with their decisions on what, how much, when and how they purchase, consume, use and get rid of products. Consequently, changing and influencing individual consumer behaviour is also considered to have great potential for supporting sustainable development. This is also evident in numerous current initiatives to promote sustainable consumption (BMUB, 2016). The described behaviour – which is not sustainable or not sufficiently sustainable in terms of the model of sustainable development (or according to individually-expressed attitudes) – is discussed in the relevant research under the terms 'behavioural gap' or 'corporate social responsibility (CSR)-consumer paradox' (Carrington *et al*, 2014; Gupta and Ogden, 2009; Janssen and Vanhamme, 2015). But it is not only at the end of the value chain that buyers impact, by their behaviour, whether and to what extent contributions for sustainable development arise. Also, at the upstream stages of the value chain, pre- and post-purchase behaviours influence sustainability within the process as a whole. In this chapter, 'buyer behaviour' is used as a summary term for all factors influencing decisions and the resulting actions of buyers (whether they be private or organizational) in the pre- and post-purchase phases. The pre-purchase phase is completed with the purchase or non-purchase, the post-purchase phase comprises consumption, use and disposal.

However, previous research on sustainable buyer behaviour mainly has focused on determinants for sustainable purchase and consumption at the last stage of the value chain, while considering the processes taking place within that stream as a black box (Geiger *et al*, 2018; Lindgreen, Maon and Swaen, 2009; Lindgreen, Swaen and Maon, 2009; Martin and Väistö, 2016). This applies, for example, to adjustments by suppliers to increased sustainability awareness among end consumers and intensified sustainability marketing by retailers. How quickly, to what extent, and in what way it is responding to such changes at the end of the value chain is likely to depend, inter alia, on the relations between supply chain actors (including their relative power). However, by neglecting such processes within the value chain, the potential causes for missing drivers of sustainable buyer behaviour further up the supply chain cannot be fully identified. In particular, the role of multilevel (indirect) marketing, by which the provider addresses the customers of its customers, or suppliers of its suppliers, has barely been investigated in comparison to the traditional one-step (direct) marketing approach with regard to promoting sustainable buyer behaviour (Grunwald and Schwill, 2017; Homburg *et al*, 2014; Homburg and Wilczek, 2014).

In this context, this chapter seeks to analyse how (non-) sustainable buyer behaviour can be explained at and across different stages of the value chain, with special consideration of holistic relationship-oriented approaches. In so doing, this chapter provides a more comprehensive explanation of the behavioural gap, frequently observed at the end of the value chain, between merely expressed or normatively desired sustainable behaviour, on the one hand, and the actual realized sustainable behaviour, on the other.

In order to gain deeper insights into behavioural gaps also at upstream levels in value chains, we consider the tensions arising when stakeholders perceive a gap between a company's stated and actual behaviour with regard to CSR (Hoffmann, 2018; Maon *et al*, 2019). From this perceived gap, negative assessments, attitudes and ultimately changes in buying behaviour may arise, potentially leading to a sustainability crisis for the providers involved in the value chain (Grunwald and Schwill, 2018). Based on the analysed determinants of sustainable buyer behaviour, initial approaches for promoting sustainable buyer behaviour as part of a relationship-oriented, multi-level marketing approach are derived; further, research gaps are identified.

This chapter is structured as follows. First, we characterize sustainable buyer behaviour and the behavioural gap. Then, potential determinants of (non-)sustainable buyer behaviour in value chains are presented, integrating research on consumer behaviour, sustainability and relationship marketing and, also, sustainable supply chain management. In addition to demand-side effects, the relationships between different actors in the value chain are considered (ie the supply-side effects). Finally, implications for sustainability marketing are discussed and research propositions formulated.

Sustainable buyer behaviour and the 'behavioural gap'

Sustainable consumption can be understood as a normative model from which proposals for changing consumption and production structures and processes can be derived in order to secure their future viability by balancing ecological, social and economic goals. This guiding principle is based on the principle of intergeneration, according to which a consumer satisfies their own needs – or should satisfy them – such that the living and consumption possibilities of other people and future generations are not endangered (Balderjahn, 2013; Belz and Peattie, 2012; Hansen and Schrader, 2001).

Behaviour consistent with this framework of thought is referred to as *sustainable buyer behaviour*. This is an individual decision in favour of voluntarily assuming responsibility, deciding and acting in whole or in part for reasons of conscience (in the sense of ethical consumption). Sustainable buyer behaviour can be described as behaviour designed to (more intensely) consider the consequences of one's own buying and use behaviour on the environment, society and the economy. It is up to the buyer to become more aware of sustainability issues in their decisions and to pursue a behavioural change in favour of this principle in the pre- and post-purchase phases (Schoenheit and Schudak, 2013).

A sustainable buyer can thus be seen as an ecologically, socially and economically responsible citizen (Schoenheit and Schudak, 2013). As an ecologically conscious buyer, the person pays increased attention to environmental and climate protection issues, to environmentally compatible ingredients and packaging, and to recycling. The social dimension of sustainable buyer behaviour incorporates issues such as fair consumption (fair pay and human rights), support for a charitable purpose through the purchase of a product, and politically motivated consumption. The latter can manifest itself in a boycott of certain providers and products in response to unethical behaviour. A consumer buycott is also conceivable in which the buyer specifically supports companies with exemplary sustainable behaviour through the buyer's own purchases (Balderjahn, 2013). The economic behavioural dimension can manifest itself in the consumer's conscious restriction of consumption ('less is more', as in the concept of voluntary simplicity; Etzioni, 1998), in debt-free consumption or in collaborative consumption (ie 'sharing instead of owning'; Balderjahn, 2013). Beyond this focus on the *sustainability dimensions*, sustainable buyer behaviour can also be seen in different pre- and post-purchase phases and also in different areas of consumption (Geiger *et al*, 2018).

Based on models of buying-decision processes (Grunwald and Hempelmann, 2017), different phases of the pre- and post-purchase processes can be distinguished. Considering such models, sustainable buyer behaviour can refer to the acquisition, consumption or use and the disposal of products (Fischer *et al*, 2012; Schrader *et al*, 2013). With regard to *acquisition*, the buyer exerts influence through what they select and buy based on processes of perception and appraisal. In the pre-purchase phase, the buyer initially decides fundamentally on the quantity of goods or services for consumption and the time of consumption (depending on the economic situation). Then, the product category is selected and priorities for consumption are formed. Next, the product or brand choice is made, depending on brand preferences, brand loyalty, decision rules, and buyer expectations. In the buying phase, the buyer selects the type of store or online portal for their shopping, makes comparisons across multiple stores or portals and asks for further information, eg about the product use or product-related services. Through purchasing, swapping, sharing and renting, the buyer ascertains the availability of products, from which, in each case, different contributions to sustainability can emanate. The *usage* phase refers to the type and intensity of the actual consumption or application of the product in different situations, thereby impacting product safety and durability, for instance. *Disposal* can be affected by means of recycling, removal, bartering, giving away, selling, etc. The extensive buying-decision process described above is typical for planned and rather rationally controlled buying behaviour. However, in some cases (eg depending on the buyer's involvement and experience, the situation and the product) consumers can also adopt a much shorter process that can be called implusive, habitual or limited buying processes. In the case of impulsive buying, for example, the buyer spontaneously makes their choice without thinking about it. Attitudes are only formed – if at all – after the purchase (Kroeber-Riel and Gröppel-Klein, 2013).

The *consumption areas* of food, housing (including water and energy consumption) and mobility can be identified as the ecologically most relevant categories in terms of greenhouse gases, acidification emissions, tropospheric ozone and resource/material requirements (EEA, 2013; Geiger *et al*, 2018; Ivanova *et al*, 2015; Lorek and Spangenberg, 2001; Steen-Olsen and Hertwich, 2015). The consumption of clothing has significant socioeconomic impacts, eg on the working and living conditions of workers in the production process (Geiger *et al*, 2018).

This idealized model of sustainable buyer behaviour suggests that consumers are aware of sustainability aspects that, according to their own information on the topic, are considered important. In reality, however, consumer behaviour rarely evidences a corresponding pattern. According to a Nielsen study conducted in 2015 on 30,000 consumers from 60 countries, an average of around 26 per cent of consumers reported desiring more sustainable products (Nielsen, 2015). On the other hand, only an average of 10 per cent reported having bought a new product because of its favourable environmental attributes or because of its contribution to social responsibility. In addition to methodological issues linked to the measurement of sustainable behaviour, attitudes, buying intentions and willingness to pay (eg social desirability effects, lack of a uniform definition of sustainable buyer behaviour, see Carrington *et al*, 2014: 2760; Janssen and Vanhamme, 2015: 776), the substantive reasons for such a *behavioural gap* or *CSR–consumer paradox* – as this phenomenon is often termed – are primarily seen in the buyer's individual decision-making process (Kostadinova, 2016; Janssen and Vanhamme, 2015).

Determinants of sustainable buyer behaviour in value chains

In this part of the chapter, we first discuss the 'actor-specific' determinants; following that, we address the 'cross-stakeholder' determinants. The term 'actor-specific' refers to influences that can be attributed to a specific party (ie an actor) within the value chain. In contrast, 'cross-stakeholder' determinants are factors that exert an influence on the relations between several parties within or outside the value chain.

Actor-specific determinants

Demand-side determinants

As a framework for explaining the behavioural gap from the consumer or demand perspective, the *theory of planned behaviour* (Ajzen, 1988, 1991) is often referenced (Janssen and Vanhamme, 2015: 776). According to this theory, the behaviour of an individual can be explained by their behavioural intention – which, in turn, depends on that person's attitude towards the behaviour (ie the degree to which they evaluate the behaviour favourably or unfavourably), subjective norms (ie the perceived social pressure to perform the behaviour) and the person's perceived behavioural control (ie the belief that they have the necessary resources and opportunities to perform the behaviour) (Ajzen, 1988; Janssen and Vanhamme, 2015).

Based on this model, it can be presumed that, on the one hand – and notwithstanding positive behavioural intention – there is no actual sustainable behaviour. This often is due to contextual (situational) factors relevant for (actual) behavioural control, such as product visibility, that serve to weaken the actual behaviour (Carrington *et al*, 2010). This effect can be referred to as the *intention–behaviour gap* (Grunwald, 2016: 14). On the other hand, there may already be a lack of sufficient intention, or motivation, to exercise actual sustainable behaviour. Thus, despite a positive attitude toward sustainable behaviour, there may be an inadequate behavioural intention because significant others (eg colleagues, friends, family) expect a different action (insufficient subjective norms) and/or because the individual's options for action (ie, competencies, resources) are considered too low (insufficient perceived behavioural control). This can be referred to as the *attitude–intention gap* (Grunwald, 2016: 14). Finally, even with favourable subjective norms and perceived behavioural control, a major reason for inadequate behavioural intention may lie in negative attitudes toward sustainable behaviour – due, at least in part, to an insufficient understanding of the benefits of one's own sustainable behaviour and/or to a negative or diminished assessment of the value of same.

The theory of planned behaviour seems helpful for identifying and structuring relevant influencing factors as may impact (non-)sustainable buyer behaviour and, as well, for predicting consumers' intentions to engage in (non-)sustainable behaviour (Janssen and Vanhamme, 2015). However, the model assumes a high degree of cognitive processing by the consumer, thereby failing to adequately describe low-involvement buying behaviour where attitudes, if any, only arise after the purchase has been made. Further, attitudes addressed by the theory only relate to sustainable behaviour; the model does not include consumer attitudes toward sustainable products and/or services (Grunwald, 2016). It is therefore doubtful whether the model fully considers the factors influencing (non-)sustainable buyer behaviour or the behavioural gap. Thus, an extended approach is required to uncover further determinants that may influence consumer behaviour.

With regard to attitudes, *personal concern* for CSR-related issues (eg in the form of environmental concern) – not only with respect to the individual's own behaviour and/or others', but also towards the facts and objects (eg products) one encounters – has been shown to impact buyers' sustainable behavioural intentions (eg environmentally friendly and green intentions) and sustainable behaviours (for a review of relevant studies, see Kostadinova, 2016; Lunde, 2018). However, higher levels of personal concern for sustainability issues may also be accompanied by more *scepticism and cynicism* toward marketing claims with regard to the sustainability of a given product (Paco and Reis 2013: 147). This can result in lower levels of sustainable behaviour, both in the present and in the future (Mohr *et al*, 1998). While 'personal concern' can be understood as an affective component of one's attitude, *perception and knowledge* are cognitive components that also can influence sustainable buying behaviour. As consumers become more conscious and knowledgeable about, for example, environmental problems, they tend to act more consistently with sustainability principles (Kostadinova, 2016: 228; Peattie, 2010).

Subjective norms may be effective in impacting behavioural intentions and actual sustainable behaviour on two different levels (Minton *et al*, 2018: 401). On a macro level, norms derive from cultural standards embedded within the country in which the consumer resides (Thogersen, 2010). On a micro level, norms emerge from peer groups (Öberseder *et al*, 2011; Terry *et al*, 1999). At both levels, and between the macro and micro levels, norms may also conflict with unclear effects on behavioural intention and behaviour (Minton *et al*, 2018: 401). On the one hand, the behavioural influence of norms can be based positively, in that the consumer wants to conform to the behavioural patterns that typify their surrounding community (or a given cultural group). For example, the buyer generally wishes (consciously or unconsciously) to be rewarded by that group for practising a sustainable behaviour that is observable by others – an effect that constitues a form of reputation building. On the other hand, the influence can also work negatively, namely to avoid sanctions by the collective in case of a violation of the norms, ie to avert threatening reputational damage.

Similar to subjective norms, values – as structures of normative expectations, as conveying ideas about something desirable – also determine sustainable buyer behaviour (Kostadinova, 2016). For example, sustainable (eg pro-environmental) consumption patterns tend to be more related to altruistic and prosocial values (Stern *et al*, 1995). The buyer who must spend more money to purchase sustainable goods, and possibly receives lower quality products, can be seen as performing an altruistic behaviour in which they display favourable characteristics, such as being able to spend more money on 'green' products, and, also, donating to worthy causes (Janssen and Vanhamme, 2015: 780). As a result, the behavioural gap could be greater for products perceived by the buyer as less expensive (Janssen and Vanhamme, 2015).

Although buyers generally have formed positive attitudes towards sustainable behaviour and products and, further, their behavioural intentions are supported by subjective norms, insufficient *perceived behavioural control* may weaken their intention to behave sustainably. Factors that can contribute to an insufficient perceived behavioural control include inadequate financial or time resources and insufficient perceived consumer effectiveness (self-efficacy) (Janssen and Vanhamme, 2015: 778). In expanding the decision-making perspective underlying the theory of planned behaviour, Janssen and Vanhamme (2015) investigate the behavioural gap from various theoretical perspectives, including the social psychology lens. From this perspective, and with respect to consumer self-efficacy (influencing perceived behavioural control), they infer that the behavioural gap 'is less apparent when the consumer witnesses peers buying the CSR products/services than if there are no other consumers to be witnessed' (p 782). This holds because CSR purchases often occur in anonymous settings where the buyer cannot evaluate the impact of a purchase on the success of the CSR programme – an effect that negatively impacts self-efficacy. Besides, the habits and lifestyles of consumers, and loyalty to established brands, may have a negative impact on sustainable buyer behaviour (Kostadinova, 2016: 230; Peattie, 2010).

Supply-side determinants

The supplier (manufacturer and distributor), both directly and indirectly, impacts buyer behaviour by its (sustainable) marketing activities in the areas of product, price, distribution and communication policy. Potential barriers to a sustainable purchase with respect to the supplier's marketing, along the typical stages of a purchase decision process, are described below.

In such a process, buyers usually initially decide on the purchase quantity and time for consumption, based on their needs and their available financial and time budgets. The purchase quantity will depend mainly on the *price*. The often-higher price of sustainable offerings can restrict sustainable purchases, although a certain price premium may be tolerated (Kostadinova, 2016: 229), notably due to the signalling potential of an altruistic behaviour, as outlined above. Studies such as IFH CSR-Tracker (IFH Köln, 2011) have shown not only that many buyers perceive sustainable products as too expensive, but that the higher prices cannot be reconstructed in part, so that losses of confidence impede purchasing behaviour (IFH Köln, 2011; imug, 2014: 56). On the other hand, credibility problems can arise if the price is too low, as price is also a signal of quality for many buyers (imug, 2014). Moreover, depending on the type of benefit consumers value for the product category (ie gentleness-related versus strength-related attributes), the 'sustainable' feature of the product can act as a signal for higher quality. In some other cases (in particular when consumers value strength-related attributes), however, it can also signal a lower quality, thereby leading to lower product preferences (cf Luchs *et al*, 2010).

Unavailable or overly complex *information* about the supply and/or the benefits of sustainable products may also constitute barriers to sustainable purchases at this stage. Such factors serve to impede the subsequent step in the decision-making process (ie when the buyer selects the relevant product category and forms preferences) (Bray *et al*, 2011). Since there can be conflicting goals between the dimensions of sustainability (thus causing issues with the formation of buyer preferences), a buyer can lose orientation in a way that paralyses sustainable consumption (imug, 2014: 60). Low *availability* of sustainable products or services in terms of quantity and quality (De Pelsmacker *et al*, 2005; Vermeir and Verbecke, 2006) in this phase may also interrupt the buying process. For the formation of preferences towards sustainable products, *self-interest* may play a central role. This can involve such things as lower follow-up costs when purchasing an energy-efficient product (Ginsberg and Bloom, 2004) and a *demonstrable effect* displaying concrete behavioural impacts of individual behaviour on sustainable development, for example in the form of X tonnes of avoided waste, plastic or CO_2 (Straughan and Roberts, 1999).

In the next phase of the purchase decision-process, the product or brand choice is made based on brand preferences, brand loyalty and expectations. *Brand awareness* and *brand popularity* play a key role in forming preferences and attitudes, not only for conventional products, but also for sustainable products. By using CSR or eco-labelling, suppliers aim to assure consumers that the products are sustainably manufactured or have sustainable features (Kostadinova, 2016: 229). However, the abundance of labels can confuse the customer, who in turn is reluctant to buy sustainably (imug, 2014: 64). In addition, some labels lack *credibility and trust* in the perception of buyers, which makes it difficult for them to distinguish labels that inform from advertising statements (D'Souza *et al*, 2007; McDonald *et al*, 2009; Meyer-Höfer and Spiller, 2012).

Scepticism among buyers can also be triggered or reinforced by exaggerated, inconsistent or false sustainability claims by the provider, thus contributing to *CSR-related tensions* (Maon *et al*, 2019: 212). One issue, for example, may be perception of corporate hypocrisy (Wagner *et al*, 2009). This may be the case when stakeholders perceive a gap between stated and actual corporate behaviour with regard to CSR. In such instances, products advertised as sustainable are often increasingly avoided by the consumer, given a reduced credibility attributed to the brand(s) (Ham and Kim, 2017). This, in turn, may increase the behavioural gap with the consumer. For providers, the situation can develop into a sustainability crisis endangering the existence of the companies involved in the value chain (Grunwald and Schwill, 2018). On the other hand, reports about or the documentation of scandals, eg in food production or animal welfare, may also have a sensitizing effect on consumers and create a heightened awareness for social or environmental issues that, ultimately, can contribute to more sustainable buying behaviour (imug, 2014: 51). For the purchase of sustainable products in particular, the fulfilment of *social expectations* by the product and the supplier is important (Rokka and Uusitalo, 2008). Salience and visibility of consumption determine the influence of social comparison and imitation on consumption patterns (Janssen and Jager, 2002). In this respect, the behavioural gap could be more apparent for CSR products that do not involve any public display (Janssen and Vanhamme, 2015).

Most of the supply-related factors discussed above may already be anticipated by the buyer prior to the formation of a behavioural intention. However, situational influences exist especially in the buying phase that are not foreseeable by the buyer which can actually moderate (strengthen or weaken) the relationship between behavioural intentions and sustainable buyer behaviour. These include *external contextual factors* at the point of purchase, such as product placement, price promotions and interaction with salespeople, and *internal contextual factors* such as the consumer's mood (Carrington *et al*, 2010).

Contributions to sustainable buyer behaviour can also be based on services and *product-service systems* (PSS). Such systems can improve the satisfaction of buyers with the product, especially in the post-purchase phases of use and disposal, through improved functionalities, while at the same time reducing the environmental impacts during the entire lifecycle (Mont, 2003: 815). *Digital tools* can also provide buyers with information about the effects of their individual consumer behaviour so as to convey a demonstrable effect with respect to sustainability (Mont, 2003: 815). In terms of *distribution*, activities such as swapping, sharing, renting, etc provide options that can help increase the usage duration of resource-consuming goods (Demailly and Novel, 2014). Measures such as taking back and disposing of the product, can improve the environmental balance and provide added value for the customer. Overall, the PSS offer can reduce the behavioural gap because of the addition of new types of benefits during the use and the disposal phase. However, lack of offers or incentives, or solutions that are too complex, represent potential barriers to sustainable buyer behaviour at this stage. Moreover, the potential rebound effects related to PSS (defined as environmentally negative second-order effects of a service activity in sharing literature; Bartolomeo *et al*, 2003) should not be overlooked. For example, some consumers may care less about products when they do not own them but rather rent them (Cherry and Pidgeon, 2018). Further, take-back systems also can have negative environmental impacts if they exacerbate psychological obsolescence by offering consumers environmental and/or social justifications, as a means of mitigating any guilt they might feel about disposing of older goods in favour of new products (Bolton *et al*, 2006).

Cross-stakeholder determinants

Thus far, only influences on (non-)sustainable buyer behaviour, with a focus on the final step of the value chain at the interface of end consumers and brand manufacturers or retailers with direct contacts, have been examined. However, the true causes can lie much deeper at the upstream stages of the value chain and, above all, in the relationships among the various actors – especially as may be reflected in poor coordination between marketing (demand) and procurement (supply) (Foerstl *et al*, 2015; Kirchoff *et al*, 2011; Sheth *et al*, 2009). CSR-related tensions potentially leading to sustainability crises may point to this problem: the focal company (which owns or controls a value chain, such as a branded goods manufacturer or a large retail chain) is under direct observation of end users and other stakeholder groups (eg non-governmental organizations (NGOs)) and is directly blamed for a supposedly unsustainable behaviour, although the problems with raw material suppliers can occur at the beginning of the value chain (at a level not visible to those stakeholders). Upstream suppliers may thus have little incentive to produce in a more sustainable fashion (Koplin *et al*, 2007; Leppelt *et al*, 2013), except under the pressure of their own brand customers or retailers. This can negatively impact buying behaviour at the final stage of the value chain. Various studies (eg Leppelt *et al*, 2013; Seuring and Müller, 2008) have emphasized the need for cross-actor, relationship-oriented research on sustainability in the context of value chains, taking particular note of CSR-related tensions and sustainability crises (Maon *et al*, 2019).

In the following sections, therefore, the relationship marketing perspective is taken to delineate further possible upstream causes of the behavioural gap. Possible barriers to greater consideration of sustainability aspects at upstream stages of the value chain, as a result of a lack of demand–supply integration, can be found both externally (in the market, ie in customers or stakeholders, and in the corporate environment) and internally (within the own company) (Fawcett and Magnan, 2002; Schaltegger and Harms, 2010). Measures related to demand–supply integration to promote sustainability goals are integral parts of sustainable supply chain management (Foerstl *et al*, 2015) or sustainable supplier relationship management (Leppelt *et al*, 2013).

External factors

Missing external drivers or incentives for upstream suppliers to invest in sustainable supply chain management may be a lack of pressure from legal regulations or stakeholder influences; these are more likely to affect the end-consumer area of the supply chain (Sajjad *et al*, 2015). Since upstream suppliers are further away from the point of sale and the product brand of the original equipment manufacturer (OEM) customer (manufacturer or retailer), they are typically under low public scrutiny. They thus can feel less pressure to fully meet the expectations of end users and other stakeholders such as NGOs with regard to sustainability (Foerstl *et al*, 2015; Grunwald and Hennig, 2012; Schaltegger and Harms, 2010; Tay *et al*, 2015). Conversely, the intensity of sustainable supplier relationship management practices will increase if the risks associated with supplier misconduct are deemed high for the OEM customer (Leppelt *et al*, 2013).

As a rule, buyers of upstream supplier products in business-to-business markets are industrial buyers whose purchasing behaviour is also less emotional than rational (Eckardt, 2010). Although sustainability criteria are important, they often lag behind quality and cost criteria. External barriers, for example, include a high degree of complexity in supplier relationships; they also lack market-related information about the changing needs of indirect customers with regard to the (future) desired sustainability characteristics and are faced with price pressure from direct customers.

Internal factors

Internal factors can concern the relationships between directly adjoining value chain partners (such as first-tier suppliers) and OEM customers or can also refer to indirect relationships between actors further up and down in the value chain (such as end users and suppliers). Internal barriers with respect to direct actor relationships include, eg, incompatibilities in the strategic direction and organization of the collaborating value chain partners, associated high implementation costs (including additional staff costs for training and audits) or lack of management support (Aregon *et al*, 2011; Bruel *et al*, 2017; Giunipero *et al*, 2012). According to the HEC/EcoVadis barometer carried out on 120 companies/buyers in 2017 (Bruel *et al*, 2017), the biggest obstacles preventing companies from more effectively engaging in supply chain and procurement sustainability are, by order: (1) a lack of internal resources (quoted as an obstacle by 57 per cent of companies in 2017, against only 28 per cent in 2013); (2) difficulty tracking supplier sustainability performance (for 37 per cent of companies); (3) concerns around cost (for 33 per cent of companies); and (4) lack of executive or board support (quoted as an obstacle by only 24 per cent of companies in 2017, against 50 per cent in 2013).

Also relevant is the degree to which sustainability goals are already an integral part of the corporate strategies in terms of the CSR of the partners involved. In this regard, Leppelt *et al* (2013: 100) posit that the existence of practices on sustainable supplier relationship management is positively associated with the definition and implementation of a harmonized corporate sustainability strategy. In particular, if the focal company or the OEM customer actively communicates sustainability for market positioning and is listed in a sustainability index, an increase in sustainable supplier relationship management activity is assumed; conversely, the lack thereof constitutes a barrier to further demand–supply integration (Leppelt *et al*, 2013: 101). Another internal aspect concerns the risks related to disclosure of previously internal data, which can increase dependence on value chain partners (Grunwald and Ostendorf, 2012: 191; Schaltegger and Harms, 2010: 10). This also addresses different power relationships, for example, between a large OEM customer and a smaller first-tier supplier (or downstream user) located in the middle of the supply chain, which may leave the supplier with little scope for proactive sustainable supply chain management due to restrictive requirements of the OEM customer or retailer (Grunwald and Hennig, 2014: 62).

An internal lack of drivers involves mainly the type of products (eg components) offered and their visibility to end users; this concerns indirect actor relationships. The less visible the product component in the final product is to the end user, the lower the motivation of the upstream suppliers to invest more in sustainable supply chain management. This holds because the sustainability related risks for the suppliers and their OEM customers are reduced (Foerstl *et al*, 2015: 83). On the other hand, also relevant is the extent to which the direct customer (eg an OEM customer) benefits from the sustainable properties of the primary product. As a result of the transition to light materials, less packaging and energy-efficient components, production costs, transport and handling costs can be saved and the sales and competitive situation improved (Foerstl *et al*, 2015: 84). If there are no such savings for the customer, the potentials associated with sustainable supply chain management are also lower for the upstream suppliers.

Implications for sustainability marketing and propositions for future research

From the analysis of the demand-side determinants, already some approaches for sustainability marketing can be derived from the theory of planned behaviour. A productive starting point is to strengthen the behavioural intentions of consumers by improving the attitude toward sustainable behaviour (or sustainable products) and by strengthening subjective norms.

On the other hand, one can try to reduce the intention-behaviour-gap by enhancing perceived behavioural control. Drawing on Fishbein's (1963, 1967) multiattribute model, the three determinants of behavioural intention can each be conceptualized by the individual's belief or perception concerning the behaviour's potential outcomes and the existence of potential social norms and potential obstacles or conditions for displaying the behaviour (cognitive component). These cognitive components are each weighted by subjective evaluations of these factors (affective component). Thus, marketing measures to promote sustainable buyer behaviour should take into account the criteria of: (1) *visibility*, including the perception of sustainable product use, behavioural consequences, and reference persons or peer groups and opportunities for action; and (2) *relevance*, comprising the assessment of sustainable behaviour for the customer himself and for important reference persons or society. In addition, (3) *trust* (eg based on supplier or product qualities as well as one's own abilities and possibilities) can be seen as a factor supporting visibility and relevance; this should be considered when planning sustainable marketing activities. On the one hand, many sustainability characteristics are so-called credence attributes (Grunwald and Schwill, 2017; Nelson, 1970), implying that buyers usually cannot verify the presence of properties such as 'eco', 'fair trade', 'no child labour' at a reasonable cost (either before or after purchase). On the other hand, but also linked to it, many consumers also lack confidence in their own abilities and potential to really put into practice a positive attitude towards sustainability (presumption of ineffectiveness) (Balderjahn, 2013).

Consumer trust can be delivered through a closer link between external and internal marketing as part of an identity-oriented sustainability marketing concept. Externally, sustainable products should provide added value for consumers, such that higher quality is perceived based on actual higher quality. Corporate communications should be trustworthy and bring out product benefits in a realistic and practical ('measurable'), understandable way. However, firms will be distrusted in their sustainability promise if their own employees are treated unethically or if employees do not act sustainably. Therefore, internal branding, eg incorporating employee-volunteering components, could play an important role in effective sustainability marketing (Jarvis, 2009). To enhance consumers' confidence in their own abilities and possibilities to act more sustainably, the role of marketing, above all, can be seen in terms of educating consumers about sustainability issues. If companies and marketing managers, in particular, can contribute to developing consumer sustainability literacy, both the cognitive aspects of consumer attitudes (as relate to visibility) and the affective aspects (as relate to relevance) will be developed. In this manner, consumer attitudes toward sustainable products can be improved, thereby contributing to reducing the behavioural gap. Sustainability marketing should, first of all, examine which one of the three factor groups – namely visibility, relevance and trust – is expected to have the greatest influence on (non-)sustainable behaviour in the respective consumer segment. From such a root-cause analysis, goals and requirements for the design of marketing measures to overcome the behavioural gap can be derived in a second step (Grunwald, 2016).

With increasing consumer demands for sustainably produced products and increasingly sustainable buyer behaviour, the pressure on upstream suppliers to invest more in sustainable supply chain management is also growing. Similar claims are also passed on to them by the brand manufacturers or retailers, often in the context of sustainability certifications (Foerstl *et al*, 2015) or 'negative lists', with which distributors (eg of consumer products) make specifications to their suppliers, ie which ingredients should not be preserved in articles (Grunwald and Hennig, 2012). Increased incentives for proactive engagement in sustainable supply chain management also exist in a negative way, namely to protect against public accountability in sustainability crises of branded goods manufacturers or retailers (Closs *et al*, 2011; Grunwald and Hennig, 2014). As a result, the opportunities for a proactive sustainable supply chain management for upstream suppliers to increase and strengthen the quality of relationships with their customers through sustainable production and product design are becoming more and more evident, thus increasing their competitiveness and performance (Foerstl *et al*, 2015). By taking ecological and social aspects into consideration, innovative product and service characteristics and processes can also be developed (Grunwald and Hennig, 2012).

One promising approach for improving the perception and positioning of one's own achievements in the area of sustainability in order to exploit the full potential of increased sustainable supply chain management engagement is *multilevel (indirect) marketing*, by which upstream suppliers direct marketing measures to the customers of their own customers (Grunwald, 2018; Homburg *et al*, 2014; Homburg and Wilczek, 2014; Kleinaltenkamp and Saab, 2009). This approach also includes multilevel market research activities in order to be able, as a supplier, to analyse the needs of indirect customers more promptly and more precisely (Kirchoff *et al*, 2011). With this approach, the supplier can increase the visibility of their own components in the final product for end consumers, thereby triggering a pull effect in the value chain (Homburg *et al*, 2014) – but also strengthening the sustainability performance, sales opportunities and competitiveness of the OEM customer (Foerstl *et al*, 2015). For example, upstream suppliers can leverage retailers' sustainability demand and packaging specifications by working closely with retailers. Alternatively, the supplier can also service a lucrative customer segment, which appreciates the advantages of its sustainable components produced in a sustainably oriented upper supply chain. Potentials also arise through the strengthening of employer attractiveness, since the integration of sustainability aspects also addresses potential applicants in the procurement area (Schaltegger and Harms, 2010).

Although in the original concept and definition of multilevel marketing the focus is on the downstream direction, within the context of sustainability its focus should be expanded to considering the upstream direction, ie from customers to suppliers' suppliers. This is particularly important for the study of CSR-related tensions and sustainability crises in which, as touched on earlier, consumers often mistrust companies from which they buy products because of scandals about how they were produced (for instance, when consumers discover the use of forced or child labour in mining or in agricultural production at the origin of the supply chain). Industrial customers should thus develop marketing measures (eg information, training sessions) across the upstream part of their value chain, considering not only their direct suppliers, but also suppliers' suppliers.

However, research gaps exist with regard to the mechanisms of multilevel marketing and the conditions under which multilevel marketing may reduce the behavioural gap and promote sustainable buyer behaviour at the end of the value chain (Grunwald, 2018):

1 *Which measures of multilevel marketing are most effective in influencing sustainable behaviour in the value chain and reducing the behavioural gap? For example, what contribution can multilevel marketing make to reducing a potential bullwhip effect of sustainable products?* Based on a literature review and a qualitative empirical study, Homburg *et al* (2014) provide a systematization approach for multilevel marketing measures, which distinguishes three relevant types of activities: (1) direct customer downstream support (eg indirect market research, downstream analysis of product requirements, product customization, educational training, process optimization); (2) cooperative indirect customer marketing (eg ingredient branding, trade shows, sales force visits, co-development of products or product applications); and (3) independent indirect customer marketing (eg classic or online media brand communication, educational

or technical services, co-development of products and product applications) (Homburg *et al*, 2014: 74). The effects of such measures on sustainable buying behaviour and their potential to reduce the behavioural gap should be further analysed and supplemented with an analysis of upstream marketing activities.

2 *How can multilevel marketing be used in dealing with CSR-related tensions, corporate irresponsibility and sustainability crises that reveal perceived behavioural gaps on the supply side? What lessons can be learned from this regarding the reduction of behavioural gaps on the demand side?* Measures of multilevel sustainability marketing, especially in the underexplored research fields of CSR-related tensions, corporate irresponsibility and sustainability crises, could provide deeper insights into the potentials and mechanisms of proactive and reactive CSR (Grunwald and Schwill, 2018). This could help in dealing with such forms of negative publicity by positively influencing sustainable buying behaviour and ultimately reducing behavioural gaps. In addition to value chain partners, such an analysis should also include external stakeholders who exert an impact on the value chain (eg interested parties and secondary stakeholders). Potentially, conclusions can be drawn from this also for impacting sustainable buying behaviour in the absence of negative CSR-related publicity.

3 *Under what conditions do measures of multilevel marketing promote or hinder sustainable behaviour at the end of the value chain?* Consistent with some of the aforementioned results of research on sustainable supply chain management, potential moderators of the effects of indirect sustainability marketing could be external with respect to value chain characteristics such as product value-related factors (eg product value contribution for direct and indirect customers) and power-related factors (eg relative power of the B2B supplier and indirect customers) (Homburg *et al*, 2014). Internal moderators relating to the B2B supplier's professionalization of indirect customer approaches could consist in structure-related factors (eg the allocation of vertical responsibility and cross-linking of vertical responsibility) as well as process-related factors (eg network relationship management and network performance measurement) (Homburg *et al*, 2014). Here, the potential resistance to multi-stage marketing in the value chain must be taken into account, in particular the acceptance of direct customers. Empirical research results, yet unrelated to sustainability, indicate that the acceptance of the direct customers is positively influenced by open communication with them about the strategy and the contribution

to their own benefit as well as the knowledge that their own customers are also open to being approached by the indirect suppliers. On the other hand, the acceptance of direct customers is lower if they have greater market power compared to the supplier (Homburg and Wilczek, 2014). These factors should be further empirically analysed in the context of sustainability marketing.

Although in the concept of multilevel marketing the focus is on actors of the value chain, the range of actors should be expanded in the context of sustainability (Seuring and Müller, 2008).

Due to the wide range of issues that should be examined (eg environmental concerns, social issues such as child labour or forced labour, ethical issues or integrity issues), a longer part of the value chain needs to be considered in addition to stakeholders outside the value chain such as NGOs or the media. Although such stakeholders do not always provide critical resources for the actors within the value chain, they often have sufficient organizational capacity to build up the potential for sanctions (Fischer, 2017), eg as in the case of sustainabiliy crises, and/or the potential for supporting the company's sustainability strategy via their specific expertise and their perceived organizational legitimacy in their consumers' eyes.

Conclusion

Thus far, sustainable buyer behaviour has predominantly been examined from the consumer perspective and has focused on a so-called behavioural gap between actual and manifested sustainable behaviour at the bottom of the value chain. Potential causes for insuffient sustainable behaviour on the demand side are seen especially in a low personal concern, scepticism and cynicism towards sustainability issues, insufficient perception and knowledge, inadequate pressure (or support) from peer groups or reference persons, conflicting values and various factors that can be subsumed under a low (perceived) behavioural control such as inadequate resources and self-efficacy. Determinants on the supply side are associated with an inadequate product price or quality, insufficient or complex information, low availability of sustainable offerings, low brand awareness and brand popularity as connected with the company's brand marketing, as well as contextual factors at the point of purchase. Inconsistencies in the CSR-related marketing of the provider, revealing gaps between stated and actual sustainability performance (as an equivalent of the behavioural gap on the demand side) are identified as a potential source of consumer distrust and CSR-related tensions. These can be seen as precursors of sustainability crises, with negative impacts on sustainable buying behaviour. CSR-related tensions and sustainability crises are identified as still relatively unexplored research fields that should be addressed by future research contributions with regard to explaining (non-)sustainable buyer behaviour.

Overall, however, previous buyer behaviour research has tended to focus on the actors with direct customer contact at the end of the value chain. At this point, this chapter examines further causes for (non-)sustainable buyer behaviour at the upstream stages of the value chain also, especially considering the direct and indirect relationships of the value chain partners. Research contributions in the field of sustainable supply chain management have identified some external and internal factors such as the lack of stakeholder influences and opportunities for reputation building as well as competitive opportunities at the product and process level, which impact supplier sustainability and demand–supply integration, thereby potentially influencing sustainable buyer behaviour at the end of the value chain.

In the value chain context, the approach of multilevel (indirect) marketing appears promising, which also gives suppliers at the upper end or middle of the value chain possibilities to make their sustainability contributions more visible to customers' customers, thereby exploiting the full potential of a proactive sustainable supply chain management. Analysing the options for action and the effects of multilevel marketing with regard to influencing sustainable consumer behaviour at the end of the value chain also represents a research field that is still underdeveloped, both theoretically and empirically. Within the framework of the project academy of the German Research Foundation (DFG) on the topic of sustainability in global value chains, a research framework and empirical pre-studies are conceived to analyse sustainable multilevel marketing in the context of CSR-related tensions and sustainability crises.

References

Ajzen, I (1988) *Attitudes, Personality, and Behaviour*, Dorsey Press, Chicago

Ajzen, I (1991) The theory of planned behaviour, *Organizational Behaviour and Human Decision Processes*, **50**, pp 179–211

Aregon, B, Gunasekaran, A and Spalanzani, A (2011) Sustainable supply management: An empirical study, *International Journal of Production Economics*, **140** (1), pp 168–82

Balderjahn, I (2013) *Nachhaltiges Management und Konsumentenverhalten*, UTB, Constance and Munich

Bartolomeo, DM, Dal Maso, D, De Jong, P, Eder, P, Groenewegen, P, Hopkinson, P and Slob, A (2003) Eco-efficient producer services: What are they, how do they benefit customers and the environment and how likely are they to develop and be extensively utilised? *Journal of Cleaner Production*, **11** (8), pp 829–37

Belz, F-M and Peattie, K (2012) *Sustainability Marketing: A global perspective*, 2nd edn, Wiley, Chichester

BMUB – Bundesministerium für Umwelt, Naturschutz, Bau und Reaktorsicherheit (ed) (2016) Nationales Programm für nachhaltigen Konsum – Gesellschaftlicher Wandel durch einen nachhaltigen Lebensstil, Berlin

Bolton, E, Cohen, JB and Bloom, PN (2006) Does marketing products as remedies create 'get out of jail free cards'? *Journal of Consumer Research*, **33** (1), pp 71–81

Bray, J, Johns, N and Kilburn, D (2011) An exploratory study into the factors impeding ethical consumption, *Journal of Business Ethics*, **98** (4), pp 597–608

Bruel, O, Menuet, O and Thaler, P-F (2017) [accessed 23 September 2020] *Scaling Up Sustainable Procurement: A new phase of expansion must begin – White paper based on the 2017 HEC/EcoVadis Sustainable Procurement Barometer, 7th Edition*, HEC, Paris [Online] https://aim-progress.com/files/22/2017-hec-ecovadis-sp-barometer-7th-edition.pdf (archived at https://perma.cc/XQ69-PH6P)

Carrington, MJ, Neville, BA and Whitwell, GJ (2010) Why ethical consumers don't walk their talk: Toward a framework for understanding the gap between the ethical purchase intentions and actual buying behaviour of ethically minded consumers, *Journal of Business Ethics*, **97** (1), pp 139–58

Carrington, MJ, Neville, BA and Whitwell, GJ (2014) Lost in translation: Exploring the ethical consumer intention–behaviour gap, *Journal of Business Research*, **67** (1), pp 2759–67

Cherry, CE and Pidgeon, NF (2018) Why is ownership an issue? Exploring factors that determine public acceptance of product-service systems, *Sustainability*, **10** (7), p 2289, 10.3390/su10072289

Closs, DJ, Speier, C and Meacham, N (2011) Sustainability to support end-to-end value chains: The role of supply chain management, *Journal of the Academy of Marketing Science*, **39** (1), pp 101–16

De Pelsmacker, P, Janssens, W, Sterckx, E and Mielants, C (2005) Consumer preferences for the marketing of ethically labelled coffee, *International Marketing Review*, **22** (5), pp 512–30

Demailly, D and Novel, A-S (2014) *The Sharing Economy: Make it sustainable*, Studies N°03/14, IDDRI, Paris, France

D'Souza, C, Taghian, M, Lamb, P and Peretiatko, R (2007) Green decisions: Demographics and consumer understanding of environmental labels, *International Journal of Consumer Studies*, **31** (4), pp 371–376

Dubois, G, Sovacool, B, Aall, C, Nilsson, M, Barbier, C, Herrmann, A, Bruyère, S, Andersson, C, Skold, B, Nadaud, F, Dorner, F, Richardsen Moberg, K, Ceron, JP,

Fischer, H, Amelung, D, Baltruszewicz, M, Fischer, J, Benevise, F, Louis, VR and Sauerborn, R (2019) It starts at home? Climate policies targeting household consumption and behavioural decisions are key to low-carbon futures, *Energy Research and Social Science*, **52**, pp 144–58

Eckardt, GH (2010) *Business-to-Business-Marketing*, Schäffer-Poeschel, Stuttgart

EEA (European Environment Agency) (2013) *Environmental Pressures from European Consumption and Production: A study in integrated environmental and economic analysis, Technical report No 2/2013*, EEA, Copenhagen

Etzioni, A (1998) Voluntary simplicity: Characterization, select psychological implications, and societal consequences, *Journal of Economic Psychology*, **19**, pp 619–43

Fawcett, SE and Magnan, GM (2002) The rhetoric and reality of supply chain integration, *International Journal of Physical Distribution and Logistics Management*, **32** (5), pp 339–61

Fischer, D, Michelsen, G, Blättel-Mink, B and Di Giulio, A (2012) Sustainable consumption: How to evaluate sustainability in consumption acts, in *The Nature of Sustainable Consumption and How to Achieve It: Results from the focal topic 'From knowledge to action – new paths towards sustainable consumption'*, ed R Defila, A Di Giulio and R Kaufmann-Hayoz, Oekom, Munich, pp 67–80

Fischer, K (2017) *Corporate Sustainability Governance. Nachhaltigkeitsbezogene Steuerung von Unternehmen in einer globalisierten Welt*, Springer, Wiesbaden

Fishbein, M (1963) An investigation of the relationships between beliefs about an object and the attitude toward the object, *Human Relations*, **16**, pp 233–40

Fishbein, M (1967) Attitude and the prediction of behaviour, in *Readings in Attitude Theory and Measurement*, ed M Fishbein, Wiley, New York

Foerstl, K, Azadegan, A, Leppelt, T and Hartmann, E (2015) Drivers of supplier sustainability: Moving beyond compliance to commitment, *Journal of Supply Chain Management*, **51** (1), pp 67–92

Geiger, SM, Fischer, D and Schrader, U (2018) Measuring what matters in sustainable consumption: An Integrative framework for the selection of relevant behaviours, Sustainable *Development*, **26** (1), pp 18–33

Ginsberg, JM and Bloom, PN (2004) Choosing the right green marketing strategy, *MIT Sloan Management Review*, **46** (1), pp 79–84

Giunipero, LC, Hooker, RE and Denslow, D (2012) Purchasing and supply management sustainability: Drivers and barriers, *Journal of Purchasing and Supply Management*, **18** (4), pp 258–69

Grunwald, G (2016) Nachhaltiges Käuferverhalten zwischen Bekundung und Kaufrelevanz: Erklärungsansätze und Marketingimplikationen, Antrittsvorlesung an der Hochschule Osnabrück, Fakultät Management, Kultur und Technik, 27 April 2016, Lingen/Ems

Grunwald, G (2018) [accessed 23 September 2020] Nachhaltiges Käuferverhalten in der Wertschöpfungskette: Determinanten und Marketingimplikationen,

Projektantrag im Rahmen der DFG-Projektakademie [Online] http://gepris.dfg.de/gepris/projekt/419736677 (archived at https://perma.cc/3QBX-43WB)

Grunwald, G and Hempelmann, B (2017) *Angewandte Marketinganalyse: Praxisbezogene Konzepte und Methoden zur betrieblichen Entscheidungsunterstützung*, De Gruyter, Berlin/Boston

Grunwald, G and Hennig, P (2012) Beiträge der REACH-Umsetzung zur CSR-Strategie, *Zeitschrift für Wirtschafts- und Unternehmensethik* (Journal for Business, Economics and Ethics), **13** (1), pp 82–91

Grunwald, G and Hennig, P (2014) Impacts of the REACH candidate list of substances subject to authorisation: The reputation mechanism and empirical results on behavioural adaptations of German supply chain actors, *Journal of Business Chemistry*, **11** (2), pp 53–66

Grunwald, G and Ostendorf, RJ (2012) Verankerung von REACH in der Unternehmensstrategie: Alternative Ansätze zur ökologischen Positionierung im Wettbewerb, Umweltwirtschaftsforum, **20** (2), pp 189–95

Grunwald, G and Schwill, J (2017) *Beziehungsmarketing: Gestaltung nachhaltiger Geschäftsbeziehungen – Grundlagen und Praxis*, Schäffer-Poeschel, Stuttgart

Grunwald, G and Schwill, J (2018) Managing latent corporate sustainability crises: The effects of crisis content and CSR specifity, in *Global Marketing Conference (GMC) at Tokyo Proceedings, 26–29 July, Global Alliance of Marketing and Management Associations (GAMMA), Changwon National University*, ed JChoi, Changwon, Korea, pp 280–90

Gupta, S and Ogden, DT (2009) To buy or not to buy? A social dilemma perspective on green buying, *Journal of Consumer Marketing*, **26** (6), pp 376–91

Ham, C-D and Kim, J (2017) The role of CSR in crises: Integration of situational crisis communication theory and the persuasion knowledge model, *Journal of Business Ethics*, **158** (2), pp 353–72

Hansen, U and Schrader, U (2001) Nachhaltiger Konsum – Leerformel oder Leitprinzip? in *Nachhaltiger Konsum. Forschung und Praxis im Dialog*, ed U Schrader and U Hansen, Campus, Frankfurt/Main, pp 17–45

Hoffmann, J (2018) Talking into (non) existence: Denying or constituting paradoxes of corporate social responsibility, *Human Relations*, **71** (5), pp 668–91

Homburg, C and Wilczek, H (2014) Mehrstufiges Marketing: Erfolgswirkungen und Erfolgsfaktoren, IMU Research Insights, 021, Working Paper, Institut für Marktorientierte Unternehmensführung, Universität Mannheim

Homburg, C, Wilczek, H and Hahn, A (2014) Looking beyond the horizon: How to approach the customers' customers in business-to-business markets, *Journal of Marketing*, **78** (5), pp 58–77

IFH Köln (Institut für Handelsforschung) (2011) CSR-Tracker – Basisreporting, 2, Welle 2011, Cologne

imug (Institut für Markt-Umwelt-Gesellschaft) (2014) Nachhaltiger Konsum: Schon Mainstream oder noch Nische? imug Konsumstudie im Auftrag der REWE Group, Hannover

Ivanova, D, Stadler, K, Steen-Olsen, K, Wood, R, Vita, G, Tukker, A and Hertwich, EG (2015) Environmental impact assessment of household consumption, *Journal of Industrial Ecology*, **20** (3), pp 526–36

Janssen, C and Vanhamme, J (2015) Theoretical lenses for understanding the CSR–consumer paradox, *Journal of Business Ethics*, **130** (4), pp 775–87

Janssen, MA and Jager, W (2002) Stimulating diffusion of green products: Co-evolution between firms and consumers, *Journal of Evolutionary Economics*, **12** (3), pp 283–306

Jarvis, C (2009) [accessed 23 September 2020] The 3 basic steps to create trust through corporate social responsibility, Fast Company [Online] https://www.fastcompany.com/1323260/3-basic-steps-create-trust-through-corporate-social-responsibility (archived at https://perma.cc/6VZQ-CDW7)

Kirchoff, JF, Koch, C and Nichols, BS (2011) Stakeholder perceptions of green marketing: The effect of demand and supply integration, *International Journal of Physical Distribution and Logistics Management*, **41** (7), pp 684–96

Kleinaltenkamp, M and Saab, S (2009) *Technischer Vertrieb: Eine praxisorientierte Einführung in das Business-to-Business-Marketing*, Springer, Berlin/Heidelberg

Koplin, J, Seuring, S and Mesterharm, M (2007) Incorporating sustainability into supply management in the automotive industry: The case of the Volkswagen AG, *Journal of Cleaner Production*, **15** (11–12), pp 1053–62

Kostadinova, E (2016) Sustainable consumer behaviour: Literature overview, *Economic Alternatives*, **2**, pp 224–34

Kroeber-Riel, W and Gröppel-Klein, A (2013) *Konsumentenverhalten*, 10th edn, Vahlen, Munich

Leppelt, T, Foerstl, K, Reuter, C and Hartmann, E (2013) Sustainability management beyond organizational boundaries: Sustainable supplier relationship management in the chemical industry, *Journal of Cleaner Production*, **56**, pp 94–102

Lindgreen, A, Maon, F and Swaen, V (2009) Guest editorial: Corporate social responsibility in the supply chain, *Supply Chain Management: An international journal*, **14** (2), pp 71–74

Lindgreen, A, Swaen, V and Maon, F (2009) Editorial: Corporate social responsibility within the organization, *Corporate Reputation Review*, **12** (2), pp 83–86

Lorek, S and Spangenberg, JH (2001): Indicators for environmentally sustainable household consumption, *International Journal of Sustainable Development*, **4** (1), pp 101–20

Luchs, MG, Naylor, RW, Irwin, JR and Raghunathan, R (2010) The sustainability liability: Potential negative effects of ethicality on product preference, *Journal of Marketing*, **74** (5), pp 18–31

Lunde, MB (2018) Sustainability in marketing: A systematic review unifying 20 years of theoretical and substantive contributions (1997–2016), *AMS Review*, **8** (3), pp 85–110

Maon, F, Vanhamme, J, De Roeck, K, Lindgreen, A and Swaen, V (2019) The dark side of stakeholder reactions to corporate social responsibility: Tensions and micro-level undesirable outcomes, *International Journal of Management Reviews*, **21** (2), pp 209–30

Martin, DM and Väistö, T (2016) Reducing the attitude–behaviour gap in sustainable consumption: A theoretical proposition and the American electric vehicle market, in *Marketing in and for a Sustainable Society (Review of Marketing Research, 13)*, ed NK Malhotra, Emerald Group Publishing, Bingley, pp 193–213

McDonald, S, Oates, C, Thyne, M, Alevizou, P and McMorland, L-A (2009) Comparing sustainable consumption patterns across product sectors, *International Journal of Consumer Studies*, **33** (2), pp 137–45

Meyer-Höfer, M von and Spiller, A (2012) *Anforderungen an eine nachhaltige Land- und Ernährungswirtschaft: Die Rolle des Konsumenten*, KTBL Schrift 500: Steuerungsinstrumente für eine nachhaltige Landwirtschaft – Stand und Perspektiven, Neu-Ulm, pp 7–16

Minton, EA, Spielmann, N, Kahle, LR and Kim, C-H (2018) The subjective norms of sustainable consumption: A cross-cultural exploration, *Journal of Business Research*, **82**, pp 400–08

Mohr, LA, Eroglu, D and Ellen, PS (1998) The development and testing of a measure of skepticism toward environmental claims in marketers' communications, *Journal of Consumer Affairs*, **32** (1), pp 30–55

Mont, O (2003) Editorial for the special issue of the *Journal of Cleaner Production* on product service systems, *Journal of Cleaner Production*, **11** (8), pp 815–17

Nelson, P (1970) Information and consumer behaviour, *Journal of Political Economy*, **78** (2), pp 311–29

Nielsen (2015) [accessed 23 September 2020] Looking to achieve new product success? Listen to your consumers – Global Product Innovation Survey 2015 [Online] https://www.nielsen.com/uk/en/insights/report/2015/looking-to-achieve-new-product-success/ (archived at https://perma.cc/72LL-LWPG)

Öberseder, M, Schlegelmilch, BB and Gruber, V (2011) Why don't consumers care about CSR? A qualitative study exploring the role of CSR in consumption decisions, *Journal of Business Ethics*, **104** (4), pp 449–60

Paco, AMF and Reis, R (2013) Factors affecting skepticism toward green advertising, *Journal of Advertising*, **41** (4), pp 147–55

Peattie, K (2010) Green consumption: Behaviour and norms, *Annual Review of Environmental Ressources*, **35**, pp 195–228Robertson, TS, Zielinski, J and Ward, S (1984) *Consumer Behaviour*, Scott, Foresman and Company, Glenview, IL

Rokka, J and Uusitalo, L (2008) Preference for green packaging in consumer product choices: Do consumers care? *International Journal of Consumer Studies*, **32** (5), pp 516–25

Sajjad, A, Eweje, G and Tappin, D (2015) Sustainable supply chain management: Motivators and barriers, *Business Strategy and the Environment*, **24**, pp 643–55

Schaltegger, S and Harms, D (2010) Sustainable supply chain management: Praxisstand in deutschen Unternehmen, Center for Sustainability Management (CSM) e.V., Lüneburg

Schoenheit, I and Schudak, A (2013) [accessed 23 September 2020] Indikatoren für Nachhaltigen Konsum – Abschlussbericht, imug Institut, Hannover [Online] https://www.imug.de/fileadmin/user_upload/Downloads/imug_institut/Schoenheit_Schudak_2013_Indikatoren_Nachhaltiger_Konsum_BLE.pdf (archived at https://perma.cc/62RG-MM68)

Schrader, U, Liedtke, C, Lamla, J, Arens-Azevedo, U, Hagen, K, Jaquemoth, M, Kenning, P, Schmidt-Kessel, M and Strünck, C (2013) Verbraucherpolitik für nachhaltigen Konsum –Verbraucherpolitische Perspektiven für eine nachhaltige Transformation von Wirtschaft und Gesellschaft: Stellungnahme des wissenschaftlichen Beirats Verbraucher- und Ernährungspolitik beim BMELV – German Federal Ministry for Food, Agriculture and Consumer Protection, Berlin

Seuring, S and Müller, M (2008) From a literature review to a conceptual framework for sustainable supply chain management, *Journal of Cleaner Production*, **16** (15), pp 1699–710

Sheth, JN, Sharma, A and Iyer, GR (2009) Why integrating purchasing with marketing is both inevitable and beneficial, *Industrial Marketing Management*, **38** (8), pp 865–71

Steen-Olsen, K and Hertwich, EG (2015) Life cycle assessment as a means to identify the most effective action for sustainable consumption, in *Handbook of Research on Sustainable Consumption*, ed LA Reisch and J Thøgersen, Edward Elgar Publishing, Cheltenham, pp 131–44

Stern, P, Dietz, T and Guagnano, G (1995) The new ecological paradigm in social-psychological context, *Environment and Behaviour*, **27** (6), pp 723–43

Straughan, RD and Roberts, JA (1999) Environmental segmentation alternatives: A look at green consumer behaviour in the new millennium, *Journal of Consumer Marketing*, **16** (6), pp 558–75

Tay, MY, Rahman, AA, Aziz, YA and Sidek, S (2015) A review on drivers and barriers towards sustainable supply chain practices, *International Journal of Social Science and Humanity*, **5** (10), pp 892–97

Terry, DJ, Hogg, MA and White, KM (1999) The theory of planned behaviour: Self-identity, social identity and group norms, *British Journal of Social Psychology*, **38** (3), pp 225–44

Thogersen, J (2010) Country differences in sustainable consumption: The case of organic food, *Journal of Macromarketing*, **30** (2), pp 171–85

Vermeir, I and Verbeke, W (2006) Sustainable food consumption: Exploring the consumer 'attitude–behavioural intention' gap, *Journal of Agricultural and Environmental Ethics*, **19** (2), pp 169–94

Wagner, T, Lutz, RJ and Weitz, BA (2009) Corporate hypocrisy: Overcoming the threat of inconsistent corporate social responsibility perceptions, *Journal of Marketing*, **73** (6), pp 77–91

Tactical planning measures for sustainable and efficient international transportation networks 09

MICHAEL DIRCKSEN

Introduction

International trade is growing and, accordingly, so is the demand for transport. On a national level, there exists a binary relationship between tonne-kms and gross domestic product (GDP), and this can be extended to a three-way relationship with the international perspective of the trade multiplier (McKinnon, 2017: 82–83). On a global level, transport, storage and communication costs are growing in line with the GDP in sum; however, disaggregating this data shows that in some countries, the share of transport, storage and communication costs of the GDP have decreased, while in other countries the opposite can be measured (see Figure 9.1). In addition, consumption expenditures and international trade are growing in most countries (United Nations Department of Economic and Social Affairs, 2018: 301–17; Airbus SAS, 2018: 18).

Figure 9.1 Expenditure on transport, storage and communication and GDP

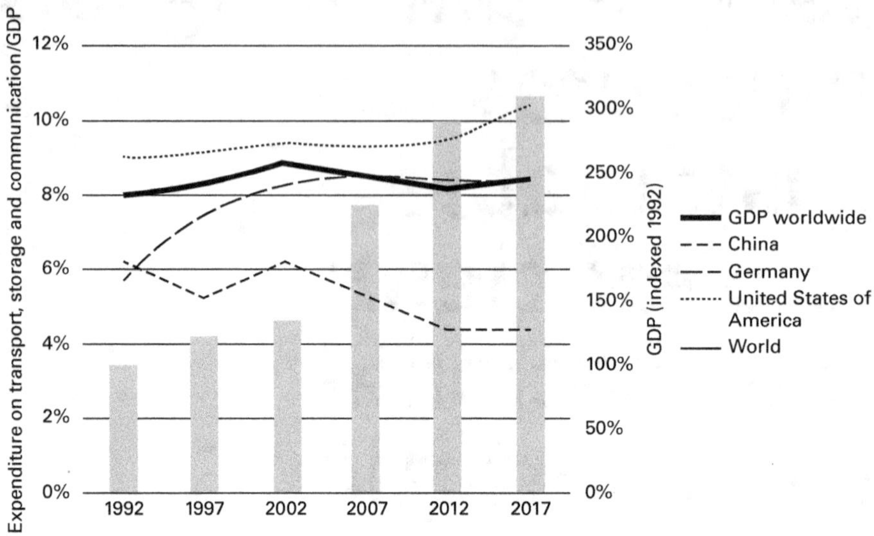

SOURCE Own, based on data published by United Nations Conference on Trade and Development, 2019a, 2019b

No global data are available on transport demand. Container freight volume (+ 4.8 per cent in 2017) and air freight volume (+9.0 per cent in 2017) have increased internationally, whereas road and rail volume are only estimated on a national level, showing growth rates of between 2.1 per cent and 6.4 per cent in the EU, Russia, and the USA (International Transport Forum, 2018: 1).

Beside the economic perspective, the ecological view on our behaviour is gaining increasing attention. With growing transport demand, the energy consumption of the transport sector grows as well (EIA, 2018: 127). Since the Earth Summit climate conference held in Rio de Janeiro in 1992, ecological targets have been detailed step by step. Measured from the base year of 1995, the overall target of the European Community is a greenhouse gas emissions reduction of 80–95 per cent by 2050 (European Commission, 2018: 4). For the transport sector in Germany, different scenarios have been calculated to achieve this goal. Suggested measures are a modal shift, energy consumption reduction, low-emission drive systems, and emission-neutral fuels (Hasler, 2019: 3; Rolle, 2018: 167). However, green initiatives should be aligned with the market focus on efficiency to obtain a holistic view (Höglund, 2016: 12). A study by the Confederation of Germany Industry (BDI) revealed a disillusioning picture: at least 80 per cent of investments in green alternatives yield no positive return under current circumstances (Rolle and Nuyken, 2019: 1).

A review of the literature reveals numerous definitions of sustainability that consider different objectives. The most frequently quoted definition comes from the UN World Commission on Environment and Development (WCED): 'development that meets the needs of the present without compromising the ability of future generations to meet their own needs' (World Commission on Environment and Development, 1987). In keeping with this definition, the present author understands sustainability as operating practices of a value-creation system that meet the needs of present users with respect to costs and service level without compromising the ability of future generations to meet their own needs, particularly with regard to scarce natural resources. Sustainable operating practices support ecological, human and economic health and endurance. Regarding sustainability, the focus of this chapter lies on CO_2 emissions. CO_2 is one of six greenhouse gases of the UN Kyoto protocol, and it accounts for 90–95 per cent of emissions in the logistics sector (McKinnon, 2017: 36).

The goal of this chapter is to evaluate the potential of sustainable tactical planning measures in transportation networks. This requires the consideration of economic and environmental factors in decision-making situations. The first part describes the different logistical functions and planning phases to gain a common understanding of the decision-making field. The evaluation aspects for costs, time and CO_2 emissions are then defined. With those evaluation aspects different measures within the tactical planning field can be evaluated. Those measures are distinguished in investment decisions or regarding ongoing managerial or operational tasks. The first part shows the impact of investments using the return on investment (ROI), and in the last section an applied approach is used to develop holistic ways of evaluating managerial and operational tasks in transportation networks.

Logistics functions in international transport networks

While there is no difference in the basic problems of national and international logistics, there are particular frameworks that lead to a greater complexity and higher risks for international logistic processes (Flaherty, 1996: 281; Stock and Lambert, 2001: 376; Schieck, 2008: 70; Pfohl, 2010: 337). In general, international logistics is characterized by a high degree of complexity, since companies mostly accept national boundaries and organize their planning on a country-specific basis (Mayer *et al*, 2009: 33; Bretzke,

2010: 164). The key tasks of international logistics are processing, warehousing and transport (Specht and Fritz, 2005: 115). The impact of the framework conditions on these areas should therefore be focused on during planning.

Order processing

On the one hand, processing is concerned with company-internal processes and, on the other hand, it interacts with external actors. As borders are crossed, companies must deal with custom authorities. However, the import regulations and processes in the target country play a decisive role in expenditures and lead times (Organisation for Economic Co-operation and Development, 2003: 4–5; Lewis, 2009: 6–7). Due to these basic conditions, customs represents a significant part of the lead time and must be integrated into the planning procedure as a central evaluation parameter.

Transport

Depending on the respective processes and distribution structures, transport options must be evaluated in advance as part of the planning process. Since a directly comparable abstraction of specific variables cannot be achieved, detailed knowledge of the conditions, prices and terms is indispensable (Klatt, 1997: 1209; Wildemann, 2010: 214).

In terms of transport weight, ocean shipping is the most significant carrier, with a share of 90 per cent of international goods transport (International Chamber of Shipping, 2019). The advantage of ocean transport lies mainly in the vast quantity of goods that can be transported over great distances. The internationally significant operating mode of liner shipping is mainly deployed in container traffic, with the providers of line shipping services facing an anonymous transport market on the demand side (Böhme, 1997: 544). Airfreight comprises 35 per cent of transport volume based on value; however, this still accounts for only 1 per cent of the worldwide movement of goods. Just 50 per cent of airfreight volume is transported in 'freight-only' aircraft, since the joint transport of passengers and freight offers the advantage of more flight routes (Airbus SAS, 2018: 129; Crabtree *et al*, 2018: 7). Regarding rail transport, trends show that the use of carriers in modern logistical concepts is restricted to regular block trains between well-developed handling centres. The complexity increases noticeably in an international context due to technical specifications and case-specific applications and their organization (Kummer, 2010: 131). It is established that there are only a few states where road transport is not the dominant mode of inland transport. The supply side of transport services can be described as 'atomized' in most countries, since it is dominated by many small and medium-sized companies. Aside from vehicles and various actors, on the infrastructural level, road freight transport requires roads and transhipment facilities (Aberle, 2009: 162–67).

Warehousing and transhipment

The number of warehouses depends on the geographical size of the logistical area, the expected response time of the demanders, the value of the goods stored, the lead time, and the respective transport costs (Ihde, 1991: 44). The basic decision about storage in a region is primarily influenced by the expected supply service. However, bundling effects that can be realized by temporal decoupling of supply from transport can also lead to warehousing (Bretzke, 2010: 172–82). In addition to warehousing costs, the geographical location plays a part in the planning process. During the planning phase, it is possible to establish the point at which minimal total costs are achieved. Detailed location factors and local conditions are excluded in early planning stages and postponed to later concrete planning and implementation processes, since they are highly difficult to parameterize (Gudehus, 2005: 386; Bretzke, 2010: 163; Schieck, 2008: 348).

Decisions concerning transhipment are like those on warehousing due to the similar process integration of these functions. The differentiating attribute is that for transhipment, the function of storage is replaced by a short time buffer. Primary unloading and loading procedures as well as sorting tasks are the foreseen activities. Transhipment points are often multimodally connected to fulfil the tasks in intermodal transport chains (Rodemann *et al*, 2018: 128–37).

Planning processes

Success in national and international competition is defined by the competitive advantages of business activities. Among the primary activities in the value chain is distribution logistics, which is closely related to customers and can therefore generate competitive advantages directly (Porter, 2010: 1–3). For internal customers, such as the functions of purchasing and production, logistics supports and creates indirect value. As a performance indicator from both perspectives, the service level represents the key or crucial worth of the assessment of a logistical system: it shows the value or the share of orders that are delivered within an agreed or planned time frame (Gudehus, 2005; Chopra and Meindl, 2016; Wildemann, 2010) for external and internal customers.

Considering the scope of decisions regarding the dimensions of time, management level, importance for the company and degree of aggregation, the planning process can be differentiated into the strategic, the tactical and the operational level (Günther and Tempelmeier, 2016: 22; Klein and Scholl, 2012: 19–20). General policies are developed on the highest level: strategic planning. Exemplary decisions in the field of logistics concern the design of physical transport networks and their evolution. Further examples are the location planning of major facilities, the acquisition of major resources, and the definition of broad service and tariff policies (Crainic, 2003: 461). In general, the goals and therefore the tasks are multifarious and need to be defined, for example in order to support the competitive strategy (Schulte, 2013: 56–58). For tasks that are identified as being served by own assets, the planning scope includes the determination of the number of assets of each type, the period of deployment and depreciation, and the way the vehicles are financed, maintained and serviced (Wieberneit, 2007: 78; Seiler, 2012: 68).

Following the described methodology, the strategic planning sets the framework for the tactical planning level. Tactical planning with the medium-term time horizon aims to determine the fleet size, the allocation of properties, and the utilization of existing resources (Crainic, 2003: 461; Klein and Scholl, 2012: 20; Fleischmann and Kopfer, 2018: 72). The decisions aim to achieve the best possible performance of the whole system regarding service level and cost. Concrete planning issues are frequency and scheduling decisions, traffic distribution, terminal policies, and balancing strategies for empties (Crainic, 2003: 479–481; Seiler, 2012: 69; Wieberneit, 2007: 81–82). Therefore, products, materials, customers, facilities, and suppliers are assigned to transport concepts to develop and establish a mid-term load plan within the transport network (Seiler, 2012: 68).

Bringing into account specific and incidental transport demands or other issues, local management performs the operational (short-term) planning. Important operational decisions concern the implementation and adjustment of schedules for services, crews and maintenance activities; the routing and dispatching of vehicles and crews; and the dynamic allocation of resources (Crainic, 2003: 461; Fleischmann and Kopfer, 2018: 72).

In addition to the strategic, tactical and operational level, several mixed forms are described in the literature, and the allocation of the tasks and issues is heterogeneous. In this chapter, the following scope is suggested: tactical planning is the determination and scheduling of the immediate activities required in achieving the objectives of strategic planning (Klein and Scholl, 2012: 20). For this purpose, the phase includes decisions about investment and disinvestment of assets following the strategic principles and defines guidelines and concepts based on forecasted transport demands. The goal is to achieve an optimal service level with the most efficient input and output relation of the logistics functions considering the dimensions of costs, time and sustainability.

Definition of assessment dimensions

Determination of costs

Due to the different cost calculation models of the logistical functions and target conflicts between cost elements – for example, transportation costs vs inventory costs – the target function for the optimization is not linear (Chopra and Meindl, 2016: 428). For the customers, operators have developed different service types to fulfil heterogeneous transport demands, such as less-container-load (LCL) for smaller transportation demands instead of full-container-load (FCL). The movement of the decoupling point by a delivery warehouse enables the implementation of a customer-neutral replenishment process to achieve bundling effects. The costs for inventory are moving antithetical to the fixed order costs, whereby they can be decreased by ordering smaller replenishment lots. To follow the idea of the total cost optimum, the order lot size should be calculated using the trade-off between the fixed replenishment cost factors and the inventory and warehousing costs (Thonemann and Albers, 2010: 198).

In addition to the described transportation, warehouse and transhipment, the tie up capital needs to be considered. The capital charge in the warehouse is calculated by the average stock level multiplied by the production price plus the costs of operation according to the total costs of ownership (TCO) approach (Schulte, 2013: 303). The capital costs during transportation are dependent on the product value during transport and the transportation time. In conclusion, only the total cost of the transportation chain, including transportation, inventory, warehousing, customs, and transhipment costs, is relevant to the decision. Table 9.1 provides an overview of different transport and transhipment costs, separated into the make and buy perspectives.

Table 9.1 Exemplary cost factors of logistic functions

Element	BUY: Transportation mode or service type	BUY: Cost factor	MAKE: Cost factor
Pre-carriage on road	Sea freight – LCL	Rate per m^3 charge weight per region depending on departure seaport	Load volume / total load volume of vehicle × variable costs per vehicle km + fixed costs
	Sea freight – FCL	Fixed rate per container per region depending on departure seaport	TEU / total TEU × variable costs per vehicle km + fixed costs
	Airfreight	Rate per kg charge weight per region depending on departure airport	Load volume / total load volume of vehicle × variable costs per vehicle km + fixed costs
Customs export and import	All service types	Per entry	Per entry
Transhipment (before and after main run)	Sea freight – LCL	Rate per m^3 charge weight per trade lane	Usually no self-entry
	Sea freight – FCL	Fixed rate per container per seaport	
	Airfreight	Included in the main run rate	
Main run	Sea freight – LCL	Rate per m^3 charge weight per trade lane	
	Sea freight – FCL	Fixed rate per container per trade lane	
	Airfreight	Rate per kg charge weight per trade lane	
On-carriage to warehouse or delivery from port/airport to the destination on the road	Sea freight –LCL	Rate per m^3 charge weight per region depending on arrival seaport	Load volume / total load volume of vehicle × variable costs per vehicle km + fixed costs
	Sea freight – FCL	Fixed rate per container per region depending on arrival seaport	TEU / total TEU per vehicle × variable costs per vehicle km + fixed costs
	Airfreight	Rate per kg charge weight per region depending on arrival airport	Load volume / total load volume of vehicle × variable costs per vehicle km + fixed costs
Delivery from warehouse to the final destination	Road – groupage	Cost per charge weight cluster and distance cluster (matrix tariff)	Load volume / total load volume of vehicle × variable costs per vehicle km + fixed costs

Determination of time

Delivery or replenishment time is an important factor on the service level of the logistic system. Shorter lead times reduce the bounded capital in the supply chain and increase flexibility. The choice of transport mode has a large impact on the travelling time of the goods, but intermodal chains are often necessary to realize door-to-door movement. In addition, administrative tasks or regulations such as customs procedures or order processing times and material handling increase the total lead time after the transport demand occurs. For the physical movement, the availability of transport assets at the point of loading needs to be ensured, and the transit time must be calculated. Transhipment, cargo consolidation, and external circumstances such as traffic jams or weather conditions affect the calculation as well. Service providers normally offer various operation times for the service, and customers can often choose between service models with different transport times. Usually, a higher operational flexibility for the service provider means lower costs.

Besides the service level, the lead time also affects costs for warehousing. Uncertainty regarding the demand and the volatility of lead times needs to be handled. In addition, the frequency of delivery also influences the period of certainty. Those effects are compensated by security stocks to avoid a lack in the delivery capability. Because of the higher stock level, the bounded capital in the supply chain increases and leads to higher capital costs. Finally, the possibility to move the order penetration point in the delivery process after a possible storage procedure enables a reduction in the customer-related delivery time. It should be mentioned that production-related activities, known as value-adding services, can also be operated in the warehouse to move the order penetration point backwards.

Determination of CO_2 emissions

Different uncoordinated efforts by standards agencies, industry bodies, and governments have led to many approaches and methodologies to measure emissions within logistics processes. Furthermore, companies have developed their own approaches due to the lack of guidance on measurement, analysis, and reporting (Auvinen *et al*, 2014: 42–44). Hence, steps have been taken to reduce this diversity to harmonize carbon accounting in the logistics sector (McKinnon, 2017: 38). The acceptance of EN 16258 as the first standard focusing on emission calculation for transports was the reason for

Table 9.2 Exemplary calculation methods of CO_2 emissions

Function / Factor	Sea freight	Airfreight	Road	Rail	Transhipment harbour	Transhipment airport	Warehousing
Volume	Calc volume per container and no of containers [1], [3]	Ton [2]	Ton [1]	Ton [4]	Calc volume per container [1]	Ton [7]	Square metre [7]
Bridged difference	Actual distance [3]	Great circle distance [2]	Distance [3]	Distance separated in electrified and diesel tracks [3]	Picked volume / total volume [7]	Picked volume / total volume [7]	Time used [1]
Consumption factor	FCL: global default value container vessel [3] for LCL: multiply with average payload [8]	Global default value hybrid aircraft [3]	Per truck; average payload EU [3], [5]	Per waggon; average payload EU [3]	Energy consumption (electric power, gas, oil) [7], [8]	Energy consumption (electric power, gas, oil) [7], [8]	Energy consumption (electric power, gas, oil) [7], [8]
Emission factor	International factor [4] – CO_2 – well to wheel	International factor [4] – CO_2 – well to wheel	Regional emission factors [6] – CO_2 – well to wheel	Regional emission factors separated diesel and electric [3] – CO_2 – well to wheel	International factor [4]	Average factor [7]	Average factor [7]

SOURCE [1] Dircksen (2012), [2] International Air Transport Association (undated), [3] EcoTransIT World Initiative (2018), [4] Greene and Lewis (2016), [5] Wilmsmeier and Spengler (2015: 6), [6] Deutsches Institut für Normung (2013), [7] Rüdiger *et al* (2016: 891–94), [8] Schmied and Knörr (2013: 56–58) establishing it as a central methodological item (Deutsches Institut für Normung, 2013). This emphasis has been further supported by the broad acceptance of the standard for transports inside and outside Europe. However, further efforts will have to tackle current restrictions, such as the ambiguity in the choice of transportation system, the differentiation in case of combined transports, and the lack of emission accountability with respect to functions other than transportation, such as warehousing and transmission (Auvinen *et al*, 2014: 44–45). Regarding the additional functions in the transportation chain, fewer data sources and calculation methodologies exist for the emissions generated. One example is the environmental performance indicator (EPI), which is a process-oriented approach and considers the main functions with the variables of energy, maintenance and packaging. Those variables are multiplied by the number of processed or stored items and packages, with less differentiation by activity, scale and type (Rüdiger *et al*, 2016: 892–94). The more heterogeneous the product range, the more difficult the allocation exercise becomes (McKinnon, 2017: 41–42).

Following the essential logistical functions, the bridged differences are a gap between supply and demand in the dimensions of time, distance and quantity, which are fulfilled by transportation, warehousing, transhipment and stock picking (Gudehus, 2005: 8).

Characterization of evaluation aspects

As previously mentioned, the internalization of external CO_2 emissions in transport logistics is a common topic in several societies (Rothengatter, 2015: 415). A holistic view is inhibited by the missing direct link inside logistic targets between CO_2 emissions and the traditional optimization dimensions of cost, time and quality. McKinnon, Greening and Cebon categorize measures and development options by CO_2 abatement potential and ease of implementation under the estimated factors of technological level, economic benefits and political regulations. In addition, the authors have distinguished technological and operational means (see Figure 9.4 – font style) (McKinnon, 2017: 260; Greening, 2016: 5–6; Cebon, 2016: 3–4). The measures can additionally be characterized according to the tactical planning phase (see Figure 9.4 – frames).

For the measures of rescheduling and nomination of deliveries, the adjusted service strategy and the competitive strategy need to be aligned (Schulte, 2013: 58). The adjustment of these measures should therefore be considered at the strategic level. Supply chain collaboration is a relationship approach that involves performing tasks collectively within the value chain. These tasks can be joint procurement, distribution, warehousing, research and development, and much more. The concept of collaborative planning, forecasting and replenishment (CPFR) aims at a strategic and long-term foundation of the processes (Völker and Neu, 2008: 11; Chopra and Meindl, 2016: 273–74).

Predictive analytics describes the use of data mining or machine learning methods to develop prediction models. Those concepts can be used for transportation, for example, to relocate the fleet, to avoid delays, to fulfil the demand of market, or to take weather forecasts into account. It seems almost self-evident that these technologies have a deep impact on logistic processes and have a huge optimization potential, but the initial implementation is complex and should therefore be assigned to the strategic level (Meyer and Reese, 2018; Kröckel, 2019: 27; Wehberg, 2019: 377).

The tactical planning measures can be examined using various economic valuation methods. For one-time investments in fixed assets, replacement decisions or decisions about their modification, the economic and ecological return can be calculated against the input factors (see Figure 9.4 – frame: tactical level – investment decision) (Lücke, 2002: 403–04). In contrast, the evaluation needs to be changed to the goal of optimum overall costs in the case of ongoing managerial or operational measures and tasks (see Figure 9.4 – frame: tactical level – managerial or operational tasks) (Chopra and Meindl, 2016: 428–37).

Calculation of investment measures

Investments in vessels, aircraft and trains are limited to specialized transport or courier, express and parcel (CEP) operators that offer their service to the market. Shippers, logistic planners and supply chain managers normally cannot influence the emissions directly and deal with the offered prices. In addition, investment decisions are not made on the tactical level. Hence, the focus of this section is on road transport or, more specifically, the investment in trucks.

For calculations, a baseline must be developed. Therefore, the cost allocation for the different components to operate a truck are an important aspect. Table 9.3 shows an example calculation for a long-distance 40-ton Euro VI truck with a total driving performance of 130,000 km annually (Bundesverband Güterkraftverkehr Logistik und Entsorgung eV, 2019).

Figure 9.2 Comparison of decarbonization measures in terms of carbon abatement potential and ease of implementation. Clustered by development means (font style) and planning level (frames)

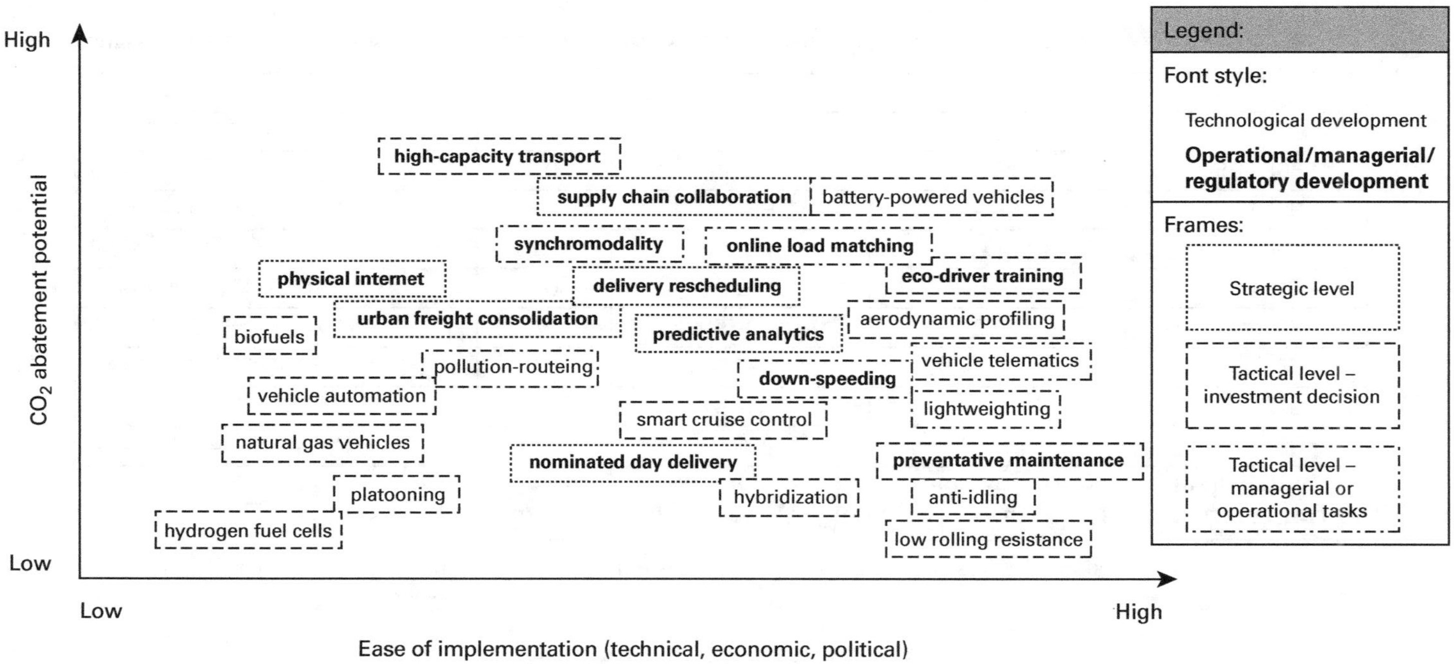

SOURCE Own based on McKinnon (2017: 260); Greening (2016: 5–6); Cebon (2016: 3–4)

Table 9.3 Exemplary calculation of annual truck transport costs (for detailed allocation see Appendix I)

	Share in %	Cost / year [EUR] (baseline diesel)	Cost / year [EUR] (baseline toll)	Cost / year [EUR] (calculated)
Personnel costs with expenses	34.2	61,996	61,335	61,666
Diesel/fuel costs	24.9	45,156	44,674	44,915
Depreciation (fixed and variable)	8.4	15,263	15,101	15,182
Additional operating costs	7.8	14,103	13,985	14,028
Additional fixed holding costs	6.0	10,804	10,689	10,746
Toll	9.6	17,384	17,199	17,292
Administrative overhead	9.1	16,568	16,392	16,480
Total per year	100.0	181,275	179,343	180,309
Avg costs EUR / km				1.39 EUR
Avg costs w/o toll EUR / km				1.25 EUR

SOURCE Own, based on shares published by Bundesverband Güterkraftverkehr Logistik und Entsorgung eV (2019)

Here the cost per year is scaled up based on two dimensions: on the one hand (third column – baseline diesel), the average monthly diesel fuel cost for a bulk purchaser in 2018 (Bundesverband Güterkraftverkehr Logistik und Entsorgung eV, 2018) and the total kilometres driven by trucks monthly in 2018 (Bundesamt für Güterverkehr, 2018), to a weighted average value of 1.037 EUR per litre; and on the other hand (fourth column – baseline toll), the toll costs in Germany of about 0.13 EUR per kilometre for the aforementioned 40-ton Euro VI truck. Comparing both results, a difference of only 1.1 per cent shows the validity of the approach. The calculated costs (fifth column – calculated costs) are used for further analyses in this chapter.

The CO_2 emissions of a 40-ton Euro VI truck can be calculated with the average fuel consumption about 33.5 litres per 100 km (Bundesverband Güterkraftverkehr Logistik und Entsorgung eV, 2019) multiplied with the CO_2 factor well-to-wheel of 3.17 kg/l CO_2 (Deutsches Institut für Normung, 2013: 23) to 138 tons for an annual distance of 130,000 km.

The aerodynamics of a truck can be improved with additional spoilers and covers, which reduce the wind resistance during the ride. The additional investment costs of 3,500 EUR are offset by fuel and equivalent CO_2 emissions of 5 per cent (Wittenbrink, 2011: 95–86). The delivery or transport time is not affected by this measure. Due to the decrease in fuel consumption, the cost per year can be reduced by 1,355 EUR, which means an ROI in 31 months. The CO_2 emissions can by reduced by 7 tons per year.

Low rolling resistance, eco-driver training, anti-idling, preventive maintenance and other comparable measures can be evaluated using a similar approach. In some decisions, other costs shown in Table 9.3 are also affected and need to be considered. For replacement purchasing, for instance to replace the fuel (natural gas vehicles, hydrogen fuel cells, hybridization or battery-powered vehicles) or high-capacity transport (HCT) vehicles, attention must be paid to depreciation. This aspect can be appointed by a fixed factor, affected by the age, and a variable factor, driven kilometres, or by a mixture of both. In Germany, from the official depreciation rules, a truck should be in use for nine years or have driven 600,000 km (Bruhn *et al*, 2005: 197; Bundesministerium der Finanzen (Berlin), 2000). In the calculation model (shown in Table 9.3), the depreciation is calculated 50:50, which means an acquisition value of 103,354 EUR in sum for the exemplary diesel truck and the trailer. Investments in new drive systems need to be weighted this way as well.

Currently, the average age of a truck on German roads is increasing (2010: 7.6 years; 2019: 8.0 years) (Kraftfahrt-Bundesamt, 2019), but the majority of these trucks are already in the highest emission class, EURO IV (see Figure 9.3). In addition, the data show that especially for large trucks with five or more axles, the share in the EURO IV class is significant at three-quarters, measured by kilometres driven (see Figure 9.4). These numbers indicate the willingness to invest in state-of-the-art technologies triggered by the reduction of fuel consumption and cost advantages with the differentiation of toll rates (Schuckert, 2016: 5; Toll Collect GmbH, 2019).

Figure 9.3 Distribution of pollutant classes measured in kilometres driven in Germany by country of registration

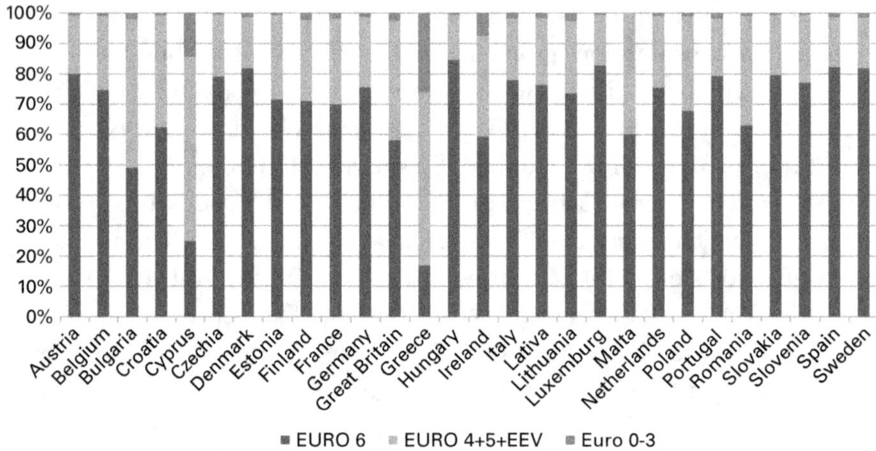

SOURCE Own calculation with data from the Bundesamt für Güterverkehr (2018)

Figure 9.4 Distribution of pollutant classes measured in kilometres driven in Germany by number of axles

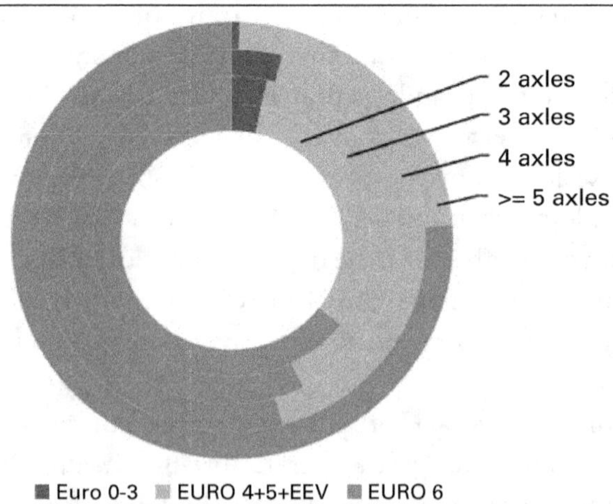

SOURCE Own calculation with data from the Bundesamt für Güterverkehr (2018)

Planning managerial or operational tasks

Various issues affect the success of transportation. For example, demand fluctuation, problems in supply, traffic, and laws make the different planning phases complex. Those effects can be recognized in performance indicators such as load factor, fill rates, high transport costs, high emissions, and excessive inventory holding (Mangan *et al*, 2012: 131). Regarding the utilization factors for airfreight, no resilient market evaluations or estimations have been published. A figure by Lufthansa shows a load factor of 66.4 per cent of freight aircraft for 2018, measured by transported tons without volume constraints (dpa, 2019). Furthermore, the freight volume transported in the belly hold of hybrid aircraft – which means the necessary consideration of passengers in the calculation – is also missing. However, for various reasons, McKinnon assumes that there are very few 'empty' operations. Loading volume is high due to belly freight and the hub and spoke networks. In addition, the high operational costs of a flight force operators to practise market supply (McKinnon, 2017: 137–38). For rail transportation, the data availability is like that of air transportation: no comparable data has been globally published (McKinnon, 2017: 135). EcoTransit estimates the loading factor (LF) and the empty trip factor (ETF) from the European rail market situation considering different values for various train types. The LF ranges from 50 per cent to 100 per cent, and the ETF from 20 per cent to 100 per cent (EcoTransIT World Initiative, 2018: 58).

For container shipping, two perspectives on the utilization must be considered. The load factor of container vessels, measured by the number of TEU transported, is estimated to be 70 per cent worldwide (EcoTransIT World Initiative, 2018: 75–76; BSR, 2014: 1–4). Empty runs do not need to be considered, as voyages in round trips are the common state of business. Nevertheless, the utilization can differ on the journeys between the harbours (Lee and Meng, 2015: 166). The fill rate represents the utilization of the containers and is influenced by the demanders of the transport. However, global evaluations are missing, and EcoTransit recommends a factor of 10 tonnes per twenty foot equivalent unit (TEU) for statistics due to two influencing factors. First, not only heavy containers can be transported due to the payload in tons deadweight (tdw) of the vessels (for example, MSC Megamax-24 vessels with 228,149 tdw and 23,000 TEU means 9.9 tons/TEU (Hannemann, 2019)). Second, light goods are restricted by volume (EcoTransIT World Initiative, 2018: 104).

For trucks, different studies have been published and need to be differentiated regarding empty runs and fill rate. McKinnon estimates empty runs to represent between one quarter and one third of the total truck kms (McKinnon, 2017: 42), while Eurostat shows a heterogeneous picture, ranging from 44 per cent in Cyprus to 22 per cent in Germany and 6 per cent in Belgium, measured using total truck-kms (Eurostat, 2019). For other countries, values have been estimated with an average of around 30 per cent, though in developing countries it is often significantly higher (McKinnon, 2017: 133–134; Smart Freight Center, 2016: 1). Regarding the fill rate, the large number of different truck types and the multidimensional consideration of the filling degree in volume, weight and loading devices pose immense difficulties for the desired comparison. For Europe, the average freight volume per transport has been calculated to be 13.7 tons, while numbers concerning other limiting factors are not available (Eurostat, 2019; McKinnon, 2017: 133).

The previous paragraphs have shown the difficulties in measuring a performance indicator presumed to be easy. Nevertheless, all numbers show improvement potential targeting full utilization. In fact, the utilization factor is only a secondary measure or a result and not a determination aspect for transport planning. For air, rail and sea freight, the supply is realized in anonymous markets, so that shippers cannot directly influence the capacities. Thus, the tactical planning is based on the offers and the assignment. Facing the tactical planning, different measures such as down-speeding and synchromodality must be implemented for the operational realization.

In container shipping, transport offers with lower speed (slow steaming) can be found in the market. Normally, the fuel use and emissions per ton-mile are roughly proportionally connected to the percentage of speed reduction, but the offered transport tariffs are not affected (International Maritime Organization, 2015: 54–55). Besides the extra costs for additional vessels of the operators to ensure frequency (Lee and Meng, 2015: 292), the shippers need to calculate with longer lead times for the transport. This influences the capital costs for the stocks in transit as well as the inventory costs in the warehouse (Dircksen, 2012: 154–58). As a first evident result, slow-steaming has no positive effect on the aspect of time or cost, but on CO_2 emissions.

Regarding road transportation, an effective measure for down-speeding is to adjust the existing speed limiters of trucks (Dünnebeil *et al*, 2015: 24). Studies have shown a reduction of fuel consumption by 3.4 per cent with a speed reduction from 85 to 80 km/h (Dünnebeil *et al*, 2015: 86). Following the calculations in Table 9.1, this means a fuel cost reduction of 1,527 EUR and extra costs for the driver of 3,854 EUR. In addition, the fixed depreciation increases by 474 EUR and the additional fixed holding costs by 877 EUR, because more trucks are required. An increase in the inventory costs only needs to be considered for transports longer than one day. The resulting negative cost impact of 3,678 EUR yearly leads to a reduction in emissions of about 5 tons per annum. Reflecting on the methodology, it is important to note the assumption that personnel costs per annum will increase. This effect occurs when marginal speed reduction affects productivity, which is often unobservable in practice (McKinnon, 2017: 175).

Transport modes have different advantages and disadvantages which can be combined into an optimal transport network, using the strength of the modes for the different tasks (Rodemann *et al*, 2018: 42–83; Schulte, 2013: 175–90). The described concept of intramodality is extended by a higher flexibility regarding changes, inventory management and service levels to an overall concept called synchromodality (alice, 2015: 11; Dong *et al*, 2018: 5). Some exemplary analyses of different transport chains for Asian-European services are shown in Table 9.4.

The values in Table 9.4 give a first idea of the potential for the configuration of transport chains. Bearing in mind the described complexity of transport planning, deeper analyses need to be conducted. For the tactical planning phase, feasible and realistic models need to be used to provide an appropriate framework for operational transport planning and execution. This can be done by the examination of realistic case studies. As an example in this chapter, a supply chain from Brazil to a German market is introduced, based on a case study by Dircksen and Feldmann (2019). The product is a plastic spare part with a consumption rate of one item per car per year. The total demand is allocated to the 10 largest cities in Germany (Statistisches Bundesamt, 2017: 30). The final destination for the transportation chain is a single distribution centre in each city with a constant demand based on 50 calendar weeks. Table 9.5 provides the parameters for the product to be distributed.

Table 9.4 Indexed emissions and cost and time factors for door-to-door from Central China to Western Europe

Description	Rail	Air	Sea
CO_2 emissions kg CO_2/ton	270	5.727	391
Transit time in days	22	4	38
Cost (indexed to 100)	100	474	50

SOURCE Own calculation based on DB Schenker (2013: 8–11)

Table 9.5 Case study: overview of company-specific input parameters

Description	Value	Unit
Total demand per year	6,253,342	products
Products per pallet	3,120	units
Weight per pallet	312	kg
Volume per pallet	0.77	m^3
Price/value of one product	3.50	€
Capital commitment rate	15	%

SOURCE Dircksen and Feldmann (2019)

For the configuration of the supply chain, four different scenarios are calculated: sea freight (FCL) and airfreight, both with a warehouse in the target country, and direct delivery via sea freight (LCL) or airfreight. In all scenarios, transport inside Germany is carried out by trucks. Customs procedures and transhipment of goods are also considered. Stocks are located at the transport-optimal warehouse location calculated using the Steiner Weber approach (Domschke and Drexl, 1996). In the scenarios with the warehouse, the inventories enable the implementation of a customer-neutral replenishment process to achieve bundling effects. To reduce CO_2 emissions and transport costs per part, the FCL containers are filled with the maximum number of pallets.

The result for the transportation chain based on FCL sea freight is 27 containers per year and an average stock level of 115,803 pieces. The warehousing costs are calculated based on the floor space used per m^2. In addition to transportation, warehousing, and transhipment costs, the products in the value chain tie up capital during transportation and warehousing. The capital charge in the warehouse is calculated by multiplying the average stock level by the production price plus the costs of operation according to the total costs of ownership (TCO) approach (Schulte, 2013: 303). The capital costs during transportation are dependent on the product value during transport and the transportation time.

Table 9.7 shows the result of the practical application for the supply chain from Brazil to a German market.

Scenarios for pollution-routeing in international transport networks can be measured with the same approach as the concept of synchromodality due to the similar planning perspective. Exemplary case studies showed a minimal cost effect with significant CO_2 reductions changing the target function of route optimization methods to ecological aspects (Figliozzi, 2010; Palmer and Piecyk, 2010; Liu *et al*, 2014).

Table 9.6 Costs of alternatives for export from Brazil to Germany

Structuring alternative / Cost element [costs in EUR/year]	FCL with warehouse	Airfreight with warehouse	LCL	Airfreight
Road (precarriage)	5,996	15,515	41,340	15,515
Customs clearance (export)	2,579	644	47,767	6,439
Transshipment	6,586		10,546	
Sea freight	15,660		79,900	
Airfreight		525,210		525,210
Transshipment	6,750		51,000	
Customs clearance (import)	675	707	3,102	7,070
Road (replenishment)	14,607	68,778		
Warehousing	62,359	6,176		
Road (distribution)	70,479	70,479	63,800	68,778
Capital charge (transport)	326,285	103,450	419,495	93,800
Capital charge (stocks)	65,834	9,645		
Total	**577,810**	**800,604**	**716,950**	**716,812**

SOURCE Own calculation based on Dircksen and Feldmann (2019)

Table 9.7 Overview results of alternatives for export from Brazil to Germany

Element \ Structuring alternative	FCL with ware-house	Airfreight with ware-house	LCL	Airfreight
Costs (EUR/year)	577,810	800,604	716,950	716,812
Delivery time (days)	1	1	46	10
Emissions (tons CO_2/year)	88,4	4870.8	81,0	4,861.6

SOURCE Own calculation adapted from Dircksen and Feldmann (2019)

Conclusion

The topic of this chapter was the sustainable tactical planning of transportation networks, which requires consideration of economic and environmental factors in decision-making situations. The first part described the different logistical functions and the different planning phases. To meet its objective, this chapter presented some approaches to the holistic evaluation of logistical measures to improve the economic efficiency and the ecological impact of international transportation networks. Starting with a first categorization of different measures, single investments were distinguished from continuous measures. For single investments, the holistic goal is to gain a short-term ROI under the restriction of the service level for the internal and the external customers. In addition, CO_2 emissions were calculated. For managerial or operational tasks, the evaluation aspects need to be integrated into the ongoing decision basis. Therefore, the tactical planning can provide evaluated approaches to organize the transport network with the mid-term perspective and to support operational tasks. All in all, this chapter showed that a clear decision base can be developed to achieve the overall goal of a sustainable and efficient transport network. In addition, it demonstrated the inevitable circumstance that the basic conditions, variables and evaluation aspects must be clearly defined to be able to make holistic decisions.

Further research is proposed for the integration of CO_2 emissions into economic decision-making models. A further standardization of the CO_2 calculation is also suggested. In addition, technological, operational, managerial and regulatory development will change the evaluation variables, and new measures will also arise.

References

Aberle, G (2009) *Transportwirtschaft: Einzelwirtschaftliche und gesamtwirtschaftliche Grundlagen, Wolls Lehr- und Handbücher der Wirtschafts- und Sozialwissenschaften*, 5th edn, Oldenbourg, München

Airbus SAS (2018) [accessed 23 September 2020] *Global Networks, Global Citizens: Global market forecast 2018–2037, Airbus Global Market Forecast (GMF)*, Blagnac Cedex, France [Online] https://www.airbus.com/content/dam/corporate-topics/publications/media-day/GMF-2018-2037.pdf (archived at https://perma.cc/F7BN-FC5D)

alice (Alliance for Logistics Innovation through Collaboration in Europe) (2015) [accessed 23 September 2020] *Corridors, Hubs and Synchromodality: Research and innovation roadmap* [Online] http://www.etp-logistics.eu/wp-content/uploads/2015/08/W26mayo-kopie.pdf (archived at https://perma.cc/9DH9-VNXW)

Auvinen, H, Clausen, U, Davydenko, I, Diekmann, D, Ehrler, V and Lewis, A (2014) Calculating emissions along supply chains: Towards the global methodological harmonisation, *Research in Transportation Business and Management*, **12**, pp 41–46

Böhme, H (1997) Linienschifffahrt, in *Vahlens großes Logistiklexikon*, ed J Bloech and GB Ihde, Verlag Franz Vahlen, München, pp 544–46

Bretzke, W-R (2010) *Logistische Netzwerke*, Springer-Verlag, Heidelberg

Bruhn, H, Perseke, J and Vaterrodt, P (2005) *Güterverkehr-Spedition-Logistik: Kaufmännische Steuerung und Kontrolle*, 1 Aufl, Bildungsverlag EINS, Troisdorf

BSR (CleanCargo Working Group) (CCWG) (2014) [accessed 23 September 2020] *Global Maritime Trade Lane Emissions Factors* [Online] https://www.bsr.org/reports/BSR_CCWG_Trade_Lane_Emissions_Factors.pdf (archived at https://perma.cc/NH8P-S6NV)

Bundesamt für Güterverkehr (2018) [accessed 23 September 2020] Monatliche Mautstatistik für Dezember [Online] https://www.bag.bund.de/SharedDocs/Downloads/DE/Statistik/Lkw-Maut/18_Monatstab_12.html?nn=2221970 (archived at https://perma.cc/SL3G-QQZC)

Bundesministerium der Finanzen (Berlin) (2000) [accessed 23 September 2020] *AfA-Ta-bel-le für die all-ge-mein ver-wend-ba-ren An-la-ge-gü-ter, § 193ff AO § 7 Abs 1 EStG* [Online] https://www.bundesfinanzministerium.de/Content/DE/Standardartikel/Themen/Steuern/Weitere_Steuerthemen/Betriebspruefung/AfA-Tabellen/Ergaenzende-AfA-Tabellen/AfA-Tabelle_AV.html (archived at https://perma.cc/DM4T-QTJ4)

Bundesverband Güterkraftverkehr Logistik und Entsorgung (BGL) eV (2018) [accessed 23 September 2020] Dieselpreis-Information (Großverbraucher) [Online] https://www.bgl-ev.de/images/downloads/dieselpreisinformation.pdf (archived at https://perma.cc/648J-HLVE)

Bundesverband Güterkraftverkehr Logistik und Entsorgung (BGL) eV (2019) [accessed 23 September 2020] Modellrechnungen zur Kostenentwicklung – Hinweise zu den Modellrechnungen [Online] https://www.bgl-ev.de/web/der_bgl/informationen/zusatzinformationen_zum_kostenentwicklungsrechner.htm (archived at https://perma.cc/FJ46-KJSL)

Cebon, D (2016) *Technology Options for Decarbonizing Road Freight: The future role of trucks for energy and environment*, IEA, Brüssel

Chopra, S and Meindl, P (2016) *Supply Chain Management: Strategy, planning, and operation, Always learning*, 6th edn, Pearson, Boston

Crabtree, T, Hoang, T, Tom, R and Gregg, G (2018) [accessed 23 September 2020] *Boing World Air Cargo Forecast 2018–2037*, Boeing, Seattle [Online] https://www.boeing.com/resources/boeingdotcom/commercial/about-our-market/cargo-market-detail-wacf/download-report/assets/pdfs/2018_WACF.pdf (archived at https://perma.cc/6HNX-2E6T)

Crainic, TG (2003) Long-haul freight transportation, in *Handbook of Transportation Science: International series in operations research and management science*, 2nd edn, ed RW Hall, Kluwer Academic Publishers, Boston, pp 451–516

DB Schenker (2013) [accessed 23 September 2020] *Get Your Business Rolling With Innovative Rail Logistics Solutions Between China and Europe: Trans Eurasian rail logistics*, DB Schenker, Essen [Online] https://www.dbschenker.com/resource/blob/489220/e3caffd7ced19e657ea7f60be0823f9b/china-rail-data.pdf (archived at https://perma.cc/6HQ7-BXJC)

Deutsches Institut für Normung (2013) *Methode zur Berechnung und Deklaration des Energieverbrauchs und der Treibhausgasemissionen bei Transportdienstleistungen (Güter- und Personenverkehr): Deutsche Fassung EN 16258:2012 German version EN 16258:2012 Version allemande EN 16258:2012 / Methodology for Calculation and Declaration of Energy Consumption and GHG Emissions of Transport Services (freight and passengers) / Méthodologie pour le calcul et la déclaration de la consommation d'énergie et des émissions de gaz à effet de serre (GES) des prestations de transport (passagers et fret) Deutsche Norm*, März 2013, Berlin

Dircksen, M (2012) Prozessorientiertes Entscheidungsmodell zur Planung der internationalen Distributionslogistik, Zugl: Zittau, Internat Hochsch-Inst, Diss, 2012, Cuvillier, Göttingen

Dircksen, M and Feldmann, C (2019) *Holistic Evaluation of the Impacts of Additive Manufacturing on Sustainability, Distribution Costs, and Time in Global Supply Chains*, Transportation Research Procedia (TRPRO), Mumbai

Domschke, W and Drexl, A (1996) *Standorte, Oldenbourgs Lehr- und Handbücher der Wirtschafts- und Sozialwissenschaften*, vol 3, 4th edn, Oldenbourg, München

Dong, C, Boute, R, McKinnon, A and Verelst, M (2018) Investigating synchromodality from a supply chain perspective, *Transportation Research Part D: Transport and environment*, **61**, pp 42–57

dpa (2019) [accessed 23 September 2020] Lufthansa bleibt Europas größte Fluggesellschaft, *Handelsblatt*, 10 January [Online] https://www.handelsblatt.com/unternehmen/handel-konsumgueter/airline-lufthansa-bleibt-europas-groesste-fluggesellschaft/23850854.html (archived at https://perma.cc/SCB6-3TD2)

Dünnebeil, F, Reinhard, C, Lambrecht, U, Kies, A, Hausberger, S and Rexeis, M (2015) [accessed 23 September 2020] *Zukünftige Maßnahmen zur Kraftstoffeinsparung und Treibhausgasminderung bei schweren Nutzfahrzeugen*, Dessau-Roßlau [Online] http://www.umweltbundesamt.de/publikationen/zukuenftige-massnahmen-zur-kraftstoffeinsparung (archived at https://perma.cc/RS47-XR9C)

EcoTransIT World Initiative (EWI) (2018) [accessed 23 September 2020] *Ecological Transport Information Tool for Worldwide Transports: Methodology and data*, Berne, Hannover, Heidelberg [Online] https://www.ecotransit.org/download/EcoTransIT_World_Methodology_Data_Update_2018.pdf (archived at https://perma.cc/WUJ2-2AL7)

EIA (US Energy Information Administration) (2018) [accessed 23 September 2020] *International Energy Outlook 2018* [Online] https://www.eia.gov/outlooks/ieo/pdf/transportation.pdf (archived at https://perma.cc/4DD6-D6X8)

European Commission (2018) [accessed 23 September 2020] *A European Strategic Long-Term Vision for a Prosperous, Modern, Competitive and Climate Neutral Economy, COM(2018) 773 final* [Online] https://eur-lex.europa.eu/legal-content/EN/TXT/PDF/?uri=CELEX:52018DC0773&from=EN (archived at https://perma.cc/ZJ57-9GN6)

Eurostat (2019) [accessed 23 September 2020] *Road Freight Transport by Characteristics of Journeys* [Online] https://ec.europa.eu/eurostat/statistics-explained/images/f/f6/SE_Journeys_charact_2017-update.xlsx (archived at https://perma.cc/3DCN-GF4M)

Figliozzi, M (2010) Vehicle routing problem for emissions minimization, *Transportation Research Record: Journal of the Transportation Research Board*, **2197** (1), pp 1–7

Flaherty, MT (1996) *Global Operations Management, McGraw-Hill Series in Management*, 2nd edn, McGraw-Hill, New York,

Fleischmann, B and Kopfer, H (2018) Transport- und Tourenplanung, in *Planung logistischer Systeme*, *Fachwissen Logistik*, ed H Tempelmeier, Springer Vieweg, Berlin, pp 71–98

Greene, S and Lewis, A (2016) [accessed 23 September 2020] *GLEC Framework for Logistics Emissions: Methodologies*, 1st edn, Amsterdam [Online] https://www.smartfreightcentre.org/en/how-to-implement-items/what-is-glec-framework/58/ (archived at https://perma.cc/5GAN-MXG9)

Greening, P (2016) *Proven Strategies to Enable More Efficient and Low-Carbon Logistics: The future role of trucks for energy and environment*, IEA, Brüssel

Gudehus, T (2005) *Logistik: Grundlagen, Strategien, Anwendungen*, 3rd edn, Springer-Verlag, Berlin

Günther, H-O and Tempelmeier, H (2016) *Produktion und Logistik: Supply chain und operations management*, 12, verbesserte Auflage, BoD – Books on Demand, Norderstedt

Hannemann, R (2019) [accessed 23 September 2020] MSC Gülsün [Online] http://www.ship-db.de/nawbn.php?wbn_nr=SSHK2248010 (archived at https://perma.cc/W3GR-KPYD)

Hasler, J (2019) [accessed 23 September 2020] *Analyse der Klimapfade Verkehr 2030*, Berlin [Online] https://bdi.eu/publikation/news/analyse-der-klimapfade-verkehr-2030/ (archived at https://perma.cc/2WPR-HMUJ)

Höglund, M (2016) *Drive the Shift Toward Sustainable Transport: The future role of trucks for energy and environment*, IEA, Brüssel

Ihde, GB (1991) *Transport, Verkehr, Logistik: Gesamtwirtschafliche Aspekte und einzelwirtschaftliche Handhabung, Vahlens Handbücher der Wirtschafts- und Sozialwissenschaften*, 2nd edn, Vahlen, München

International Air Transport Association (IATA) Montreal, Canada (undated) [accessed 23 September 2020] *Recommended Practice 1678: CO_2 emissions measurement methodology* [Online] https://www.iata.org/en/programs/cargo/sustainability/carbon-footprint/ (archived at https://perma.cc/232N-5KNL)

International Chamber of Shipping (2019) [accessed 23 September 2020] Key facts [Online] https://www.ics-shipping.org/shipping-facts/key-facts (archived at https://perma.cc/3VX2-5QC9)

International Maritime Organization (2015) [accessed 23 September 2020] *Third IMO GHG Study 2014* [Online] http://www.imo.org/en/OurWork/Environment/PollutionPrevention/AirPollution/Documents/Third%20Greenhouse%20Gas%20Study/GHG3%20Executive%20Summary%20and%20Report.pdf (archived at https://perma.cc/MGG5-Z6S3)

International Transport Forum (2018) [accessed 23 September 2020] *Key Transport Statistics: 2017 data* [Online] https://www.itf-oecd.org/sites/default/files/docs/key-transport-statistics-2018.pdf (archived at https://perma.cc/E6RA-K3TV)

Klatt, S (1997) Verkehrsqualität, in *Vahlens großes Logistiklexikon*, ed J Bloech and GB Ihde, Beck [ua], München, pp 1208–11

Klein, R and Scholl, A (2012) *Planung und Entscheidung: Konzepte, Modelle und Methoden einer modernen betriebswirtschaftlichen Entscheidungsanalyse, Vahlens Handbücher der Wirtschafts- und Sozialwissenschaften*, 2 Aufl, Franz Vahlen, München

Kraftfahrt-Bundesamt (2019) [accessed 23 September 2020] Bestand in den Jahren 2010 bis 2019 nach ausgewählten Fahrzeugklassen mit dem Durchschnittsalter der Fahrzeuge [Online] https://www.kba.de/DE/Statistik/Fahrzeuge/fahrzeuge_node.html (archived at https://perma.cc/PHB7-RW33)

Kröckel, J (2019) *Data Analytics in Produktion und Logistik*, 1 Auflage, Vogel Communications Group GmbH & Co KG, Würzburg

Kummer, S (2010) *Einführung in die Verkehrswirtschaft, Betriebswirtschaftslehre*, vol 8336, 2nd edn, Facultas Verlag, Wien

Lee, C-Y and Meng, Q (eds) (2015) *Handbook of Ocean Container Transport Logistics: Making global supply chains effective, International Series in Operations Research and Management Science*, volume 220, Springer, Cham

Lewis, G (2009) The impact of ICT on customs, *World Customs Journal*, **3** (1), pp 3–11

Liu, W-Y, Lin, C-C, Chiu, C-R, Tsao, Y-S and Wang, Q (2014) Minimizing the carbon footprint for the time-dependent heterogeneous-fleet vehicle routing problem with alternative paths, *Sustainability*, **6** (7), pp 4658–84

Lücke, W (2002) Investitionsplanung, in *Handbuch Logistik, Engineering online library VDI-Buch*, ed D Arnold, H Isermann and A Kuhn, Springer-Verlag, Berlin, pp 403–07

Mangan, J, Lalwani, CS, Butcher, T and Javadpour, R (2012) *Global Logistics and Supply Chain Management*, 2nd edn, Wiley, Chichester

Mayer, S, Thiry, E and Cay-Bernhard, F (2009) *Supply Chain Excellence Amidst the Global Economic Crisis: 6th European AT Kearney/ELA logistics study 2008/2009 – Summary of study results July 2009*, Techn Univ, Inst für Betriebswirtschaftslehre, Darmstadt

McKinnon, A (2017) *Decarbonising Logistics: An internal perspective*, Kogan Page, London

Meyer, W and Reese, H (2018) [accessed 23 September 2020] *Künstliche Intelligenz als Innovationsbeschleuniger in Unternehmen* [Online] https://www.pwc.de/de/digitale-transformation/ki-als-innovationsbeschleuniger-in-unternehmen-whitepaper.pdf (archived at https://perma.cc/9PAN-8AWH)

Organisation for Economic Co-operation and Development (2003) [accessed 23 September 2020] *Trade Facilitation: The benefits of simpler, more transparent border procedures, Policy brief* [Online] http://www.oecd.org/regreform/facilitation/8920454.pdf (archived at https://perma.cc/Y65F-U7VW)

Palmer, A and Piecyk, M (2010) [accessed 23 September 2020] *Time, Cost and CO_2 Effects of Rescheduling Freight Deliveries* [Online] http://www.greenlogistics.org/SiteResources/15thLRN/Palmer%20and%20Piecyk.pdf (archived at https://perma.cc/78T9-WZAJ)

Pfohl, H-C (2010) *Logistiksysteme: Betriebswirtschaftliche Grundlagen*, 8th edn, Springer-Verlag, Berlin

Porter, ME (2010) *Wettbewerbsvorteile: Spitzenleistungen erreichen und behaupten*, 7th edn, Campus Verlag, sl, Frankfurt

Rodemann, H, Jong, FD, Ruijgrok, K and Verweij, K (2018) *The Vitality of Intermodal Transport*, 1st edn, InterRoJo Publications, Barendrecht

Rolle, C (2018) [accessed 23 September 2020] *Klimapfade für Deutschland* [Online] https://bdi.eu/media/publikationen/?publicationtype=Studien#/publikation/news/klimapfade-fuer-deutschland/ (archived at https://perma.cc/4MU7-MERS)

Rolle, C and Nuyken, P (2019) [accessed 23 September 2020] *Maßstäbe einer CO_2-Bepreisung*, Berlin [Online] https://bdi.eu/media/publikationen/?publicationtype=Positionen#/publikation/news/massstaebe-einer-co2-bepreisung/ (archived at https://perma.cc/L6BC-SWV2)

Rothengatter, W (2015) Approaches to internalisation of transport externalities, in *Handbook of Research Methods and Applications in Transport Economics and Policy*, ed C Nash, Edward Elgar Publishing, Cheltenham, pp 403–17

Rüdiger, D, Schön, A and Dobers, K (2016) Managing greenhouse gas emissions from warehousing and transshipment with environmental performance indicators, *Transportation Research Procedia*, 4, pp 886–95

Schieck, A (2008) *Internationale Logistik: Objekte, Prozesse und Infrastrukturen grenzüberschreitender Güterströme*, 1st edn, Oldenbourg, München

Schmied, M and Knörr, W (2013) [accessed 23 September 2020] *Berechnung von Treibhausgasemissionen in Spedition und Logistik gemäß DIN EN 16258*, 2nd edn [Online] https://www.dslv.org/dslv/web.nsf/gfx/8F102DF8C3E4A2F141257BB7007779CB/$file/DSLV-Leitfaden%20Berechnung%20von%20THG-Emissionen%20Stand%2003-2013.pdf (archived at https://perma.cc/6VWU-6Z5W)

Schuckert, M (2016) *Daimler's advances in fuel efficiency and zero emission activities: The future role of trucks for energy and environment*, IEA, Brüssel

Schulte, C (2013) *Logistik: Wege zur Optimierung der Supply Chain, Vahlens Handbücher der Wirtschafts- und Sozialwissenschaften*, 6th edn, Franz Vahlen, München

Seiler, T (2012) *Operative Transportation Planning: Solutions in consumer goods supply chains, Contributions to Management Science*, 2012 edition, Physica-Verlag HD, Heidelberg

Smart Freight Center (2016) [accessed 23 September 2020] *Barriers for Carriers to Adopt Fuel-Saving Technologies and Measures* [Online] https://www.smartfreightcentre.org/pdf/Barriers-for-Carriers-SFC-Final-Dec2016.pdf (archived at https://perma.cc/F3WD-HU6M)

Specht, G and Fritz, W (2005) *Distributionsmanagement, Kohlhammer Edition Marketing*, 4th edn, Kohlhammer, Stuttgart

Statistisches Bundesamt (2017) *Statistisches Jahrbuch Deutschland 2017*, 1, Auflage, Wiesbaden

Stock, JR and Lambert, DM (2001) *Strategic Logistics Management, The McGraw-Hill/Irwin Series in Marketing*, 4th edn, McGraw-Hill/Irwin, Boston

Thonemann, U and Albers, M (2010) *Operations Management: Konzepte, Methoden und Anwendungen, Wi – Wirtschaft*, 2nd edn, Pearson Studium, München

Toll Collect GmbH (2019) [accessed 23 September 2020] Mautsätze pro Kilometer ab 01 Januar 2019 [Online] https://www.toll-collect.de/de/toll_collect/bezahlen/maut_tarife/maut_tarife.html (archived at https://perma.cc/2BLZ-ZARC)

United Nations Conference on Trade and Development (UNCTAD) (2019a) *Gross Domestic Product: GDP by type of expenditure, VA by kind of economic activity, total and shares, annual: Gross domestic product (GDP)*, UNCTAD

United Nations Conference on Trade and Development (2019b) *Gross Domestic Product: GDP by type of expenditure, VA by kind of economic activity, total and shares, annual: Item: Transport, storage and communications (Code: 51)* ISIC Rev3, divisions 60–64, UNCTAD

United Nations Department of Economic and Social Affairs (2018) *Statistical Yearbook 2018 Edition*, 61st issue, United Nations Publication, New York

Völker, R and Neu, J (2008) *Supply Chain Collaboration: Kollaborative logistik-konzepte fr̈ third- und fourth-tier-zulieferer*, Springer-Verlag, Heidelberg

Wehberg, G (2019) Logistik 40 – die sechs Säulen der Logistik in der Zukunft, in *Logistik der Zukunft – logistics for the future: Logistics for the future*, 8, aktualisierte und erweiterte Auflage, ed I Göpfert, Springer Gabler, Wiesbaden, pp 367–96

Wieberneit, N (2007) Service network design for freight transportation: A review, *OR Spectrum*, **30** (1), pp 77–112

Wildemann, H (2010) *Logistik Prozeßmanagement, TCW*, vol 19, 5th edn, TCW Transfer-Centrum-Verl, München

Wilmsmeier, G and Spengler, T (2015) Towards benchmarking energy consumption in container terminals, *Maritime and Logistics Bulletin*, July

Wittenbrink, P (2011) *Transportkostenmanagement im Straßengüterverkehr: Grundlagen, Optimierungspotenziale, Green Logistics*, 1st edn, Betriebswirtschaftlicher Verlag Dr Th Gabler / GWV Fachverlage GmbH Wiesbaden, Wiesbaden

World Commission on Environment and Development (1987) *Our Common Future*, Oxford University Press, Oxford

Appendix I

Table 9.8 Appendix I

<table>
<tr><th colspan="3">Cost categories 'Bundesverband Güterverkehr'</th><th colspan="2">Allocation in this chapter</th></tr>
<tr><th colspan="2"></th><th>Share in %</th><th></th><th>Share in %</th></tr>
<tr><td rowspan="3">Personal costs without expenses</td><td>Wage</td><td>24.51</td><td rowspan="4">Personnel costs with expenses</td><td rowspan="4">34.2</td></tr>
<tr><td>Social insurance</td><td>5.69</td></tr>
<tr><td>Others</td><td>1.02</td></tr>
<tr><td>Personal costs – expenses</td><td>Expenses</td><td>2.98</td></tr>
<tr><td colspan="2">Fuel costs</td><td>24.91</td><td>Fuel costs</td><td>24.9</td></tr>
<tr><td colspan="2">Depreciation (km based)</td><td>4.21</td><td rowspan="2">Depreciation (km and time)</td><td rowspan="2">8.4</td></tr>
<tr><td colspan="2">Depreciation (time-related)</td><td>4.21</td></tr>
<tr><td rowspan="6">Vehicle operating costs</td><td>Additional fuel costs (Adblue)</td><td>0.33</td><td rowspan="6">Additional operating costs</td><td rowspan="6">7.8</td></tr>
<tr><td>Lubricants</td><td>0.55</td></tr>
<tr><td>Vehicle cleaning</td><td>0.59</td></tr>
<tr><td>Tires</td><td>1.66</td></tr>
<tr><td>Maintenance and repair</td><td>4.38</td></tr>
<tr><td>Others</td><td>0.27</td></tr>
<tr><td rowspan="5">Fixed asset costs</td><td>Debt financing costs</td><td>0.74</td><td rowspan="5">Additional fixed asset costs</td><td rowspan="5">6.0</td></tr>
<tr><td>Inspection fees</td><td>0.24</td></tr>
<tr><td>Taxes</td><td>0.51</td></tr>
<tr><td>Insurance</td><td>3.15</td></tr>
<tr><td>Others</td><td>1.32</td></tr>
<tr><td colspan="2">Toll (km related)</td><td>9.59</td><td rowspan="2">Toll</td><td rowspan="2">9.6</td></tr>
<tr><td colspan="2">Toll (related)</td><td>0.00</td></tr>
<tr><td rowspan="2">Administrative overhead</td><td>Personal costs</td><td>5.03</td><td rowspan="2">Administrative overhead</td><td rowspan="2">9.1</td></tr>
<tr><td>Asset costs</td><td>4.11</td></tr>
</table>

SOURCE Own based on Bundesverband Güterkraftverkehr Logistik und Entsorgung eV (2019)

PART THREE
Actions to continuously improve sustainability in global value chains

There is an increasing demand for a stronger inclusion of the social dimension in the overall concept of sustainability (Seuring and Müller, 2008; Wu and Pagell, 2011). This is reflected in some studies on the design of supply chains, which are increasingly taking up both the economic and social dimensions (Xia *et al*, 2015). However, even in these publications, the focus is, once again, not on a comprehensive parallel examination of all three dimensions. The need to explore more specific implementation possibilities and practical solutions through research in the field of SSCM was highlighted in 2014 in the issue celebrating the 50th anniversary of the *Journal of Supply Chain Management*. It explicitly called for more research on new practices and processes to create truly sustainable (economically, ecologically and socially successful) value chains (Pagell and Shevchenko, 2014). This shows that new insights into the approaches by which sustainability can be successfully implemented in all three dimensions are of great interest for both practice and research (Yawar and Seuring, 2017). The practices and strategies for sustainable supply chains have evolved and constitute a major part in corporate competitive andvantage, although suppliers are still critical in view of the success of SSCM implementation projects. Supply chain managers need to recognize opportunities to integrate sustainability in an organization, understand the foundational elements of SSCM and have the skills to operationalize them (Zimon *et al*, 2019).

References

Pagell, M and Shevchenko, A (2014) Why research in sustainable supply chain management should have no future, *Journal of Supply Chain Management*, **50** (1), pp 44–55

Seuring, S and Müller, M (2008) From a literature review to a conceptual framework for sustainable supply chain management, *Journal of Cleaner Production*, **16** (15), pp 1699–710

Wu, Z and Pagell, M (2011) Balancing priorities: Decision-making in sustainable supply chain management, *Journal of Operations Management*, **29** (6), pp 577–90

Xia, Y, Zu, X and Shi, C (2015) A profit-driven approach to building a people-responsible supply chain, *European Journal of Operational Research*, **241** (2), pp 348–60

Yawar, SA and Seuring, S (2017) Management of social issues in supply chains: A literature review exploring social issues, actions and performance outcomes, *Journal of Business Ethics*, **141** (3), pp 621–43

Zimon, D, Tyan, J and Sroufe, R (2019) Implementing sustainable supply chain management: Reactive, cooperative, and dynamic models, *Sustainability*, **11** (24), p 7227

Biomimetic principles for improved organizational information processing

10

Toward sustainable supply chains

LYDIA BALS

Introduction

Resource depletion and increasing environmental disruption are contributing to growing social and ecological tensions, requiring a societal discussion about the necessity of long-term conservation of livelihoods (BMU, 2012; ODI *et al*, 2012). In this context, the concept of sustainability or sustainable development (WCED, 1987) which was shaped by the World Commission on Environment and Development in 1987 gains in importance (Günther, 2008). It comprises the continuous improvement of quality of living of current as well as future generations, creating sustainable communities, capable of developing the ecological and social innovation potential besides efficient use of resources. Wealth, environmental protection and social coherence should be ensured in this way (Gregori and Wimmer, 2011).

Due to increasing outsourcing and globalization, today's supply chains are constantly changing, becoming increasingly complex and developing into global networks (Linton *et al*, 2007; Carter and Rogers, 2008). Already by 2013, the yearly published baseline report of the World Business Council for Sustainable Development (WBCSD) demanded that companies adopt a broader perspective on sustainability, as the greatest sustainability impacts do not result within single companies, but aggregated in their respective supply chains (WBCSD, 2013). Whereas in the past usually single (or multiple) business competitors were in focus, nowadays it is mostly vertically disaggregated supply chains that compete with each other (Li *et al*, 2006). At the same time, companies belong to a variety of these competing supply chains. Against this competitive background, the question arises how such optimization potential of vertical cooperation beyond company borders across the supply chain between retailer, wholesaler, manufacturer and suppliers of components and raw material can be realized successfully and be controlled and tracked from an entrepreneurial point of view (Miemczyk *et al*, 2012).

This increased significance of analysing integrated supply chain processes is not only reflected in regular scientific publications in which research on global and sustainable supply chains, eg, is denoted as a game-changing megatrend (Dittmann, 2013; Ellinger and Richey, 2013), but has also found its way into many political agendas around the world. For example, the EU defines sustainable development as one of the pillars of the Europe 2020 strategy and the United Nations highlights how important the function of supply chain management is within the economy for enabling more sustainable products and processes (UNGC, 2015). The approval of the 2030 Agenda for Sustainable Development by the United Nations (UN General Assembly, 2015) and the agreement on a new climate and energy policy in 2015 (UN, 2015) by the international community foster the realization of the concept of sustainability, together with the CSR Guidelines of the EU (2014/95/EU) (European Parliament and Council, 2014) with which large companies are obliged to extend their management reports and group management reports from 2017 on. In addition to the political responsibility of governments, it explicitly seeks to make companies contribute to the realization of social and ecological goals. The scope of responsibility is clearly defined: it covers the entire supply chain (BMZ, 2015).

Due to these developments, the concept of sustainable supply chain management (SSCM) has further evolved also in research over recent years. SSCM has been defined by Seuring and Müller (2008: 1700) as follows:

> [SSCM is the] management of material, information and capital flows as well as cooperation among companies along the supply chain while taking goals from

all three dimensions of sustainable development, ie, economic, environmental and social, into account which are derived from customer and stakeholder requirements.

In order to tackle the challenges of establishing sustainability in global supply chains, functional silo mentality must be overcome. Still, cooperation measures beyond single company borders in most cases are limited to bilateral cooperation in the context of sustainability between buyer and seller. Despite the increased popularity of sustainable manufacturing processes as cradle-to-cradle (McDonough and Braungart, 2013), circular economy, closed-loop supply chains (Schenkel *et al*, 2015) and other approaches for a holistic management of material cycles, the integrated SSCM across several value creation levels remains still unexplored to a large extent (Wilhelm *et al*, 2016) so that the holistic integration of sustainability along the global supply chain remains an up-to-date challenge across industries and sectors (Sarkis, 2003; Pagell and Shevchenko, 2014).

Therefore, an integrated view is important to cope with the aforementioned sustainability issues – as they often originate in intransparent information flows and lack of cooperation within and between organizations. To study solutions from natural systems might lead to transferable measures, and new technologies like blockchain etc could support such measures. This approach is based in biomimicry or biomimetics, a method imitating techniques and processes of nature to achieve effectiveness, efficiency and sustainability (Benyus, 1997). It has already been noted that in natural ecosystems there often can be observed an interplay of bottom-up and top-down control dynamics, whereas in supply chains there is a consumer-driven situation with majorly top-down control (Wallner and Herbst, 2014). Interestingly, new technologies enabling more transparency into supply chains are currently evolving, eg using blockchain technology for improved tracking of sustainability parameters for retailers (CBInsights, 2018). More specifically, blockchain technology has been increasingly highlighted to help sustainability in supply chains by ensuring transparency, traceability and security (Saberi *et al*, 2018).

The central idea of the research presented here is to study solutions from natural systems to current business problems and identify transferable measures for SSCM. The focal units of analysis are inter- and intra-organizational designs and how they can adopt principles from natural systems in terms of increased cellularity and modularity, leveraging management innovations as well as newly developing technologies that allow more decentral information processing (eg blockchain technology) in order to arrive at a more holistic approach to managing according to economic, environmental and social criteria simultaneously. The theoretical lens for this research is information processing theory (IPT) (Galbraith, 1970, 1973, 1977; Tushman and Nadler, 1978) and the ecological information-based approach (Kharrazi *et al*, 2015).

Sustainable supply chains and the circular economy: The challenge of organizational decision making

Current research in SSCM still focuses especially on dyadic relationships between the focal buying company and the direct supplier (Wu and Pagell, 2011; Glover *et al*, 2014). However, since within global supply chains the main sustainability risks are often not to be found in the field of direct suppliers but further upstream with regard to suppliers of raw materials (Grimm *et al*, 2014; Mena *et al*, 2014, Wilhelm *et al*, 2016), measures on dyadic level often are insufficient in order to improve sustainability performance in vertically dissaggregated global supply chains significantly and holistically (Tachizawa and Wong, 2014).

Furthermore, sustainability in the context of supply chain has been researched sparsely with respect to the three dimensions part of the definition – ie economic, environmental and social issues, also referred to as *triple bottom line* (TBL) (Elkington, 1998). In the last ten years greater focus on the social dimensions in the implementation of the concept of sustainability has been demanded more and more (Seuring and Müller, 2008; Wu and Pagell, 2011). This is reflected in several recent studies on sustainable supply chain design, which increasingly address both the economic and social dimensions, or even all three dimensions – economic, environmental and social (Bals and Tate, 2018; Xia *et al*, 2015).

Regarding the ethical aspects of global supply chains, a pertinent question is how far multinational enterprises (MNEs) with global supply chains can deal with diverse stakeholder requirements (Amaeshi *et al*, 2008; Hartmann and Moeller, 2014). Here questions about different cultural and ethical contexts come up for MNEs and how these can and must be respected, for instance when it comes to the development of corporate guidelines (codes of conduct, etc) and strategies in the context of SSCM (Pedersen and Andersen, 2006; Talaulicar, 2009; Schleper and Busse, 2013).

There is inherent tension between often conflicting economic objectives of buying companies and their suppliers that can result in ethical issues of exploitation (Schleper *et al*, 2015). Then questions arise about the interplay between the global compliance principle and the regional and national differentiations in the implementation of different aspects of sustainability. Current SSCM and sustainable-compliance research in the global context has identified several descriptive factors that can either promote or diminish the willingness to comply; among them, competitive pressure (eg Yu, 2008), stakeholder interests (eg Chung, 2014), intra-organizational conditions and processes of focal firms (eg Lund-Thomsen and Lindgreen, 2014), lacking resources on the part of the suppliers from developing countries (Lim and Philips, 2008; Andersen and Skjoett-Larsen, 2009) and a missing common understanding of the meaning of sustainability in the respective context (Busse *et al*, 2016).

This challenge of taking a holistic perspective is particularly relevant for the transformation towards a circular economy. A circular economy has been defined as an economy in which resources and material value are kept within the economy for as long as possible, and when a product reaches the end of its life, it is to be used over and over to create further value (EC, 2015). Waste and resource use are minimized. In a circular economy, factory 'waste' would become valuable input for other industrial processes and even move across industries as products are repaired, reused or upgraded or individual materials are repurposed instead of being thrown away (Preston, 2012). Based on an analysis of 114 circular economy (CE) definitions, Kirchherr *et al* (2017) concluded that the circular economy is most often characterized as a combination of reduce, reuse and recycle activities. The issue with that view is that the circular economy is not positioned as a systemic shift, which is necessary to thoroughly transform the economy. Taking the problem of electronic waste (e-waste) as an example, Ryen *et al* (2018) suggest that in order to truly transition toward a circular economy a systemic shift is required, ie the industrial ecosystem needs to emulate natural systems. This echoes with supply chain management research, which already proposed that

> traditional supply chains appear to be giving way to supply ecosystems, which represent a set of interdependent and coordinated organizations that share common adaptive challenges and that collectively shape the creation and nurturing of a sourcing base that contributes to competitive advantage and superior performance.
>
> (Ketchen *et al*, 2014: 165)

In addition to that statement, the research here seeks to extend the latter part toward including sustainability criteria in line with the transition toward a circular economy.

Organizing corporate action towards such a transition requires sound decision making and execution. As a study (based on 90 usable questionnaires) among small and medium-sized enterprises (SMEs) in Germany during 2016 illustrates, the SMEs struggled with inter-functional cooperation due to a lack of information transmission and communication issues, which led to resource wastage and higher emissions (Flämig and Kesel, 2017). They saw particular need to improve their organizational structures and processes in terms of being able to interact and cooperate, in order to improve sustainability. In this study, they were even asked whether they would be interested in learning from nature as a blueprint for such improvements and stated they were very interested (Flämig and Kesel, 2017).

Biomimicry: An introduction

Biomimicry has been seen primarily in new product development research and practice, such as self-cleaning façade paints based on the water- and dust-repellent properties of the lotus leaf (Sivakumar *et al*, 2012), but biomimicry reaches beyond products and includes management and organizational insights from nature:

> Biomimicry is an approach to innovation that seeks sustainable solutions to human challenges by emulating nature's time-tested patterns and strategies. The goal is to create products, processes, and policies – new ways of living – that are well-adapted to life on Earth over the long haul.
>
> (Biomimicry Institute, 2017)

Illustrating the biomimetic perspective, an example based on the work on stromatolites by Atkinson and Williams (2009) is discussed in relation to transferability to the business context of British Telecom (BT) like this:

> Stromatolites are colonies of bacteria that self-assemble into rock formations in tidal salt flats. Each stromatolite can make independent decisions, while maintaining communication with the colony. The workload is shared among all colony individuals. Stromatolites breed rapidly, and quickly develop resistance

> to antibiotics and other threats by developing new genes. Ian Marshall plans to incorporate these principles into the next wave of BT network management. Like the stromatolites, each element of BT's network will be able to make independent decisions, yet will remain fully communicative with neighbours. Workload – ie, incoming calls – will be spread evenly through the network. And in a process mimicking natural selection, desirable services will be quickly distributed to BT customers, while undesirable services die out.
>
> (AskNature, 2017)

Another example from nature for how organizational modularity is leveraged is amoeba management, created by Kyocera, and it:

> begins with dividing an organization into small units called 'amoebas'. Each amoeba leader is responsible for drafting plans and goals for the unit. Amoebas achieve their goals through collaboration and the hard efforts of all their amoeba members. In this system, every employee plays a major role and voluntarily participates in managing the unit, achieving what is known as 'Management by All'.
>
> (Kyocera, 2019)

At the same time, this highlights an organizational approach that represents 'extreme decentralization – with thousands of small, customer-focused business units' (Adler and Hiromoto, 2012: 83). Taking a slightly broader perspective, another biomimetic example of particular interest for this research is slime mould. Slime mould has two distinct phases in its lifecycle, as when there is abundant food it exits as independent amoeba, but when food becomes scarce 'the previously independent amoeba begin to act as a coherent whole' (Robinson, 2018). This suggests that the biomimetic context could also offer insights not only into organizational structures, but also the dynamics that enable effective decentral organization.

With relation to establishing a circular economy, Tate *et al* (2019) recently highlighted several biomimetic principles based on how forests establish circular material systems. Among those principles, particularly relevant to this research are principle 2, 'In order to transition to a circular value system, decomposers need to manage information and material flows in an integrated way', and principle 6, 'In order to transition to a circular value system, the ecosystem needs reliable, decentralized information storage' (Tate *et al*, 2019).

Information processing in organizations and organizational design

The theoretical lens for this research is information processing theory (IPT). IPT evolved in the 1970s with an intra-organizational focus, in response to organizational design problems of large firms (Galbraith, 1970, 1973). It was later extended to a dyadic, inter-organizational level to assess buyer–supplier relationships (Bensaou and Venkatraman, 1995). Information processing encompasses the gathering, interpreting and synthesizing of information (Tushman and Nadler, 1978). IPT is concerned with the link between environmental uncertainty and a firm's information processing needs, as well as with the question of how firms can cope with these needs (Bensaou and Venkatraman, 1995; Galbraith, 1977). Uncertainty as the root cause of information processing needs is 'the difference between the amount of information required to perform the task and the amount of information already possessed by the organization' (Galbraith, 1973: 5). Uncertainty tends to be augmented by complexity (ie, the plurality of relevant factors) and dynamism (ie, a measure of temporal change) (Duncan, 1972). Later studies acknowledged different types (sources) of uncertainty, all of which augment information processing needs (Bensaou and Venkatraman, 1995). In supply chain management related research, the relation of information processing needs and organizational designs have been subject to investigation (Trautmann, Bals and Hartmann, 2009; Trautmann, Turkulainen, Hartmann and Bals, 2009).

In this research, the focus is on how companies strive for TBL sustainability and are faced with uncertainty about the attainment of those goals. In order to cope with this uncertainty more effectively and efficiently, in terms of corporate decision making, questions of organization design arise.

Organizational designs can vary in a number of macro-level structural elements and micro-level characteristics, influenced by various contingency factors (Bals *et al*, 2018). Such designs evolved in management literature, from functional, divisional, to horizontal overlays and matrix structures in a first era, to horizontal organization designs with team and process-based emphasis during a second era (starting in the 1980s), and moving to organizational boundaries opening up (from the mid-1990s onwards) in a third era, creating even hollow organizations with the majority of their processes outsourced, and modular organizations (though modularity often being interpreted as product-centric, as will be discussed further below) and finally shifting towards a need to partner with entities over whom there is no direct control (Anand and Daft, 2007). These designs influence how organizational decision making takes place, eg with relation of internal versus external boundaries (Bals and Turkulainen, 2017) and in the face of the above mentioned differing levels of uncertainty.

Volberda *et al* (2013), for example, have highlighted that in order for companies to improve innovation, productivity and competitiveness, one important source is how they innovate their actual management approach (Volberda *et al*, 2013). Such alternative approaches to management have been coming up in recent decades under the term 'management innovation' (Hargrave and Van de Ven, 2006; Van de Ven and Poole, 1995; Hamel, 2006; Kimberly, 1981), later extended to 'management practices' in order to also cover practices, processes, techniques and organizational structures 'as different facets of the rules and routines by which work gets done inside organizations' (Birkinshaw *et al*, 2008: 828). Although 'new organizational structure' (Volberda *et al*, 2013: 4) has been explicitly included in that research context (Birkinshaw *et al*, 2008; Vaccaro *et al*, 2012) as well as future research questions about management innovation in an inter-organizational relations were stated (Volberda *et al*, 2013), it has unfortunately received scant subsequent research attention (Hollen *et al*, 2013, are a notable exception for the inter-organizational context). Moreover, most of this research is rooted in comparing the 'old' approaches to 'new' approaches of *human* organization of corporations. Therefore, the aforementioned biomimetic example about stromatolites already highlights an interesting perspective beyond that – how about emulating other species' or even ecological systems' tried and tested solutions? The stromatolites, for example, highlighted the benefits of a *modular* organization.

Although it was anticipated as early as the late nineties that in the knowledge age organizations would turn to more 'cellular form' (Miles *et al*, 1997), when looking at management research on cellularity or modularity, the majority of publications on modularity take a product-centric view and classically argue that organizational modularity results from product modularity and that these are linked tightly, oftentimes looking at industry level (Schilling and Steensma, 2001; Sanchez and Mahoney, 1996). The stromatolites, for example, challenge such a product-centric view, highlighting that a modular organization might have benefits already at their very level of existence, being part of a certain ecological niche. The latter is mentioned here because, as they form part of the tidal community, they get their share of the benefits (eg nutrients, ability to procreate), but also on their own do not harm their surroundings and do not produce any 'waste' in the current industrial sense of 'polluting' their surroundings. Instead of focusing on products, it might make sense to focus on process level. Also in management research, Campagnolo and Camuffo (2009: 277) have raised the question whether product and organizational architectures might indeed not always confer, but rather be affected by, diverse 'independent factors', and they ask, 'Does the adoption of a process perspective facilitate the definition of modules, interfaces and standards at the organizational level?' Also in this direction, Bals and Turkulainen (2017) have highlighted that organizations can be designed using activity-oriented, facilitating modularity.

Another motivation to further explore opportunities for organizational modularity is that it can be linked to the development of ambidexterity (March, 1991; Chandrasekaran *et al*, 2011; Kristal *et al*, 2010). Product and organizational modularity can facilitate flexibility; organizational modularity allows the firm to make greater use of contingent workers and outsourcing (Schilling and Steensma, 2001; Bals and Turkulainen, 2017) and product modularity allows resources and capabilities to be quickly linked together in a new way (Hoetker, 2006). Hence, new things can be done quickly. This links to traditional operations management dimensions of volume flexibility and product flexibility (Hayes and Wheelwright, 1984; Vickery *et al*, 1999). Simultaneously, however, modularity can be linked to higher efficiency as activity-based organization as a modular form of organization means that some activities are managed centrally at the global level, reducing the effort and costs needed for coordination (Bals and Turkulainen, 2017; Turkulainen and Ketokivi, 2012; Lawrence and Lorsch, 1967; Galbraith, 1973). Thus, modularity also increases efficiency. Taken together, organizational modularity can be a source of ambidexterity.

At the same time, information processing abilities of companies are currently changing. With decentral information processing possibilities of new emerging technologies such as blockchain technology (Lockl *et al*, 2018), the means to move away from hierarchical decision-making processes become available. Invented as a distributed ledger to make intermediaries obsolete and work as a backbone of the cryptocurrency bitcoin (Beck *et al*, 2018; Risius and Spohrer, 2017), blockchain technology could transform process management and foster a paradigm shift from central control towards decentral coordination (Lockl *et al*, 2018). Fittingly, it has been highlighted that '[d]ecentralization is an essential characteristic of blockchain technology' (Kouhizadeh and Sarkis, 2018: 2). Although blockchain technology is the main example mentioned here, Kaufmann and Portmann

(2015), for example, present research on biologically inspired information systems, eg mentioning IBM's vision of an organic, self-organization approach to IT systems management inspired by the autonomic nervous system. Or a combination of various technologies under the headline of internet of things (IoT), such as RFID and sensor technologies, suggested by the World Economic Forum to be a sustainability game-changer in order to accelerate progress on the Sustainable Development Goals (SDGs) of the United Nations (WEF, 2018). Such approaches will be scrutinized further as this research progresses, with regard to its applicability to enable decentral information processing in supply chains for the attainment of sustainability-related performance objectives. When considering what performance objectives these are, this will require a further review of criteria beyond classical economic sustainability criteria, to also include environmental sustainability criteria (eg the OECD criteria of regeneration, substitutability, assimilation and avoidance of irreversibility; OECD, 2001) and social sustainability criteria (Bals and Tate, 2018; Tate and Bals, 2018).

As highlighted in the introduction and previous paragraph, this research is concerned with how organizational design approaches mimicking solutions from the natural world could help address the challenges of sustainable supply chain management. This gives this research an inter-firm, network, even system scope. Therefore, there is need to incorporate insights on sustainable supply chain design (Bals and Tate, 2018) and foster a supra-firm design (Mathews, 2012) towards more sustainable supply chains, or actually sustainable supply systems.

Therefore, the main idea is to bridge between traditional IPT and the ecological information-based approach; as Kharrazi *et al* (2015: 806) summarize:

> High levels of efficiency tend to weaken the system's ability to respond to shocks or disruptions to its internal flows, whereas high levels of redundancy are costly to maintain and thereby tend to weaken the system's internal development and its ability to distribute flows in an orderly way. Therefore, from the perspective of the ecological information-based approach, sustainability is achieved when the system maintains robust delivery (ie, the intensive dimension) while also achieving a reduction in the total usage of resource (ie, the extensive dimension).

Therefore, in order to arrive at truly sustainable business systems, it stands to reason that both the intensive and extensive dimensions – and how to improve them – could be operationalized for information processing in businesses. As highlighted above, one current key concept identified to achieve this balance between intensity and extensiveness – in the context of managing supply systems for sustainability – at this point is organizational modularity.

Nevertheless, as this research is still ongoing, a variety of concepts and also biomimetic sources of inspiration – beyond stromatolites and amoebas – are still subject to further scrutiny. This will be outlined in the final section.

Conclusion: Toward biomimetic principles for information processing

Regarding the envisioned methodological approach to take this research further, the current standpoint is twofold. First, empirically, the next step is to identify empirical contexts (ideally both in nature and business, but at least in the former) suitable for further analysis. These contexts (or this context) might then be approached with a case study research approach (Ketokivi and Choi, 2014; Yin, 2013; Ellram, 1996). Second is to apply the methodology of metaphorical transfer (Chen *et al*, 2013; Tsoukas, 1991; Garud and Kortha, 1994), taking the analogies from the natural context and transferring them to the business context in a rigorous manner. Whether case study research and metaphorical transfer will be combined or only a suitable empirical context for metaphorical transfer be identified and then utilized for the transfer, is currently being evaluated.

As this research is still ongoing, the current hypotheses are working hypotheses, guiding the further analysis of literature and scoping of the exact empirical context. Regarding current hypotheses, the main ones concern 1) the need to improve information processing in organizations by challenging traditional (ie hierarchical) designs; 2) the benefit of modularity/cellular design for achieving both intensity and extensiveness, here a broad range of objectives, such as TBL performance. Here, it is worth mentioning that organizational design for improved decision making in general could profit from a biomimetic approach, but this research specifically centres on TBL considerations in global supply chains. Conversely, the results of this research provide insights for future research beyond that specific context.

Hypothesis 1: Hierarchical structures hinder decision making for TBL performance

Hypothesis 2: Modular/cellular designs facilitate decision making for TBL performance

Table 10.1 Potential empirical contexts from a biomimetic perspective

Natural example	Main findings/relevant subjects (excerpts)	References
Ants (army-ant colony), bees (honeybee colony), dogs (African wild dogs)	'Team effectiveness in swarms like bees, colonies of ants, schools of fish, flocks of birds, and fireflies flashing synchronously are all as a result of highly coordinated behaviors that emerge from collective, decentralized intelligence.' 'effectiveness of teams was equal to mastery of each individual x coordination x communication (collective intelligence)'	Mashingaidze, 2015
Ants (army-ant colony), bees (honeybee colony)	Flexible work organization	Fewell, 2015
Natural information systems like electrical charges, hormones, DNA, pheromones, electromagnetic waves (nervous system, immune system, human societies, ant colonies)	Theoretical framework to address the three major aspects of biomimetic information systems: user experience, information processing, and management cybernetics	Kaufmann and Portmann, 2015
Ants, termites, bees, etc	Self-organization, resilience, and swarm intelligence. Mentions special appeal of the approach to learn from nature when it comes to economic tensions, related to increasing complexity, uncertainties and accelerated change	Ferdinand *et al*, 2012

Table 10.1 highlights the empirical contexts in nature that come into question from a broad literature review with particular focus on biomimetic insights for organizational issues. The search terms used were: Biomimicry, Biomimetics, Biolog* analogy business, Organization + Nature oder + Biolog*; Organization*

Design + Nature oder + Biolog*; Information* Process* + Nature oder + Biolog*; Biomimicry in/+ organizations, Biomimicry in/ + Business; biopreneuring; biologically inspired design/ bio-inspired; Business biomimetics/biomimicry. And additionally in German: Bionik; Biolog* Organisationsform*; Bionik + Wirtschaft; Wirtschaftsbionik.

Although this search yielded a wide variety of publications, the majority of them were product-centric, either discussing the specific application of a natural inspiration for a product (eg termite mounds as the inspiration for climate controlled buildings; Turner and Soar, 2008), or how biomimicry from a methodological angle can spur creativity for new product development in research and development (Kennedy *et al*, 2018).

The next steps involve 1) the further development of the organization design framework under development in order to highlight the contribution of this research for decision making for TBL sustainability as specifically as possible, 2) the empirical context to study (potentially both in the biological and business contexts) and 3) further development – and extension – of the preliminary hypotheses.

References

Adler, RW and Hiromoto, T (2012) Amoeba management: Lessons from japans Kyocera, *MIT Sloan Management Review*, **54** (1), pp 83–89

Amaeshi, KM, Osuji, OK and Nnodim, P (2008) Corporate social responsibility in supply chains of global brands: A boundaryless responsibility? Clarifications, exceptions and implications, *Journal of Business Ethics*, **81** (1), pp 223–34

Anand, N and Daft, RL (2007) What is the right organization design? *Organizational Dynamics*, **36** (4), pp 329–44

Andersen, M and Skjoett-Larsen, T (2009) Corporate social responsibility in global supply chains, *Supply Chain Management: An international journal*, **14** (2), pp 75–86

AskNature (2017) [accessed 23 September 2020] Bacterial colonies that form stromatolites self-assemble by making independent decisions while maintaining communication [Online] https://asknature.org/strategy/colonies-self-assemble/#.WNa2MvnhBb0 (archived at https://perma.cc/V7HF-JX86)

Atkinson, S and Williams, P (2009) Quorum sensing and social networking in the microbial world, *Journal of the Royal Society Interface*, **6** (40), pp 959–78

Bals, L and Tate, WL (2018) Sustainable supply chain design in social businesses: Advancing the theory of supply chain, *Journal of Business Logistics*, **39** (1), pp 57–79

Bals, L and Turkulainen, V (2017) Achieving efficiency and effectiveness in purchasing and supply management: Organization design and outsourcing, *Journal of Purchasing and Supply Management*, **23** (4), pp 256–67

Bals, L, Laine, J and Mugurusi, G (2018) Evolving purchasing and supply organizations: A contingency model for structural alternatives, *Journal of Purchasing and Supply Management*, **24** (1), pp 41–58

Beck, R, Müller-Bloch, C and Leslie King, J (2018) Governance in the blockchain economy: A framework and research agenda, *Journal of the Association for Information Systems*, **19** (10), pp 1020–34

Bensaou, BM and Venkatraman, VN (1995) Configurations of interorganizational relationships: A comparison between US and Japanese automakers, *Management Science*, **41** (9), pp 1471–92

Benyus, J (1997) *Biomimicry: Innovation inspired by nature*, William Morrow and Company, New York

Biomimicry Institute (2017) [accessed 23 September 2020] What is biomimicry? [Online] http://biomimicry.org/what-is-biomimicry (archived at https://perma.cc/PEJ6-Z4E5)

Birkinshaw, J, Hamel, G and Mol, MJ (2008) Management innovation, *Academy of Management Review*, **33** (4), pp 825–45

BMU (Bundesministerium für Umwelt, Naturschutz und Reaktorsicherheit) (2012) Deutsches Ressourceneffizienzprogramm (ProgRess), Programm zur nachhaltigen Nutzung und zum Schutz der natürlichen Ressourcen, Berlin

BMZ (Bundesministerium für wirtschaftliche Zusammenarbeit und Entwicklung) (2015) [accessed 23 September 2020] Der Weg zur Agenda 2030 für nachhaltige Entwicklung [Online] http://www.bmz.de/de/themen/2030_agenda/ (archived at https://perma.cc/5DDN-XXC5)

Busse, C, Schleper, MC, Niu, M and Wagner, SM (2016) Supplier development for sustainability: Contextual barriers in global supply chains, *International Journal of Physical Distribution and Logistics Management*, **46** (5), pp 442–68

Campagnolo, D and Camuffo, A (2009) What really drives the adoption of modular organizational forms? An institutional perspective from Italian industry-level data, *Industry and Innovation*, **16** (3), pp 291–314

Carter, CR and Rogers, DS (2008) A framework of sustainable supply chain management: Moving toward new theory, *International Journal of Physical Distribution and Logistics Management*, **38** (5), pp 360–87

CBInsights (2018) [accessed 23 September 2020] How retailers are using blockchain, AI, and more to improve supply chain sustainability [Online] https://www.cbinsights.com/research/sustainability-retail-supply-chain-expert-intelligence/ (archived at https://perma.cc/R9XD-Q3EX)

Chandrasekaran, A, Linderman, K and Schroeder, R (2011) Antecedents to ambidexterity competency in high technology organizations, *Journal of Operations Management*, **30** (1–2), pp 134–51

Chen, YS, Rungtusanatham, MJ, Goldstein, SM and Koerner, AF (2013) Theorizing through metaphorical transfer in OM/SCM research: Divorce as a metaphor for strategic buyer–supplier relationship dissolution, *Journal of Operations Management*, **31** (7–8), pp 579–86

Chung, S (2014) Explaining compliance: A multi-actor framework for understanding labour law compliance in China, *Human Relations*, **68** (2), pp 237–60

Dittmann, JP (2013) *Supply Chain Transformation: Building and executing an integrated supply chain strategy*, McGraw-Hill, New York

Duncan, RB (1972) Characteristics of organizational environments and perceived environmental uncertainty, *Administrative Science Quarterly*, **17** (3), pp 313–27

EC (European Commission) (2015) [accessed 23 September 2020] Circular economy package: Questions and answers [Online] http://europa.eu/rapid/press-release_MEMO-15-6204_en.htm (archived at https://perma.cc/8FZV-932U)

Eisenhardt, KM (1989) Building theories from case study research, *Academy of Management Review*, **14** (4), pp 532–50

Elkington, J (1998) *Cannibals with Forks*, New Society Publishers, Gabriola Island, BC

Ellinger, A and Richey Jr, RG (2013) Some ideas and guidance for prospective IJPDLM authors, *International Journal of Physical Distribution and Logistics Management*, **43** (3)

Ellram, LM (1996) The use of the case study method in logistics research, *Journal of Business Logistics*, **17** (2), p 93

European Parliament and Council (2014) [accessed 1 October 2020] Directive 2014/95/EU [Online] http://data.europa.eu/eli/dir/2014/95/oj (archived at https://perma.cc/527G-YL5X)

Ferdinand, JP, Petschow, U, Gleich, AV and Seipold, P (2012) *Literaturstudie Bionik:* Schriftenreihe des IÖW

Fewell, JH (2015) Social biomimicry: What do ants and bees tell us about organization in the natural world? *Journal of Bioeconomics*, **17** (3), pp 207–16

Flämig, H and Kesel, AB (2017) Nachhaltige Gestaltung von Wertschöpfungsketten in KMU durch Nutzung von Organisationsbionik

Galbraith, JR (1970) Environmental and technological determinants of organization design, in *Studies in organization design*, ed PR Lawrence and JW Lorsch, Richard D. Irwin, Inc, Homewood, IL

Galbraith, JR (1973) *Designing Complex Organizations*, Addison-Wesley, Reading, MA

Galbraith, JR (1977) *Organization Design*, Addison-Wesley, Reading, MA

Garud, R and Kotha, S (1994) Using the brain as a metaphor to model flexible production systems, *Academy of Management Review*, **19** (4), pp 571–698

Glover, JL, Champion, D, Daniels, KJ and Dainty, AJD (2014) An institutional theory perspective on sustainable practices across the dairy supply chain, *International Journal of Production Economics*, **152**, pp 102–11

Gregori, G and Wimmer, T (2011) Grünbuch der nachhaltigen Logistik. Handbuch für die ressourcenschonende Gestaltung logistischer Prozesse, Eigenverlag Bundesvereinigung Logistik Österreich

Grimm, JH, Hofstetter, JS and Sarkis, J (2014) Critical factors for sub-supplier management: A sustainable food supply chains perspective, *International Journal of Production Economics*, **152**, pp 159–73

Günther, E (2008) *Ökologieorientiertes Management. Um-(weltorientiert) Denken in der BWL*, Lucius & Lucius Verlagsgesellschaft, Stuttgart

Hamel, G (2006) The why, what and how of management innovation, *Harvard Business Review*, **84**, pp 72–84

Hargrave, T and Van de Ven, A (2006) A collective action model of institutional innovation, *Academy of Management Review*, **31**, pp 864–88

Hartmann, J and Moeller, S (2014) Chain liability in multitier supply chains? Responsibility attributions for unsustainable supplier behaviour, *Journal of Operations Management*, **32** (5), pp 281–94

Hayes, RH and Wheelwright, SC (1984) *Restoring Our Competitive Edge: Competing through manufacturing*, John Wiley and Sons, New York

Hoetker, G (2006) Do modular products lead to modular organizations? *Strategic Management Journal*, **27** (6), pp 501–18

Hollen, RM, Van Den Bosch, FA and Volberda, HW (2013) The role of management innovation in enabling technological process innovation: An inter-organizational perspective, *European Management Review*, **10** (1), pp 35–50

Kaufmann, M and Portmann, E (2015) Biomimetics in design-oriented information systems research, in *At the Vanguard of Design Science: First impressions and early findings from ongoing research research-in-progress papers and poster presentations from the 10th International Conference, DESRIST 2015*

Kennedy, EB, Miller, DJ and Niewiarowski, PH (2018) Industrial and biological analogies used creatively by business professionals, *Creativity Research Journal*, **30** (1), pp 54–66

Ketchen Jr, DJ, Crook, TR and Craighead, CW (2014) From supply chains to supply ecosystems: Implications for strategic sourcing research and practice, *Journal of Business Logistics*, **35** (3), pp 165–71

Ketokivi, M and Choi, T (2014) The renaissance of case research as a scientific method, *Journal of Operations Management*, **32** (5), pp 232–40

Kharrazi, A, Kraines, S, Rovenskaya, E, Avtar, R, Iwata, S and Yarime, M (2015) Examining the ecology of commodity trade networks using an ecological information-based approach: Toward strategic assessment of resilience, *Journal of Industrial Ecology*, **19** (5), pp 805–13

Kimberly, JR and Evanisko, MJ (1981) Organizational innovation: The influence of individual, organizational and contextual factors on hospital adoption of technological and administrative innovations, *The Academy of Management Journal*, **24**, pp 689–713

Kirchherr, J, Reike, D and Hekkert, M (2017) Conceptualizing the circular economy: An analysis of 114 definitions, *Resources, Conservation and Recycling*, **127**, pp 221–32

Kouhizadeh, M and Sarkis, J (2018) Blockchain practices, potentials, and perspectives in greening supply chains, *Sustainability*, **10** (10), 3652, pp 1–16

Kristal, MM, Huang, X and Roth, AV (2010) The effect of an ambidextrous supply chain strategy on combinative competitive capabilities and business performance, *Journal of Operations Management*, **28** (5), pp 415–29

Kyocera (2019) [accessed 23 September 2020] What is amoeba management? [Online] https://global.kyocera.com/inamori/management/amoeba/ (archived at https://perma.cc/9PAX-ER2R)

Lawrence, PR and Lorsch, JW (1967) Differentiation and integration in complex organizations, *Administrative Science Quarterly*, **12** (1), pp 1–47

Li, S, Ragu-Nathan, B, Ragu-Nathan, TS and Rao, SS (2006) The impact of supply chain management practices on competitive advantage and organizational performance, *Omega: The international journal of management science*, **34** (2), pp 107–24

Lim, S-J and Phillips, J (2008) Embedding CSR values: The global footwear industry's evolving governance structure, *Journal of Business Ethics*, **81** (1), pp 143–56

Linton, JD, Klassen, R and Jayaraman, V (2007) Sustainable supply chains: An introduction, *Journal of Operations Management*, **25** (6), pp 1075–82

Lockl, J, Rieger, A, Fridgen, G, Röglinger, M and Urbach, N (2018) Towards a theory of decentral digital process ecosystems-evidence from the case of digital identities, *ECIS2018 Workshop on Platformization*, pp 1–2

Lund-Thomsen, P and Lindgreen, A (2014) Corporate social responsibility in global value chains: Where are we now and where are we going? *Journal of Business Ethics*, **123** (1), pp 11–22

March, JG (1991) Exploration and exploitation in organizational learning, *Organization Science*, **2** (1), pp 71–87

Mashingaidze, S (2015) Effectiveness of teams: Lessons from biomimicry, an ecological inquiry E = MC^2, *Risk Governance and Control: Financial Markets and Institutions*, **5** (3–1), pp 36–43

Mathews, JA (2012) Design of industrial and supra-firm architectures: Growth and sustainability, *Journal of Organization Design*, **1** (2), pp 42–63

McDonough, W and Braungart, M (2013) *The Upcycle*, North Point Press, New York

Mena, C, Terry, LA, Williams, A and Ellram, L (2014) Causes of waste across multi-tier supply networks: Cases in the UK food sector, *International Journal of Production Economics*, **152** (June), pp 144–58

Miemczyk, J, Johnsen, TE and Macquet, M (2012) Sustainable purchasing and supply management: A structured literature review of definitions and measures at the dyad, chain and network levels, *Supply Chain Management: An International Journal*, **17** (5), pp 478–96

Miles, RE, Snow, CS, Mathews, JA, Miles, G and Coleman Jr, HJ (1997) Organizing in the knowledge age: Anticipating the cellular form, *Academy of Management Perspectives*, **11** (4), pp 7–20

ODI, DIE, ECDPM (2012) [accessed 1 October 2020] *European Report on Development 2011–2012. Confronting Scarcity: Managing water, energy and land for inclusive and sustainable growth*, European Union, Brussels [Online] https://ecdpm.org/publications/european-report-development-2011-2012-confronting-scarcity-water-energy-land-inclusive-and-sustainable-growth/ (archived at https://perma.cc/XS5T-Q2TM)

OECD (2001) [accessed 23 September 2020] Policies to enhance sustainable development, Meeting of the OECD Council at ministerial level, 14 May [Online] https://doi.org/10.1787/9789264192683-en (archived at https://perma.cc/2QYJ-44G3)

Pagell, M and Shevchenko, A (2014) Why research in sustainable supply chain management should have no future, *Journal of Supply Chain Management*, 50 (1), pp 44–55

Pedersen, ER and Andersen, M (2006) Safeguarding corporate social responsibility (CSR) in global supply chains: How codes of conduct are managed in buyer–supplier relationships, *Journal of Public Affairs*, **6** (3–4), pp 228–40

Preston, F (2012) *A Global Redesign? Shaping the circular economy*, Chatham House, London

Risius, M and Spohrer, K (2017) A blockchain research framework, *Business and Information Systems Engineering*, **59** (6), pp 385–409

Robinson, S (2018) [accessed 23 September 2020] Learning from nature: Kyocera's amoeba management system, 10 April [Online] https://medium.com/@srerobinson/learning-from-nature-kyoceras-amoeba-management-system-483ec44428e8 (archived at https://perma.cc/EHP6-2V5Y)

Ryen, EG, Gaustad, G, Babbitt, CW and Babbitt, G (2018) Ecological foraging models as inspiration for optimized recycling systems in the circular economy, *Resources, Conservation and Recycling*, **135**, pp 48–57

Saberi, S, Kouhizadeh, M, Sarkis, J and Shen, L (2018) Blockchain technology and its relationships to sustainable supply chain management, *International Journal of Production Research*, **57** (7), pp 2117–35

Sanchez, R and Mahoney, JT (1996) Modularity, flexibility, and knowledge management in product and organization design, *Strategic Management Journal*, 17 (Special Issue: Knowledge and the Firm), pp 63–76

Sarkis, J (2003) A strategic decision framework for green supply chain management, *Journal of Cleaner Production*, **11** (4), pp 397–409

Schenkel, M, Krikke, H, Caniëls, MC and van der Laan, E (2015) Creating integral value for stakeholders in closed loop supply chains, *Journal of Purchasing and Supply Management*, **21** (3), pp 155–66

Schilling, MA and Steensma, HK (2001) The use of modular organizational forms: An industry-level analysis, *Academy of Management Journal*, **44** (6), pp 1149–68

Schleper, MC and Busse, C (2013) Towards a standardized supplier code of ethics: Development of a design concept based on diffusion of innovation theory, *Logistics Research*, **6** (4), pp 187–216

Schleper, MC, Blome, C and Wuttke, DA (2015) The dark side of buyer power: Supplier exploitation and the role of ethical climates, *Journal of Business Ethics* (in print), DOI: 10.1007/s10551-015-2681-6

Seuring, S and Müller, M (2008) From a literature review to a conceptual framework for sustainable supply chain management, *Journal of Cleaner Production*, **16** (15), pp 1699–710

Sivakumar, N, Balasubramanya, A and Sundaresan, CN (2012) Sustainable supply chain excellence: A biomimetic perspective, *IUP Journal of Supply Chain Management*, **9** (1), pp 21–39

Tachizawa, EM and Wong, CY (2014) Towards a theory of multi-tier sustainable supply chains: A systematic literature review, *Supply Chain Management: An international journal*, **19** (5/6), pp 643–63

Talaulicar, T (2009) Barriers against globalizing corporate ethics: An analysis of legal disputes on implementing US codes of ethics in Germany, *Journal of Business Ethics*, **84** (3), pp 349–60

Tate, WL and Bals, L (2018) Achieving shared triple bottom line (TBL) value creation: Toward a social resource-based view (SRBV) of the firm, *Journal of Business Ethics*, **152** (3), pp 803–26

Tate, W, Bals, L, Bals, C and Foerstl, K (2019) Seeing the forest and not the trees: Learning from nature's circular economy, *Resources, Conservation and Recycling*, **149**, pp 115–29

Trautmann, G, Bals, L and Hartmann, E (2009) Global sourcing in integrated network structures: The case of hybrid purchasing organizations, *Journal of International Management*, **15** (2), pp 194–208

Trautmann, G, Turkulainen, V, Hartmann, E and Bals, L (2009) Integration in the global sourcing organization: An information processing perspective, *Journal of Supply Chain Management*, **45** (2), pp 57–74

Tsoukas, H (1991) The missing link: A transformational view of metaphors in organizational science, *Academy of Management Review*, **16** (3), pp 566–85

Turkulainen, V and Ketokivi, M (2012) Cross-functional integration and performance – what are the real benefits? *International Journal of Operations and Production Management*, **32** (4), pp 447–67

Turner, JS and Soar, RC (2008) Beyond biomimicry: What termites can tell us about realizing the living building, *First International Conference on Industrialized, Intelligent Construction at Loughborough University*

Tushman, ML and Nadler, DA (1978) Information processing as an integrating concept in organizational design, *Academy of Management Review*, **3** (3), pp 613–24

UN General Assembly (2015) [accessed 23 September 2020] *Transforming Our World: The 2030 Agenda for Sustainable Development* [Online] https://sustainabledevelopment.un.org/post2015/transformingourworld (archived at https://perma.cc/UY32-SAB8)

UNGC (United Nations Global Compact) (2015) [accessed 23 September 2020] Supply chain sustainability [Online] www.unglobalcompact.org/what-is-gc/our-work/supply-chain (archived at https://perma.cc/94T5-TLFU)

Vaccaro, IG, Jansen, JJP, Van den Boschand FAJ and Volberda, HW (2012) Management innovation and leadership: The moderating role of organizational size, *Journal of Management Studies*, **49**, pp 28–51

Van de Ven, AH and Poole, MS (1995) Explaining development and change in organizations, *Academy of Management Review*, **20**, pp 510–40

Vickery, S, Calantone, R and Dröge, C (1999) Supply chain flexibility: An empirical study, *Journal of Supply Chain Management*, **35** (3), pp 16–24

Volberda, HW, Van Den Bosch, FA and Heij, CV (2013) Management innovation: Management as fertile ground for innovation, *European Management Review*, **10** (1), pp 1–15

Wallner, T and Herbst, A (2014) Supply chain biomimetics, *Advances in Business Management: Towards systemic approach*, 290

WBCSD (World Business Council for Sustainable Development) (2013) [accessed 23 September 2020] *Reporting Matters: Improving the effectiveness of reporting, WBCSD Baseline Report 2013* [Online] http://en.vbcsd.vn/upload/attach/WBCSD_Reporting_matters_2013_INT_PDF.pdf (archived at https://perma.cc/Z6KX-JF4Z)

WCED (World Commission on Environment and Development) (1987) *Our Common Future*, Oxford University Press, Oxford

WEF (2018) [accessed 23 September 2020] IoT for sustainable development [Online] http://widgets.weforum.org/iot4d/ (archived at https://perma.cc/SYV7-VUF6)

Wilhelm, MM, Blome, C, Bhakoo, V and Paulraj, A (2016) Sustainability in multi-tier supply chains: Understanding the double agency role of the first-tier supplier, *Journal of Operations Management*, **41** (1), pp 42–60

Wu, Z and Pagell, M (2011) Balancing priorities: Decision-making in sustainable supply chain management, *Journal of Operations Management*, **29** (6), pp 577–90

Xia, Y, Zu, X and Shi, C (2015) A profit-driven approach to building a 'people-responsible' supply chain, *European Journal of Operational Research*, **241** (2), pp 348–60

Yin, RK (2013) *Case Study Research: Design and methods*, SAGE Publications, London

Yu, X (2008) Impacts of corporate code of conduct on labor standards: A case study of Reeboks athletic footwear supplier factory in China, *Journal of Business Ethics*, **81** (3), pp 513–29

11

(How) Can research in the field of sustainable supply chain management become more forward-looking and future-shaping?

CARSTEN REUTER

Introduction: Why another approach to research for sustainable supply chain management is necessary

The growing interest in sustainably managing supply chains reflects to some extent the dramatically growing relevance for organizations to become more sustainable in order to preserve planet Earth as the habitat of humankind. While the number of publications covering sustainable supply chain management has considerably increased over recent decades, the questioning of the relevance of that research for actually impacting the way that organizations conduct their business has only recently evolved. In the article 'Why research in sustainable supply chain management should have no future', Pagell and Shevchenko (2014) echo that notion, highlighting 'that we know far more about how to adapt known practices to make a supply chain more sustainable than we know about what new practices and processes are needed to create truly sustainable supply chains' (Pagell and Shevchenko, 2014: 45). In this context, the dominating role of quite mainstream research methods that follow positivistic fundamentals and are rather analytical in nature is often quoted as preventing supply chain researchers from moving forward and 'getting ahead of practice' (Pagell and Shevchenko, 2014: 51). While the call for alternative research methods is neither novel nor limited to the field of (sustainable) supply chain management, the challenges of our time for society as a whole warrant a serious and timely debate and subsequent answers. One response to the call for alternative, ie non-mainstream, research methods has been the proposition of so-called engaged research methods where researchers turn into facilitators or agents of change instead of maintaining the role of distant observers of business practices. A 'family' of such approaches can be found under the umbrella of action research (AR). Thus, the guiding question for this chapter is, can AR be the key for research in the field of sustainable supply chain management to become more forward-looking and future-shaping?

Approaching engaged research and action research

AR has become a widely accepted, valid approach in many fields, including organizational studies (Perlow, 1999), healthcare (Tompa *et al*, 2009; Mabala and Allen, 2002) and policy development, for example. However, AR is not one clearly delineated research method, but rather 'a family of practices of living inquiry' (Reason and Bradbury, 2008: 1) with

> a participatory process concerned with developing practical knowing in the pursuit of worthwhile human purposes. It seeks to bring together action and reflection, theory and practice, in participation with others, in the pursuit of practical solutions to issues of pressing concern to people, and more generally the flourishing of individual persons and their communities.
>
> (Reason and Bradbury, 2008: 4)

The wide spectrum of AR encompasses approaches such as experimental AR, action science (rather objectivist and interventionist) and narrative inquiries, reflexive deconstruction through collaborative inquiry (postmodernism).

AR is often considered to have emerged from the pragmatist philosophy of Lewin and other social science researchers around at the end of the Second World War (Reason, 2006: 187) that recently appears to have experienced a renaissance as a response to the calls for more empiricism-based and relevant knowledge in management research (Fendt *et al*, 2008). Pragmatism intends to return to a 'proper relation between theory and praxis' (Dewey *et al*, 1904 cited in Fendt *et al*, 2008: 471). A cornerstone of pragmatism is 'the integration of theory and practice and the reintroduction of values in the realm of scientific inquiry' (Touboulic and Walker, 2016: 311). Hence, one major aspect that differentiates AR from other currently more mainstream methods is that the research is executed *with* practitioners and not only research about practice (Bradbury-Huang, 2010). This requires the researcher to step down from the ivory tower and get in close contact with so-called 'co-researchers', ie practitioners.

Despite the various appearances of AR some fundamental characteristics can be identified across the literature. On an operational level, AR consists of cycles of action and reflection, as depicted in Figure 11.1. In the action phase, co-researchers test practices and gather evidence, while the reflection stage is reserved for sensemaking, reflection and planning of further actions. Because action and reflection integrate knowing and acting, no 'gap' between knowing and doing needs to be addressed, increasing the speed of disseminating existing knowledge into practice and creating new scientific knowledge.

Figure 11.1 The action research cycle

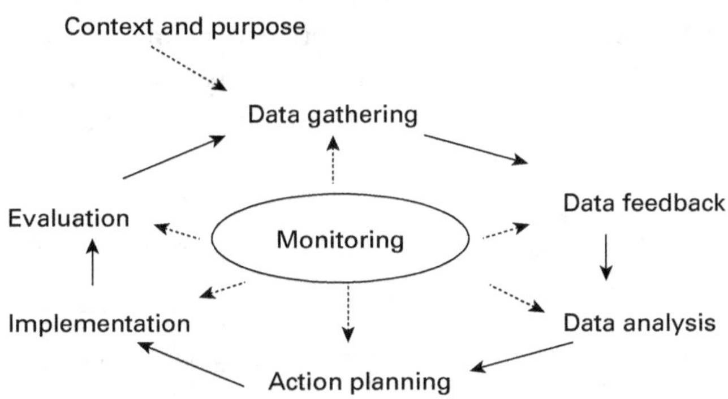

SOURCE Coughlan and Coghlan (2002: 230)

This cyclical approach without a predefined number of iterations may be one of the most irritating facts of AR for operations management (OM) researchers, who are used to a logical linear approach consisting of a stage-gated process as proposed by Flynn *et al* (1990) focused 'on the survey as the paradigm of empirical research' (see Figure 11.2). Here, the researcher is supposed to maintain a distance from the research objects and not to interfere. Considering how prominent and well received even qualitative empirical approaches have nowadays become in operations management/supply chain management, it is interesting to note the persuasive tone of this quote from 1990:

> Operations management researchers may be reluctant to undertake empirical research, due to its cost, both in dollars and time and the relative risk involved. Because empirical research may be considered 'soft', compared with mathematical modelling, it may be perceived as risky.
>
> (Flynn *et al*, 1990)

Epistemologically, AR is conceived as grounded in so-called Mode 2 knowledge production, which is defined and discussed as being antithetic to traditional Mode 1 knowledge production. In the scientific community these contrasting modes are often discussed with verve as the 'rigour–relevance gap in managerial research' (Maestrini *et al*, 2016: 289). Mode 1 advocators often propose that conducting research with practitioners poses the high risk of negatively impacting on rigour in the research process, whereas Mode 2 advocators put forward that research published in top journals in the last decade 'has been of little relevance for most practitioners' (Maestrini *et al*, 2016: 289). This echoes very well a notion from more than two decades ago by Alvesson (1996: 455): 'Practitioners seem to view the abstraction of quantified material and statistical correlations as very remote from everyday practice and therefore of little use.' It appears that scholars have

Figure 11.2 Model of rather 'mainstream' empirical research in operations management

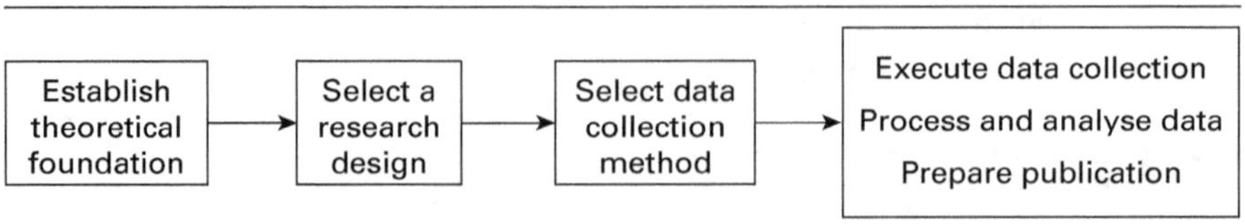

SOURCE Westbrook (1995)

Figure 11.3 Evolved model of action research in operations management

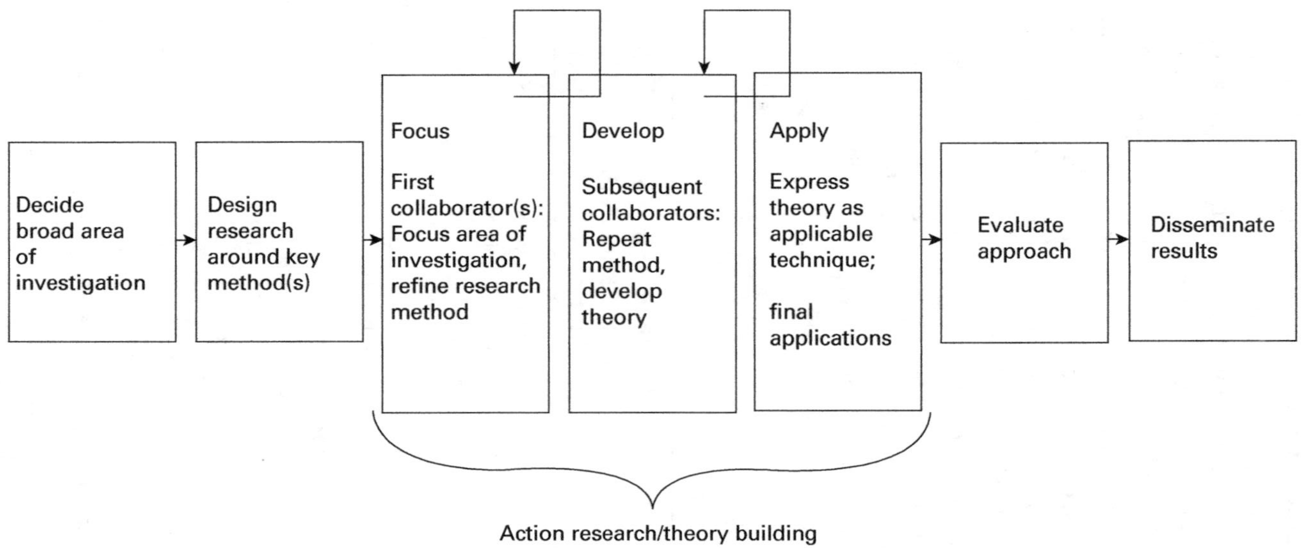

SOURCE Westbrook (1995:11)

been continuously reluctant to live-up to Kurt Lewin's maxim that 'there is nothing as practical as a good theory', ignoring the need of practice. Instead, the currently prevailing Mode 1 problems 'are set and solved in a context governed by the largely academic interests of a specific community' (Gibbons *et al*, 1994: 3) and corresponding research aims at generating context free universal knowledge. On the contrary, Mode 2 knowledge production is dependent on the collaboration among researchers and practitioners preferably in a trans-disciplinary setting. Here, the research objective does not follow a predefined academic agenda but is defined by a problem in practice, and scientific knowledge is produced in the context of an application. Or as (Reason, 2006: 188) states: 'If we start from the idea that creating knowledge is a practical affair, we will start not, as in traditional academic research, from an interesting theoretical question, but from what concerns us in practice, from the presenting issues in our lives.' The differences between mainstream positivist science (Mode 1) and AR (Mode 2) are well juxtaposed by Coughlan and Coghlan (see Table 11.1).

Table 11.1 Mode 1 vs. Mode 2 knowledge production

	Positivist science (Mode 1 knowledge production)	**Action research (Mode 2 knowledge production)**
Aim of research	Universal knowledge Theory building and testing	Knowledge in action Theory building and testing in action
Type of knowledge acquired	Universal Covering law	Particular Situational Praxis
Nature of data validation	Context free Logic, measurement Consistency of prediction and control	Contextually embedded Experiential
Researcher's role	Observer	Actor Agent of change
Researcher's relationship to setting	Detached neutral	Immersed

SOURCE Coughlan and Coghlan (2002: 224)

Action research and supply chain management

Action research is still considered underrepresented in operations management in general (Baker and Jayaraman, 2012) including supply chain management (Touboulic and Walker, 2016) and purchasing and supply management (Knight *et al*, 2016: 242), although this void had already been addressed by various academics decades ago (eg Coughlan and Coghlan, 2002; Näslund *et al*, 2010; Näslund, 2002; Westbrook, 1995). The rationale has not changed since, and AR is still contemplated to carry the potential for comprehensive insights into contextual phenomena and allow 'for relevant theory building' (Touboulic and Walker, 2016: 310). In their article named 'A relational, transformative and engaged approach to sustainable supply chain management: The potential of action research', Touboulic and Walker (2016) provide the up-to-date results of a systematic literature review of AR studies in eight major OM/SCM journals (eg *Journal of Supply Chain Management*, *Journal of Operations Management*, *Journal of Purchasing and Supply Management*) and seven sustainability/business ethics journals (eg *Journal of Business Ethics*, *Journal of Cleaner Production*, *Business Strategy and the Environment*). Accordingly, in the years 1986–2013 (no earlier articles were returned by the journals' databases) only 71 AR-related articles were published in the selected OM/SCM journals (see Figure 11.4). The authors emphasize the comparably small number of AR articles and reason 'that it [AR] is still considered as a non-traditional research approach compared to other empirical methodologies' (Touboulic and Walker, 2016: 316). The rationale may lie in the perceived riskiness of AR compared to other more mainstreamed research methods. Drawing on a number of workshops the author co-hosted together with Anne Touboulic and Lucy McCarthy in the years 2016–18, it can be stated that OM and SCM scholars perceive the challenges to outweigh the opportunities of conducting AR. In this context, a heavy emphasis is put on the challenge of publishing AR in top-tier journals, which in many instances is a prerequisite to advance the professional career.

Figure 11.4 Number of action research articles in eight major OM/SCM journals, 1986–2013

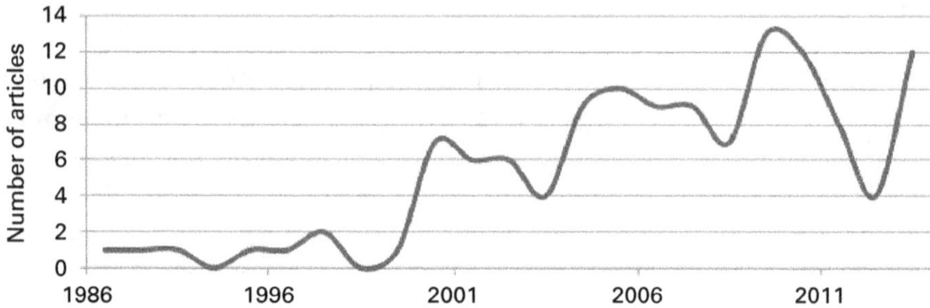

SOURCE Touboulic and Walker (2016: 316)

Action research and sustainability

While the commonly mentioned goals of AR are the enhancement of human wellbeing, emancipation, democracy and the empowerment of those involved through critical reflection (Greenwood and Levin 2007; Reason and Bradbury 2008), the explicit mentioning of sustainability remains an exception. One of these exceptions is in Kemmis (2010), who calls for 'action research for sustainability'. Following Kemmis (2010), Wittmayer and Schäpke (2014) advocate AR for sustainability based on three arguments: first, AR's orientation towards solutions; second, 'it highlights the role of research, which links different modes of science and different epistemologies based on systematic experimentation and reflexivity' (Wittmayer and Schäpke, 2014: 494); third, 'it links outcomes and research to the normative concept of sustainability' (Wittmayer and Schäpke, 2014: 494).

Further promising insights for the application of AR for sustainability come from the so-called 'Education for Sustainability' initiatives presented by Kemmis (2009):'

> Participants in these Education for Sustainability initiatives have come to *think differently* about the world and their place in it. Planet Earth is not a cornucopia of infinitely-available resources – participants understand the world in languages of ecological footprints, of 'food-miles', of sustainable agriculture, of renewable and non-renewable resources, of biodiversity and the irrevocability of its loss, and of 'reconciliation with the Earth.' Participants in these initiatives *act differently*. They reduce the size of their ecological footprint by saving energy and water, by buying local produce when they can, by helping revegetate

> degraded landscapes with indigenous plant species, by wasting less and littering not at all. And they *relate differently* to their co-inhabitants of the Earth – and not just to members of their own species. They also relate differently – more critically – to global warming sceptics and sluggish governments. They learn that changing things in the Earth can be done locally, by people acting more or less in isolation, but that changing water means acting at least on the scale of catchments, and that changing air quality means acting on a global scale. They have thus learned that they must act not only one by one, as individuals trying to make a difference, but also politically, through action in social movements. Participants in these Education for Sustainability initiatives are reconstructing the practice architectures by which our collective taken-for-granted practices are currently constructed – the ways we currently think about the world, act in it, and relate to each other and to nature. They want to change us, not just themselves, but they aim to do so by *participatory* and *democratic* means – by involving us in open discussion about the issues involved, by involving us in the process of changing the ways we use the Earth's resources and by encouraging us to join them in their advocacy for social and political change.
>
> (Kemmis, 2009: 472)

Action research for sustainable supply chain management research?

The previously cited literature review by Touboulic and Walker (2016) highlights the practical value of the few identified AR manuscripts. Out of the 13 reviewed AR papers related to sustainable SCM, seven are considered to be of high practical value (Ammenberg and Sundin (2005), Burchielli *et al* (2009), Koplin *et al* (2007), Partidário *et al* (2007), Zackrisson *et al* (2008), Golob *et al* (2014), Ribeiro and Zwirner (2010)), three of medium practical value (Mont (2004), Subramoniam *et al* (2010), Lambert *et al* (2012)) and only one (Seuring (2011)) of low practical value.

Kemmis (2010: 6–7) proposes that

> action researchers can be the yeast that helps a practice evolve in individual and collective *praxis*. They can be part of the endless production, reproduction and transformation of practices that is the process by which collective practices evolve to meet the needs, circumstances and opportunities of new times and new circumstances.

And Melnyk *et al* (2018: 187) acknowledge the potential of alternative research methods and suggest that fields outside of operations management should be seriously considered, as the following quote illustrates:

> In contrast, other empirical research methods are still in their infancy (for example, engaged research methods, such as action research, and ethnographic research) or in the growth part of their lifecycle (case research, experiments, event studies). It is critical to stay in touch with the latest theoretical and methodological developments, which often takes place in other fields, in order to sustain the quality of OSM empirical research.

What it takes to move forward

The notion 'action research for sustainability' appears to be appealing and promising not only to praxis but also to scientific practice, at least outside of the field of supply chain management. So why do scholars in the domain of SCM appear reluctant to embrace AR as another valid research approach? Bäckstrand and Halldórsson (2019) focus on the individual researcher and identify 'inconsistencies and misalignments among requirements put on the individual researcher'. Further insights are provided by Touboulic and Walker (2016) who acknowledge the advantages and challenges from applying AR in sustainable SCM (Table 11.2).

It appears that in order to move forward some fundamental changes are required. Amongst others, a reform of universities is called for, as extensively brought forward by Reason and Bradbury (2008) with quotes of contributors to their book, *The Sage Handbook of Action Research: Participative inquiry and practice*:

> Davydd Greenwood argues that we must 'move institutions of higher education in the direction of Mode 2 knowledge production, ie, the co-generative creation of "socially robust" knowledge'. John Burgoyne dreams of a business school 'in which teaching and research, action learning and action research, fuse into a combined process of mutual inquiry and learning, a meeting of critically reflective practitioner researchers and facilitators which develop themselves and their practice, contribute to, share and draw on a collective body of knowledge and understanding'. Morten Levin argues that it is vital to 'locate AR in institutions of higher education because this creates legitimacy for AR.... Institutions of higher education are probably the most fruitful arena that can connect legitimacy and diffusion'. David Coghlan points to the paradox that

Table 11.2 Advantages and challenges of applying action research in supply chain management

	Advantages	Challenges
Customer firm (large)	Engagement in research Change supporting strategic direction Supports other initiatives Reflects critically on practice	Short-term engagement on issue without long-term change Strategic direction change Suppliers get a voice Wary of critical view of researcher What happens next?
Suppliers (smaller)	Gives a voice Democracy Reflect on practice Access to research	Veiled power What happens next? Wary of research agenda View of researcher as 'knight in shining armour'
Researcher	Part of change Access to deep qualitative data Not restricted to pre-defined themes Learn to deal with sensitive issues and manage relations	Managing expectations and political aspects Address ethics and question of objectivity Feeling lost or in-between Ending the process and future of work done
SSCM field and future research	Much research focused on activities of large buying firms, AR provides a more egalitarian view of SCM Creative ways to include organizations in SSC Forward-looking research Opportunity for novel theory testing and building Impact and teaching cases	Manage engagement alongside multiple organizations: can AR be applied beyond the scope of one organization?

SOURCE Touboulic and Walker (2016: 335)

while there are continual complaints about relevance and the gap between academic research and practitioners, academic institutions continue to support a mode of research that apes the natural sciences and separates theory from practice. He argues that we must 'continue to batter at that door... however firmly it is locked and barred so that action research does not disappear' and 'publish strong action research that contains clear evidence that can be accepted in major journals'.

(Reason and Bradbury, 2008: 700–01)

Critical reflection and outlook

> The essential purpose of action research is to address issues of concern to individuals and communities in the everyday conduct of their lives. A wider purpose is to contribute to the increased well-being – economic, political, psychological, spiritual – of humanity and to a more equitable and sustainable relationship with the wider ecology of the planet of which we are an intrinsic part.
>
> (Reason, 2006: 191)

While this quote by itself brings forward the claim for action research to be worthy of consideration as a feasible approach to the sustainability related challenges of our time, the same authors intensify this notion by stating 'In the arena of sustainability, the application of action research to change in organizations could come to be useful for the broader world' (Reason and Bradbury, 2008: 86). Moreover, the above arguments have highlighted the potential of AR to contribute to (more) sustainable supply chain management as being eminent while its limited dissemination is apparent. However, the latter should not lead to the undermining of the former. Without a doubt, there are challenges inherent to applying less mainstream research methods such as AR. But it is time to acknowledge that taking mainstream routes because of the aversion of risk has not advanced the way supply chain managers and researchers deal with the sustainability challenge. What is needed is the dedication by the academic community, especially in the field of OM and SCM, to embrace AR as an alternative research approach with merit.

References

Alvesson, M (1996) [accessed 23 September 2020] Leadership studies: From procedure and abstraction to reflexivity and situation, *The Leadership Quarterly*, 7 (4), pp 455–85 [Online] https://doi.org/10.1016/S1048-9843(96)90002-8 (archived at https://perma.cc/J5KE-2N66)

Ammenberg, J and Sundin, E (2005) [accessed 23 September 2020] Products in environmental management systems: Drivers, barriers and experiences *Journal of Cleaner Production*, **13** (4), pp 405–15 [Online] https://doi.org/10.1016/j.jclepro.2003.12.005 (archived at https://perma.cc/XAP6-D98P)

Bäckstrand, J and Halldórsson, Á (2019) [accessed 23 September 2020] Engaged scholar(ship) in purchasing and supply management (PSM): Creative tension or squeezed in the middle? *Journal of Purchasing and Supply Management*, **25** (4),

100557 [Online] https://doi.org/10.1016/j.pursup.2019.100557 (archived at https://perma.cc/FA2Z-5KWU)

Baker, T and Jayaraman, V (2012) [accessed 23 September 2020] Managing information and supplies inventory operations in a manufacturing environment – Part 1: An action research study, *International Journal of Production Research*, **50** (6), pp 1666–81 [Online] https://doi.org/10.1080/00207543.2010.550697 (archived at https://perma.cc/5UHQ-NLTY)

Bradbury-Huang, H (2010) [accessed 23 September 2020] What is good action research? Why the resurgent interest? *Action Research*, **8** (1), pp 93–109 [Online] https://doi.org/10.1177/1476750310362435 (archived at https://perma.cc/5AAH-N3W7)

Burchielli, R, Delaney, A, Tate, J and Coventry, K (2009) [accessed 23 September 2020] The FairWear campaign: An ethical network in the Australian garment industry, *Journal of Business Ethics*, **90** (4), pp 575–88 [Online] https://doi.org/10.1007/s10551-010-0593-z (archived at https://perma.cc/3GJD-F4BC)

Coughlan, P and Coghlan, D (2002) [accessed 23 September 2020] Action research for operations management, *International Journal of Operations and Production Management*, **22** (2), pp 220–40 [Online] https://doi.org/10.1108/01443570210417515 (archived at https://perma.cc/PM78-Q6YU)

Fendt, J, Kaminska-Labbé, R and Sachs, VM (2008) Producing and socializing relevant management knowledge: Re-turn to pragmatism, *European Business Review*, 20, pp 471–91

Flynn, BB, Sakakibara, S, Schroeder, RG, Bates, KA and Flynn, EJ (1990) [accessed 23 September 2020] Empirical research methods in operations management, *Journal of Operations Management*, **9** (2), pp 250–84 [Online] https://doi.org/10.1016/0272-6963 (archived at https://perma.cc/JB7R-4ZHB) (90)90098-X

Gibbons, M, Limoges, C, Nowotny, H, Schwartzman, S, Scott, P and Trow, M (1994) *The New Production of Knowledge: The dynamics of science and research in contemporary societies*, Guildford, Sage

Golob, U, Johansen, TS, Nielsen, AE and Podnar, K (2014) [accessed 23 September 2020] Corporate social responsibility as a messy problem: Linking systems and sensemaking perspectives, *Systemic Practice and Action Research*, **27** (4), pp 363–76 [Online] https://doi.org/10.1007/s11213-013-9287-7 (archived at https://perma.cc/43JB-9TPA)

Greenwood, DJ and Levin, M (2007) *Introduction to Action Research*, SAGE Publications, Thousand Oaks, CA, doi: 10.4135/9781412984614

Kemmis, S (2009) [accessed 23 September 2020] Action research as a practice, based practice, *Educational Action Research*, **17** (3), pp 463–74 [Online] https://doi.org/10.1080/09650790903093284 (archived at https://perma.cc/CJB4-AFTY)

Kemmis, S (2010) [accessed 23 September 2020] What is to be done? The place of action research, *Educational Action Research*, **18** (4), pp 417–27 [Online] https://doi.org/10.1080/09650792.2010.524745 (archived at https://perma.cc/U7U3-FFU9)

Knight, L, Tate, WL, Matopoulos, A, Meehan, J and Salmi, A (2016) [accessed 23 September 2020] Breaking the mold: Research process innovations in purchasing and supply management, *Journal of Purchasing and Supply Management*, **22** (4), pp 239–43 [Online] https://doi.org/10.1016/j.pursup.2016.09.003 (archived at https://perma.cc/W37W-6FWU)

Koplin, J, Seuring, S and Mesterharm, M (2007) [accessed 23 September 2020] Incorporating sustainability into supply management in the automotive industry: The case of the Volkswagen AG, *Journal of Cleaner Production*, **15** (11–12), pp 1053–62 [Online] https://doi.org/10.1016/j.jclepro.2006.05.024 (archived at https://perma.cc/RDW6-X3GH)

Lambert, J [John], Duhon, D and Peyrefitte, J (2012) [accessed 23 September 2020] 2010 BP oil spill and the systemic construct of the Gulf Coast shrimp supply chain, *Systemic Practice and Action Research*, **25** (3), pp 223–40 [Online] https://doi.org/10.1007/s11213-011-9219-3 (archived at https://perma.cc/3LCF-3Y2S)

Mabala, R and Allen, KB (2002) [accessed 23 September 2020] Participatory action research on HIV/AIDS through a popular theatre approach in Tanzania, *Evaluation and Program Planning*, **25** (4), pp 333–39 [Online] https://doi.org/10.1016/S0149-7189(02)00044-7 (archived at https://perma.cc/ZS75-LM3X)

Maestrini, V, Luzzini, D, Shani, AB and Canterino, F (2016) [accessed 23 September 2020] The action research cycle reloaded: Conducting action research across buyer–supplier relationships, *Journal of Purchasing and Supply Management*, **22** (4), pp 289–98 [Online] https://doi.org/10.1016/j.pursup.2016.06.002 (archived at https://perma.cc/W23H-J9NN)

Melnyk, SA, Flynn, BB, and Awaysheh, A (2018) [accessed 23 September 2020] The best of times and the worst of times: Empirical operations and supply chain management research, *International Journal of Production Research*, **56** (1–2), pp 164–92 [Online] https://doi.org/10.1080/00207543.2017.1391423 (archived at https://perma.cc/Q5YT-R77W)

Mont, O (2004) [accessed 23 September 2020] Reducing life-cycle environmental impacts through systems of joint use, *Greener Management International* (45), pp 63–77 [Online] http://www.jstor.org/stable/greemanainte.45.63 (archived at https://perma.cc/EH4W-DTJA)

Näslund, D (2002) [accessed 23 September 2020] Logistics needs qualitative research – especially action research, *International Journal of Physical Distribution and Logistics Management*, **32** (5), pp 321–38 [Online] https://doi.org/10.1108/09600030210434143 (archived at https://perma.cc/F26H-JB76)

Näslund, D, Kale, R and Paulraj, A (2010) [accessed 23 September 2020] Action research in supply chain management: A framework for relevant and rigorous research, *Journal of Business Logistics*, **31** (2), pp 331–55 [Online] https://doi.org/10.1002/j.2158-1592.2010.tb00155.x (archived at https://perma.cc/Q35R-CQWY)

Pagell, M and Shevchenko, A (2014) [accessed 23 September 2020] Why research in sustainable supply chain management should have no future, *Journal of Supply Chain Management*, **50** (1), pp 44–55 [Online] https://doi.org/10.1111/jscm.12037 (archived at https://perma.cc/L3ZS-8ZY8)

Partidário, PJ, Lambert, J [Joanna] and Evans, S (2007) [accessed 23 September 2020] Building more sustainable solutions in production–consumption systems: The case of food for people with reduced access, *Journal of Cleaner Production*, **15** (6), pp 513–24 [Online] https://doi.org/10.1016/j.jclepro.2006.05.011 (archived at https://perma.cc/NFY2-R4CV)

Perlow, LA (1999) [accessed 23 September 2020] The time famine: Toward a sociology of work time, *Administrative Science Quarterly*, **44** (1), p 57 [Online] https://doi.org/10.2307/2667031 (archived at https://perma.cc/23QJ-NWGQ)

Reason, P (2006) Choice and quality in action research practice, *Journal of Management Inquiry*, **15** (2), pp 187–203 [Online] https://doi.org/10.1177/1056492606288074 (archived at https://perma.cc/8GRX-DAVF)

Reason, P, and Bradbury, H (2008) *The Sage Handbook of Action Research: Participative inquiry and practice*, 2nd edn, SAGE Publications, London

Ribeiro, MM, and Zwirner, W (2010) Applying participatory processes: Findings from a supply chain analysis on the commercialisation of paper mulberry bark in Laos, *Systemic Practice and Action Research*, **23** (4), pp 323–40 [Online] https://doi.org/10.1007/s11213-009-9162-8 (archived at https://perma.cc/JTW9-JJ89)

Seuring, S (2011) [accessed 23 September 2020] Supply chain management for sustainable products: Insights from research applying mixed methodologies, *Business Strategy and the Environment*, **20** (7), pp 471–84 [Online] https://doi.org/10.1002/bse.702 (archived at https://perma.cc/233J-6X42)

Subramoniam, R, Huisingh, D and Chinnam, RB (2010) [accessed 23 September 2020] Aftermarket remanufacturing strategic planning decision-making framework: Theory and practice, *Journal of Cleaner Production*, **18** (16), pp 1575–86 [Online] https://doi.org/10.1016/j.jclepro.2010.07.022 (archived at https://perma.cc/HQT6-F3YV)

Tompa, E, Dolinschi, R, Oliveira, C de and Irvin, E (2009) [accessed 23 September 2020] A systematic review of occupational health and safety interventions with economic analyses, *Journal of Occupational and Environmental Medicine*, **51** (9), pp 1004–23 [Online] https://doi.org/10.1097/JOM.0b013e3181b34f60 (archived at https://perma.cc/3485-M6AP)

Touboulic, A and Walker, H (2016) [accessed 23 September 2020] A relational, transformative and engaged approach to sustainable supply chain management: The potential of action research, *Human Relations*, **69** (2), pp 301–43 [Online] https://doi.org/10.1177/0018726715583364 (archived at https://perma.cc/V7PN-N4D6)

Westbrook, R (1995) [accessed 23 September 2020] Action research: A new paradigm for research in production and operations management, *International Journal of Operations and Production Management*, **15** (12), pp 6–20 [Online] https://doi.org/10.1108/01443579510104466 (archived at https://perma.cc/9R26-48GV)

Wittmayer, JM, and Schäpke, N (2014) [accessed 23 September 2020] Action, research and participation: Roles of researchers in sustainability transitions, *Sustainability Science*, **9** (4), pp 483–96 [Online] https://doi.org/10.1007/s11625-014-0258-4 (archived at https://perma.cc/66FW-VUHF)

Zackrisson, M, Rocha, C, Christiansen, K and Jarnehammar, A (2008) [accessed 23 September 2020] Stepwise environmental product declarations: Ten SME case studies, *Journal of Cleaner Production*, **16** (17), pp 1872–86 [Online] https://doi.org/10.1016/j.jclepro.2008.01.001 (archived at https://perma.cc/9FL9-WYRE)

Success factors of voluntary sustainable supply chain management sector initiatives

12

JULIA SCHWARZKOPF, KLAUS FISCHER AND MARTIN MÜLLER

Introduction

Business activities nowadays are globalized, with established diversified and global supply chains (Petersen *et al*, 2000; Gunasekaran *et al*, 2004). However, this development often comes at the cost of environmental and social damage, mainly in participating countries in the Global South (Fischer, 2020). Thus, various incidents concerning the (non-)compliance to expected minimum sustainability standards in global supply chains have been identified and published (Seuring and Müller, 2008b; Foerstl *et al*, 2010; Klein, 2010; Wolf, 2014; Amnesty International, 2017; Know the Chain, 2019; SOMO, 2016). Consequently, in academia, the focus of supply chain management was broadened by the integration of sustainability to address such issues in globalized supply chains (Seuring and Müller, 2008a; Walker and Jones, 2012; Gimenez and Tachizawa, 2012; Beske-Janssen *et al*, 2015; Ansari and Kant, 2017; Köksal *et al*, 2017).

Although we recognize that there is no unified definition of what sustainable supply chain management (SSCM) is and what it entails (Reefke *et al*, 2014), we adhere to the SSCM definition by Garcia-Torres *et al* (2019), which takes earlier well-respected definitions from Pagell and Wu (2009) and Seuring and Müller (2008b) into consideration. Garcia-Torres *et al* (2019) define '(S)SCM as the management of companies and flows (material, information and capital) throughout the SC to ensure the economic viability of the network while guaranteeing (at least) no harm to the natural and social environment' (Garcia-Torres *et al*, 2019: 87).

Due to the high complexity of globalized supply chains, SSCM is accompanied by certain challenges. One challenge is linked to achieving the transparency of supply chains, or at least of significant parts thereof, while another challenge refers to supply chains that include business activities from informal sectors, which have usually been outside the possible influence of SSCM activities (Fischer *et al*, 2009). In addition, focal companies may not feel that they have enough leverage or power to pursue SSCM activities in their supply chains. Focal companies may therefore turn to sector initiatives, which are also addressed within the SSCM literature, and practitioner-oriented company guidelines (Müller and Bessas, 2017; OECD, 2018).

The number of sustainability-oriented sector or cross-sector initiatives has thereby increased, both at international and national level, leading to quite a variety of approaches. Sector initiatives thus focus on different sustainability issues, use a variety of SSCM instruments and may show differences in their organizational or membership structure. For example, there exist rather specialized ones, focusing on certain raw material supply chains (such as the group of conflict minerals, or palm oil). Others are positioned more broadly, covering different issues and activities, such as is the case in the automotive, electronics or rail industry. While some of these broader sector initiatives (such as AIAG, 2019) address SSCM only as a sub-branch amongst others, other initiatives (such as the Joint Audit Cooperation, 2019) focus on specific aspects of SSCM. Lately, sector initiatives are even promoted within overarching policy initiatives to address certain malpractices in supply chains and have then rather a character of public–private partnerships. Here, policymakers emphasize the potential role of such initiatives in creating (more) sustainable value and supply chains. In Germany, this is, for example, the case concerning the German National Action Plan on Business and Human Rights (Auswärtiges Amt, 2016). In other cases, sector initiatives are indirectly integrated in broader policy initiatives, as for example via the OECD *Due Diligence Guidance for Responsible Supply Chains Minerals from Conflict-Affected and High-Risk Areas* (OECD, 2013), which is mentioned as an implementation guideline of the EU Conflict Minerals Regulation.

The general idea behind voluntary sector initiatives is to address the challenges of SSCM together. Sharing knowledge and experiences, as well as joining resources between the initiatives' members, can help to increase the momentum of the intended SSCM activities. Thus, if relevant players of a specific sector and value chain cooperate, the coverage of SSCM instruments might increase. For example, a sector-wide common code of conduct that is claimed by a number of focal firms from one industry is much more assertive than single specific codes from individual companies might each be. Bundled initiatives also create more clarity for the addressed value chain actors. Instead of dealing with a multitude of different, but often similar, requirements and instruments, such as self-assessment questionnaires for suppliers, sector-widely unified SSCM approaches allow varying CSR policies and requirements in the chain to be consolidated.

We can thus state that voluntary sector initiatives can potentially increase both the effectiveness as well as the efficiency of SSCM approaches. On the one hand, pooling resources, skills, and power might increase the SSCM impact compared with individual approaches. On the other hand, consolidating individual CSR policies and unifying instruments simplifies the realization of SSCM activities for all parties involved.

However, to our knowledge, no information currently exists as to whether voluntary sector initiatives can live up to the different expectations put upon them by their members, policy makers or other stakeholders. This may also be linked to the circumstance that not all stakeholders interested in the activities have formulated or addressed their expectations either.

In this chapter we aim to shed more light on the variety of sector initiatives and their work. For a first step, we define some criteria for typologizing these initiatives and will analyse how certain types of voluntary sector initiatives themselves define, and potentially measure, their success. We assume that gaining deeper insights into the success propositions of voluntary sector initiatives might contribute to paving the way for future research about the role of such initiatives in the bigger context of global sustainability governance and SSCM practices.

Typology criteria for voluntary SSCM sector initiatives

As discussed in the previous section, the number and variety of SSCM sector initiatives increased in recent years (Müller and Bessas, 2017). After proposing a definition of voluntary SSCM sector initiatives, we will therefore develop a typology to further characterize different forms of these initiatives.

We define a voluntary SSCM sector initiative as a non-compulsory organizational approach in which companies operating along a value/supply chain jointly – in some cases together with external stakeholders – establish and execute processes and/or tools for SSCM through an organization to which they declare their membership.

To characterize the different kinds of sector initiatives and attain a certain typology, we will further elaborate on the following five criteria, which refer to publicly available information:

- sector focus;
- membership base;
- governance process;
- grade of activity;
- SSCM specialization.

These critereria are not deduced from theoretical considerations, but deliver a pragmatic framework that allows a clear distinction of different types of initiatives as a precondition for developing hypotheses and future research.

Sector focus

First of all, the actors working together in a voluntary sector initiative can originate from one single industrial sector or from different sectors. While big industries such as chemicals, electronics, or automotive are often represented by specific single-sector initiatives, other industries such as fast moving consumer goods are more involved in multi-sector networks (see the presentation of initiatives in the next section). Whether an initiative is working sector-specific or cross-sectoral can depend on different factors, which could be the subject of future research: its founding history, its integration in the supply chain (top-down or bottom-up governance process, see below), or whether there are characteristic sustainability issues and challenges that are collectively relevant for a certain industry or just different industries involved.

However, independent of the membership in a single- or multi-sector initiative, those involved can be active in different industry sectors.

Membership base

Voluntary sector initiatives are often driven by so-called focal companies, which are at the centre of research within the SSCM literature (Frostenson and Prenkert, 2015). Their extraordinary role is seen to be justified by Seuring and Müller (2008b) since the focal company is the one that exercises pressure and also passes externals requirements, such as non-governmental organizations' (NGO) expectations, on its suppliers. Focal companies 'usually (1) rule or govern the supply chain, (2) provide the direct contact to the customer, and (3) design the product or service offered' (Seuring and Müller, 2008b: 1699). They have the power to determine the final product offered and are therefore also responsible for their supply chains (Seuring and Müller, 2008b; Seuring, 2011; Wang and Wood, 2016). Focal companies are thus the main actors of governance in value chains and set parameters for upstream phases of value creation (Humphrey and Schmitz, 2001).

The resulting vertical forms of chain governance (Gereffi and Lee, 2016) address internal chain actors as direct suppliers and (if possible) sub-suppliers up to the origin of value creation, such as the extraction of raw materials or the cultivation of agricultural commodities. Horizontal forms of chain governance emerge from the interaction between the chain actors and chain-external stakeholders (Gereffi and Lee, 2016), as is the case for multi-stakeholder initiatives, which are discussed in Soundararajan *et al* (2019).

For typologizing voluntary sector initiatives, it seems thus to be useful to analyse their membership bases. This allows for differentiation between those initiatives only including chain actors and those with a membership base that comprises both chain actors and external stakeholders.

Governance process

As identified by Müller and Bessas (2017) and demonstrated in Figure 12.1, sector initiatives can be differentiated by how they interact with the supply chain. Besides the question of vertical or horizontal forms of governance, depending on the membership base of an initiative, different directions of governance in the value chain occur in different initiatives.

On the one hand, there are top-down-initiatives starting from downstream companies such as brand companies and original equipment manufacturers (OEMs). They comprise, for example, industry-wide standards relevant for the upstream suppliers in that sector. On the other hand, bottom-up-initiatives start from the very bottom of the supply chains, eg at resource extraction. They are commodity-specific and provide a means of certification for particular raw materials.

For further exploring voluntary sector initiatives, it will be worth analysing which different approaches lead to which results. Thus, it may be more

Figure 12.1 Differentiation of sustainability initiatives in supply chains

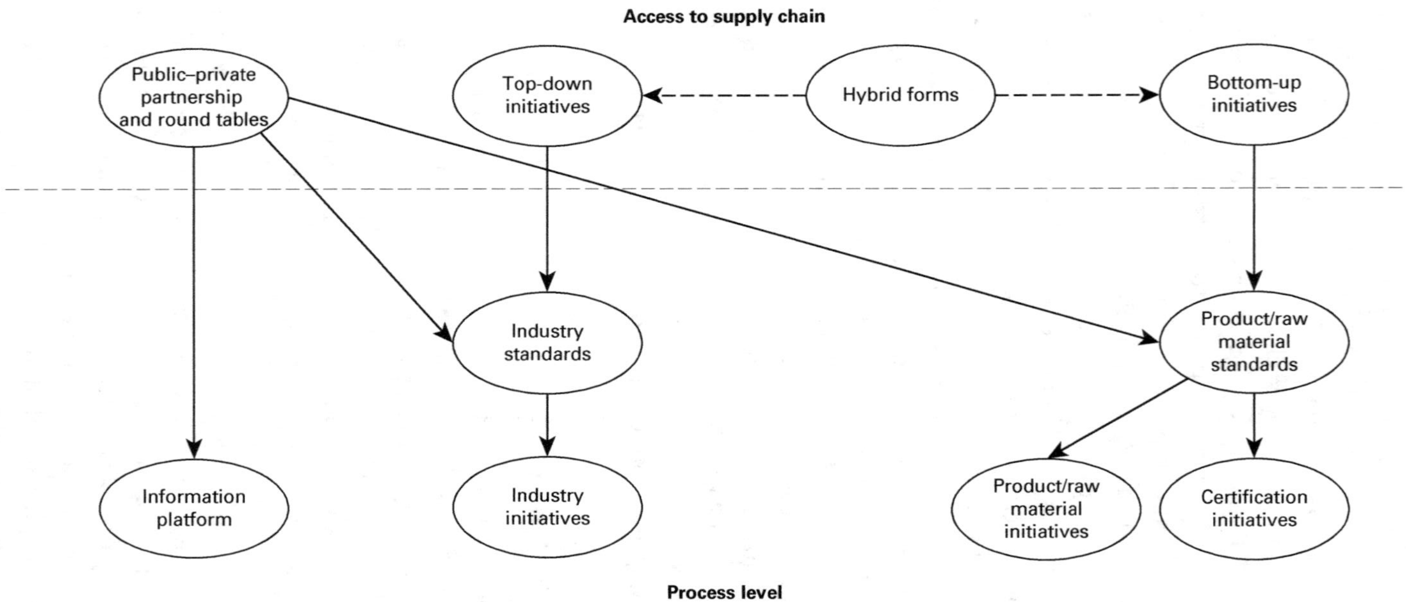

SOURCE Own translation of Müller and Bessas (2017)

effective to induce bottom-up governance processes, as they might better integrate the upstream actors in the chain and involve their requirements and expertise. Or it may be more effective to bundle the power from demand side and thus to establish top-down governance processes. However, as considered by Müller and Bessas (2017), there also exist mixed approaches. Maybe, they could integrate the advantages of both.

Grade of activity

The academic attention on SSCM is paired with increasing relevance for management practice and supported by corresponding activities in the field of SSCM (Gimenez and Tachizawa, 2012; Schöggl *et al*, 2016; Sancha *et al*, 2016; Singh and Trivedi, 2016). These activities can also be linked to stakeholder expectations demanding SSCM practices (Seuring and Müller, 2008b; Müller and Bessas, 2017). In addition, legislation on supply chain sustainability, as can be observed in the EU non-financial reporting directive (European Commission, 2014), the UK Modern Slavery Act (UK Government, 2015) or the California Transparency in the Supply Chain Act (State of California, 2010), are also demanding concrete actions from the affected companies.

Thereby, the range of possible SSCM activities is manifold, reaching from training for suppliers or buyers to the implementation of sustainability-oriented strategies, as well as risks and performance management systems, like audits, track-and-trace systems, or monitoring and sanctioning (Seuring and Müller, 2008b; Köksal *et al*, 2017; Fischer *et al*, 2018).

In this context, Reefke *et al* (2014) describe a proactive approach by suggesting a SSCM-oriented decision-making cycle, which includes the 'discovery of unsustainable areas within a SC' (Reefke *et al*, 2014: 4S) or 'the formulation of a strategy for the introduction and implementation of sustainable practices' (Reefke *et al*, 2014: 4S). Such a decision cycle is an on-going process of 'discovery–learning–strategizing–design–transformation–monitoring–control' (Reefke *et al*, 2014: 4S). It thus depends on continuous monitoring and control, which help to discover new areas of sustainability issues and to evaluate whether newly introduced practices are successful. Such a meta-approach seems to be adequate for the SSCM activities of voluntary initiatives, too.

Figure 12.2 refers to some essential SSCM activities, embedded in an ideal-typical workflow of a sector initiative.

Figure 12.2 Typical processes of sector initiatives

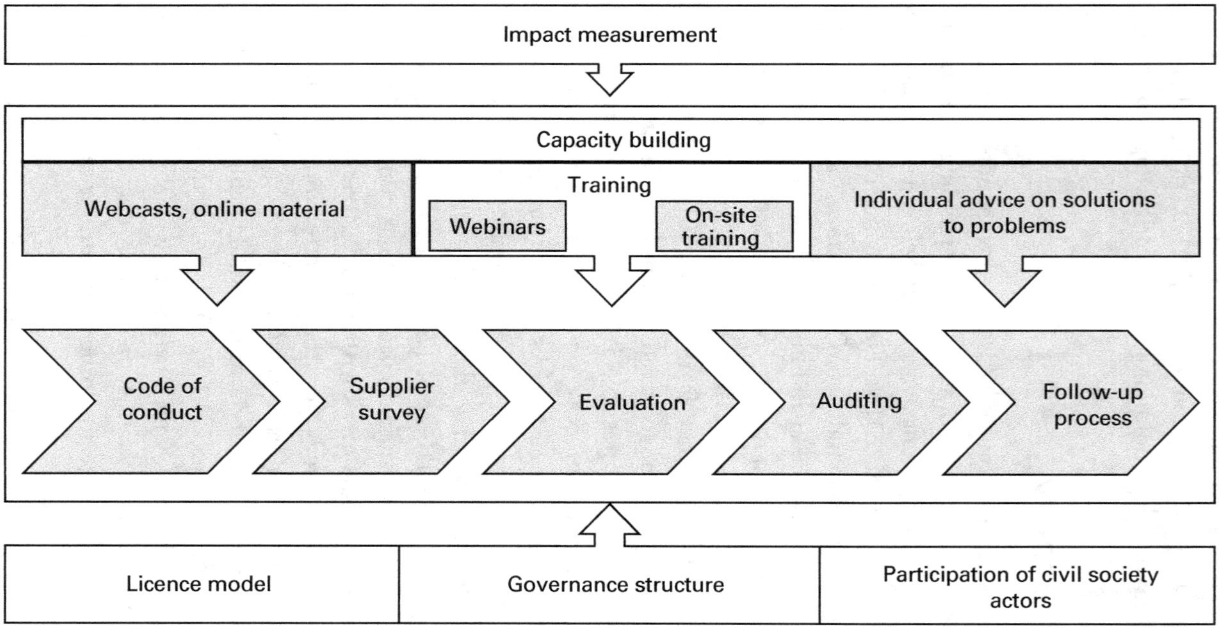

SOURCE Own translation of Müller and Bessas (2017)

While not all the elements of SSCM are necessarily addressed to the same extent by all voluntary sector initiatives, it is of interest to evaluate which of these SSCM elements are part of them. Thereby, some sector initiatives hardly go beyond activities of awareness-raising and the exchange of good practices and experiences, while others describe own measures of SSCM intervention in the chain.

For a further distinction of voluntary initiatives, we thus differentiate between those initiatives having a rather communicational character and those stating that they are implementing SSCM activities, referred to as interventional initiatives.

SSCM specialization

As one further criterion of distinction, we propose an exploration of whether the sector initiative is oriented explicitly towards SSCM or whether it deals with that approach amongst other themes and objectives. While, in the first case, SSCM is the constitutive element of the initiative and the reason for its origin, in the latter it is a subsequent 'add-on' to other activities of an existing initiative. The question is whether an existing and already well-placed initiative can deal better with SSCM objectives and can profit from its longer institutional setting, or whether SSCM achieves more penetrating power from a newly set, specialized initiative.

The aforementioned five criteria are brought together in Table 12.1, showing a first typology of voluntary SSCM sector initiatives. As the criteria are independent of each other, they can be combined freely to enable us to characterize different kinds of sector initiatives, hypothesize about possible interrelations and thus prepare for future research.

Table 12.1 Typology criteria for voluntary SSCM sector initiatives

Sector focus	Single sector	Multiple sectors
Membership base	Chain – internal	Chain – internal and external
Grade of activity	Communicational	Interventional
Governance process	Top-down (upstream)	Bottom-up (downstream)
SSCM specialization	Specialized	Non-specialized

Methodological approach and analytical framework

The analytical framework of this chapter refers to the aforementioned voluntary sector initiatives and the question of whether or not these define (and potentially measure) their success. While Müller and Bessas (2017) point out that there must be some form of impact measurement to assess the relevance and effects of voluntary initiatives concerning sustainability improvements, this will be not be addressed in this chapter for two reasons. First, to our understanding, there is so far still a missing definition on not only how to measure impact but also how to measure impact in a comparable manner, which even holds true for a comparison of focal companies (Beske-Janssen *et al*, 2015).

Second, we argue that it is valuable to explore the success propositions of voluntary sector initiatives as they are an important object of investigation by themselves. These propositions indicate the initiatives' strategic orientation and normative intentions and give insight into what their members aim to accomplish with their engagement and membership. This is, in particular, pertinent concerning their growing relevance as a tool for SSCM by focal companies, but also, as addressed above, as they are at the same time increasingly included in policy and legislative approaches.

As this is a conceptual chapter, we perform desktop research on selected voluntary sector SSCM-oriented initiatives, based on the sample of initiatives that were identified by Müller and Bessas (2017). This is done by analysing publicly available documents such as strategy statements or website presentations.

To ensure a focused analysis and to single out factors that could influence the definition of success, we selected a certain type of sector initiatives (see Table 12.2), referring to the typology criteria developed in the section above.

Table 12.2 Typology criteria addressed in desktop research (highlighted in grey)

Sector focus	Single sector	Multiple sectors
Membership base	Chain – internal	Chain – internal and external
Grade of activity	Communicational	Interventional
Governance process	Top-down (upstream)	Bottom-up (downstream)
SSCM specialization	Specialized	Non-specialized

Consequently, we are limiting our analysis to those sector initiatives that fulfill the following criteria:

- They focus on a *single sector*, eg chemicals, electronics, automotive, and do not address industries of more than one sector. However, the companies addressed by these activities, ie the suppliers, may be operating in or supplying to different sectors. This could also be true for the focal companies themselves (for example, a chemical company could be active both in the pharmaceutical sector and in the agricultural science sector).
- *The membership base contains only chain-internal actors*; thus, companies being active along a value/supply chain in the respective sector in which the initiative is working. That is, focal companies and their suppliers, which may also be a focal company themselves, are the members, but not other external (multi-)stakeholders, like civil society organizations. Therefore, initiatives like the Round Table on Sustainable Palm Oil (2019) are not in the focus of this chapter.
- *The initiatives perform interventional activities* such as a common code of conduct, supplier self-assessments, audits, supplier training or other forms of capacity building for suppliers or own staff, therefore having the potential to create an impact on the respective supply chains concerning the sustainability performance of the actors in the chain.
- *Governance processes* induced by the sector initiative are top-down and thus address upstream chain actors, starting from retailers or original equipment manufacturers. Thus, commodity-specific initiatives starting with raw material production shall not be included in the analysis.
- For the first step of exploration, *SSCM specialization is not a selection criterion*. Consequently, initiatives that are only focusing on SSCM, as well as those addressing SSCM as one subject amongst others, shall be included for further analysis.

Table 12.3 gives an overview of the originally identified initiatives from Müller and Bessas (2017), enlarged with the selection criteria above. The original initiatives were then filtered following the above-defined criteria, resulting in the inclusion of only five sector initiatives for further analysis in our chapter (see Table 12.3 for details).

Table 12.3 Overview of the sector initiatives identified by Müller and Bessas (2017); enlarged by own typology criteria

Name of initiative Year of foundation URL	Sector focus	Membership base	Grade of activity	Governance process	SSCM specialization	Further analysis?
AIM Progress 2007 https://aim-progress.com/	Multiple sectors: fast moving consumer goods, but very different goods are included	Chain – internal: Manufacturers and Suppliers	Interventional: – Capability building for suppliers – Audit recognition	Top-down (upstream)	Specialized	No
Automotive Industry Action Group (AIAG) 1982/2006 https://www.aiag.org/	Single sector: automotive	Chain – internal: Manufacturers and Suppliers	Interventional: – Not specifically focused on SSCM – Capacity building for suppliers – Common code of conduct	Top-down (upstream)	Non-specialized	Yes
Business Environmental Performance Initiative (amfori) 2014 https://www.amfori.org/	Multiple sectors: trade/retail market with companies from various sectors	Unclear. Manufacturers and single companies Unclear whether some members are in each other's supply chains	Interventional: – Auditing – Supplier performance assessment – Capacity building	Top-down (upstream)	Specialized	No
Business Social Compliance Initiative 2003	Not considered, as it is now part of amfori	–	–	–	–	–

Responsible Business Alliance (RBA) 2004 http://www.responsiblebusiness.org/	Multiple sectors: electronics, automotive, retail, toy	Manufacturers and suppliers	Interventional: – Code of conduct – Audits – Self-assessment – Capacity building	Top-down (upstream)	Specialized	No
DRIVE Sustainability 2012 https://drivesustainability.org/	Single sector: automotive	Manufacturers	Interventional: – Code of conduct – Self-assessment – Capacity building	Top-down (upstream)	Specialized	Yes
Global e-Sustainability Initiative 2008 https://gesi.org/	Multiple sectors: information and communication technology (ICT), but with members from other sectors, such as consultancy	Manufacturers and suppliers; other stakeholders	Interventional: – Self-assessment – Capacity building – Varia	Top-down (upstream)	Specialized	No

(*continued*)

Table 12.3 (Continued)

Name of initiative Year of foundation URL	Sector focus	Membership base	Grade of activity	Governance process	SSCM specialization	Further analysis?
ICTI Ethical Toy Program (formerly ICTI Care) 2003 https://www.ethicaltoyprogram.org/en/	Single sector: toys	Manufacturers, brands, retailers and civil society partners	Interventional: – Certification – Assessment – Monitoring	Top-down (upstream)	Specialized	No
Joint Audit Cooperation 2010 http://jac-initiative.com	Single sector: telecom operators	Telecom operators	Interventional: – Audits	Top-down (upstream)	Specialized	Yes
Pharmaceutical Supply Chain Initiative 2006 https://pscinitiative.org/	Multiple sectors: pharmaceutical and healthcare	Unclear Manufacturers; partners from other constituencies	Interventional: – Common principles – Audits – Capacity building	Top-down (upstream)	Specialized	No
Railsponsible 2014 http://railsponsible.org/	Single sector: rail	Railway operators and companies across the railway industry value chain	Interventional: – Assessment	Top-down (upstream)	Specialized	Yes

Responsible Sport Initiative 2016 https://www.wfsgi.org/rsi-responsible-sport-initiative/standard	Multiple sectors: sporting goods and bikes; with many sub-categories	Manufacturers and suppliers	Unclear – No clear focus on SSCM – Potentially audits	Unclear	Specialized	No
Sustainable Apparel Coalition 2010 https://apparelcoalition.org/	Multiple sectors	Brands, retailers, manufacturers; academic institutions, affiliates, governments, NGOs	Interventional: – Assessment tools	Mixed	Specialized	No
Together for Sustainability 2011 https://tfs-initiative.com/	Single sector: chemicals	Manufacturers	Interventional: – Assessment – Audit – Improvement/capacity building	Top-down (upstream)	Specialized	Yes

Results

While we reduce the number of analysed initiatives due to the formulated criteria, we positively acknowledge that all of the initial initiatives screened undertake activities on certain aspects of SSCM (see Table 12.3). Upon further analysing the publicly available documents with regard to aspects of success and the measurement thereof, it can be summarized that these initiatives provide overviews about their visions, missions and aims at a strategy level (see Table 12.4).

Table 12.4 Overview of the analysed sector initiatives and their aims/goals/visions/missions

Initiative	Aim, goal, vision, mission	Source*
Automotive Industry Action Group (AIAG)	We promote our objectives primarily by publishing standards and offering educational conferences and training.	https://www.aiag.org/about
	Automotive manufacturers and suppliers are collaborating in efforts to improve the environmental performance of their organizations.	https://www.aiag.org/corporate-responsibility/environmental-sustainability
Drive Sustainability	The mission of the partnership is to work together to improve the social, ethical and environmental performance of automotive supply chains.	https://drivesustainability.org/
	Work together on common projects in order to improve sustainability in supply chains.	https://drivesustainability.org/
	We understand supply chains are global, therefore we act as a strong promoter of standardization and harmonization of supply chain approaches to achieve long-term impact, while also maintaining independent supply chain management.	https://drivesustainability.org/vision-and-mission/

(*continued*)

Table 12.4 (Continued)

Initiative	Aim, goal, vision, mission	Source*
Joint Audit Cooperation	JAC is an association of telecom operators aiming to verify, assess and develop the corporate social responsibility (CSR) implementation across the manufacturing centres of important multinational suppliers of the information communication technology (ICT) industry.	http://jac-initiative.com/about-us/
	This approach improves the effective implementation of sustainability principles in our industry.	http://jac-initiative.com/about-us/
	JAC has the vision to be the driving force in raising sustainability and CSR awareness towards common suppliers to ensure adherence to internationally recognized standards along the ICT supply chain and upholding human rights, social, labour and environmental standards.	http://jac-initiative.com/about-us/
	Collaborative efforts from suppliers and telecom operators to verify, assess and develop sustainability standards and best practices across the different layers or tiers of the supply chain	http://jac-initiative.com/about-us/
Railsponsible	Railsponsible is an industry initiative focused on sustainable procurement, with the aim to continuously improve sustainability practices throughout the railway industry supply chain.	http://railsponsible.org/about-us/
	The initiative aims at improving environmental and social practices of companies of the railway sector and railway sector supply chain through best practice sharing and capability building. It also aims at improving efficiency in the analysis of supply chain CSR practices, and to promote greater transparency to meet increasing stakeholder requirements.	http://railsponsible.org/about-us/

(*continued*)

Table 12.4 (Continued)

Initiative	Aim, goal, vision, mission	Source*
Together for Sustainability	TfS aims to build the industry's standard for sustainable supply chains and has established a standard approach for evaluating and improving the sustainability performance of suppliers within chemical industry supply chains. Moreover, TfS assessments and audits are conducted to a pre-defined set of criteria and then shared across TfS members, improving efficiency for all involved.	https://tfs-initiative.com/about-us-2/
	TfS aims at developing and implementing a global supplier engagement programme that assesses and improves sustainability sourcing practices, including ecological and social aspects.	https://tfs-initiative.com/sustainable-supply-chains/#1473840539214-f55f9dde-3a96

***NOTE** URLs last accessed 26 August 2019. Content on these web pages may have changed since the original research project was carried out.

The five initiatives analysed in-depth overwhelmingly did not give insights on how they measure or define impact and what their current achievements are (see Tables 12.4 and 12.5). This holds true both for the overall impact of the initiatives as well as for individual SSCM-oriented activities performed by the respective initiatives (see Table 12.5). This is to some extent suprising, as several initiatives (such as Drive Sustainability or Railsponsible) state that they are using tools that allow, for example, the sustainability performance of actors along the supply chain to be assessed and improved.

Concerning the analysed sector initiatives, their publicly available descriptions of their SSCM-oriented activities are, if at all, only supported with overall numbers. Their activities are neither supported with quantitative targets, like percentage of suppliers covered or market share covered, nor with KPIs. It can therefore be concluded that either such targets do not exist or they are not made public. Also, a discussion of impacts is mostly missing, with only a brief mention in the Drive Sustainability and

Table 12.5 Overview of the activities of the analysed sector initiatives and corresponding KPIs

Initiative	Activity	KPI, numbers etc on achievements	Source*
Automotive Industry Action Group (AIAG)	AIAG supply chain sustainability elearning. This free online course highlights fundamental principles of responsible working conditions and expectations of FCA, Ford, General Motors, Honda, and Toyota and is based on the Automotive Industry Guiding Principles to Enhance Sustainability Performance in the Supply Chain.	None found on respective website.	https://www.aiag.org/store/training/details?CourseCode=ELSCS08

(*continued*)

Table 12.5 (Continued)

Initiative	Activity	KPI, numbers etc on achievements	Source*
	AIAG supply chain sustainability knowledge assessment. This free online assessment is based on the Automotive Industry guiding principles to enhance sustainability performance in the supply chain. It includes terms and knowledge common to the automotive industry and is designed to help 'on-board' employees who have been assigned to lead or champion their company's sustainability efforts.	None found on respective website.	https://www.aiag.org/store/training/details?CourseCode=SCSKA
	Water benchmarking. Assists with benchmarking water activities within manufacturing facilities and develops resources to reduce water usage.	None found on respective website.	https://www.aiag.org/corporate-responsibility/environmental-sustainability

	Energy benchmarking. Establishes benchmarks to assist the supply base in reducing energy and implement renewable electricity in their manufacturing facilities.	None found on respective website.	https://www.aiag.org/corporate-responsibility/environmental-sustainability
	Greenhouse gas reporting. Assists the supply chain with calculating and reporting greenhouse gas emissions and to develop strategies to reduce carbon footprints.	None found on respective website.	https://www.aiag.org/corporate-responsibility/environmental-sustainability
Drive Sustainability	To assess the sustainability performance of automotive suppliers, Drive Sustainability developed a common self-assessment questionnaire.	None found on respective website.	https://drivesustainability.org/compliance/
	Drive Sustainability is organizing regular supplier training series in different countries worldwide, aiming to build supplier capacity.	19 one-day training sessions with 650 participants in total; countries where training was conducted and topics covered were published in a 2018 training report.	https://drivesustainability.org/wp-content/uploads/2019/05/Training-report-final.pdf

(*continued*)

Table 12.5 (Continued)

Initiative	Activity	KPI, numbers etc on achievements	Source*
	The Raw Materials Observatory is a process to: assess the sustainability risk of the top raw materials for the automotive sector, and identify potentially impactful activities that Drive Sustainability partners could pursue collectively to address such risk.	Report on 37 jointly assessed raw materials published.	https://drivesustainability.org/raw-materials/
	In 2015 Drive Sustainability, together with Ulm University Germany, conducted research to identify what activities have the biggest sustainability impact and what is the best approach for the partnership. Data was collected from suppliers engaged in our activities, the automotive companies and other initiatives similar to Drive Sustainability. One of the main findings of the research was that suppliers need guidance and they appreciate the capacity building activities.	None found on respective website.	https://drivesustainability.org/how-we-build-our-strategy/

Joint Audit Cooperation	JAC Academy. The benefits of the recently established JAC Academy, which allows companies to train and certify in assessing and improving their supply chains, was further explored in the panel discussion lead by Wang Shi, deputy director of EHS+ Center of Nanjing University. [...] Optimize efforts and processes within a shared methodology across the supply chain	None found on respective website.	http://jac-initiative.com/2019/03/14/jac-organized-the-8th-csr-forum-in-shenzhen/
	JAC Audit Process. The JAC process is simply a coordinated on-site audit and development programme in the area of corporate social responsibility (CSR) based on a common verification, assessment and development methodology, including the follow up of corrective action plans.	The first JAC audit campaign was carried out in July 2010. Until 2017, more than 366 audits have been carried out on ICT suppliers factories located in 27 countries over the four continents of Asia, Eastern Europe, Latin America and Africa. More than 813,000 workers in total have been covered by the audits.	http://jac-initiative.com/how-it-works/ http://jac-initiative.com/results-benefits/

(*continued*)

Table 12.5 (Continued)

Initiative	Activity	KPI, numbers etc on achievements	Source*
	The Joint Audit Cooperation (JAC) considers that through the application of social responsibility standards we can enhance the economic and environmental conditions for those involved in the information and communication technology (ICT) supply chains. This includes (but is not limited to) increased efficiency and productivity for companies and suppliers, improved conditions for workers, economic development, and understanding/reducing risk to ensure continuity of supply.		http://jac-initiative.com/resources/
Railsponsible	Supplier assessment campaigns.	An annual report on the supplier assessment campaigns is published.	http://railsponsible.org/supplier-assessments/ http://railsponsible.org/download/railsponsible-annual-report-2018-2019/

	'As of March 2019 (at the end of the Railsponsible year 2018–19), a total of 1042 suppliers had been scored. Results show on average a very satisfying level of CSR performance: the average global score of Railsponsible suppliers stands at 53/100, outperforming the average global score of the EcoVadis database, which stands at 42/100.'	
	Suppliers that have responded to the Railsponsible campaign tend to be more mature than suppliers in other sectors, particularly regarding environmental and social topics. As an illustration, across all entities surveyed within the pool of Railsponsible suppliers, 52% have ISO 14001 certification level, and 62% report on energy consumption and GHG emissions. Railsponsible suppliers also generally perform significantly better on management of environmental practices, with an average score in this area that is nearly 25% above the global average. Supplier performance varies across geographical regions: on overall CSR performance,	http://railsponsible.org/download/railsponsible-annual-report-2018-2019/

(*continued*)

Table 12.5 (Continued)

Initiative	Activity	KPI, numbers etc on achievements	Source*
		North American and European suppliers (average score 55/100 and 53/100, respectively) are outperforming suppliers based in Asia (44/100). Of the suppliers assessed for Railsponsible, 623 suppliers have been scored several times by EcoVadis. The re-assessments show that 62% of Railsponsible suppliers have improved their performance compared to their previous scoring (the EcoVadis benchmark for this is 67%). While 18% of Railsponsible suppliers have decreased in score and 20% have been stable in their performance, 29% of suppliers have increased their scores by up to 5 percentage points (above the EcoVadis average of 26%).	
Together for Sustainability	The TfS approach consists of two elements: the TfS assessment conducted by EcoVadis and the TfS audit conducted by independent audit companies.	None found on respective website.	https://tfs-initiative.com/sustainable-supply-chains/#1473854170086-56d8e59f-7fa9

	Assessments: TfS selected EcoVadis, a global leader for corporate social responsibility assessments, as its partner. EcoVadis provides assessment results and scorecard ratings on a shared, web-based collaborative platform. As a prerequisite to become a member of the TfS initiative, all TfS member companies have undergone the rating procedure, which can be shared with their respective customers.	None found on respective website.	https://tfs-initiative.com/sustainable-supply-chains/#1473854170086-56d8e59f-7fa9

(*continued*)

Table 12.5 (Continued)

Initiative	Activity	KPI, numbers etc on achievements	Source*
	Audits: TfS works with independent audit companies to assess a supplier's sustainability performance against a predefined set of audit criteria tailored to the requirements of the chemical industry. Audit criteria include management, environment, health and safety, labour and human rights, and governance topics. Audits comprise on-site visits covering, for example, production facilities, warehouses and office buildings.	None found on respective website.	https://tfs-initiative.com/sustainable-supply-chains/#1473854170086-56d8e59f-7fa9
	Online training. TfS offers four online training tools which can be accessed through the TfS website.	None found on respective website.	https://tfs-initiative.com/sustainable-supply-chains/#1473855819729-4fe0def3-aaef

***NOTE** URLs last accessed 26 August 2019. Content on these web pages may have changed since the original research project was carried out.

Railsponsible initiatives. Drive Sustainability states on its website that it assessed the impacts of its activities (Drive Sustainability, 2018) while Railsponsible commits to regularly reporting 'on an aggregate view of the sustainability performance of our supply chains' (Railsponsible, 2019). However, to evaluate and assess the success and/or impact of such activities of SSCM-oriented sector initiative, such information would be needed.

Limitations and further research

Given the five typology criteria portrayed above, which can be freely combined, it is quite evident that focusing on one type of sector initiative is a limitation of our study. Additionally, as we applied these criteria on the previously identified sector initiatives from the Müller and Bessas (2017) study, the data basis was per se limited.

For further research, one could perform a more in-depth search for existing SSCM-oriented sector initiatives and enlarge the selection criteria. This would broaden the sample base and enable comparisons between different types of initiatives (eg between single and multi-sector, or top-down and bottom-up initiatives). Including cross-sector or multi-stakeholder initiatives would add more complexity to the analysis.

Additional factors such as membership models, governance structures, or intra-organizational aspects should be further analysed, too. Therefore, empirical research by document analysis could be enhanced via conducting expert interviews with company members or the facilitators to such initiatives, as eg CSR Europe (2019) or Business for Social Responsibility (2019).

In our analysis, we neglected a number of circumstances that potentially could influence the definition of success and the creation of impact of such sector initiatives. For example, we did not analyse whether or not and how these success criteria are linked to the governance structure of these initiatives (beyond the differentiation of top-down or bottom-up processes). We therefore propose to evaluate not only the governance structure of sector initiatives, but also how this structure is potentially related to success and impact. Additionally, we neglected the capabilities and individual target systems of the respective member companies, which may also influence the success propositions of such initiatives.

Conclusion and outlook

Sector initiatives are increasing in numbers and in sectors covered, especially with regard to certification and labelling schemes (Newitt, 2013), with different scopes and different activities, as outlined in our chapter. These differences are also mirrored in their definition and outlook on success.

For further research, we aim not only to deepen the understanding of success of such sector initiatives but also to identify whether or not and how they create an impact – and to understand the circumstances that support impact generation. By impact we refer to, for example, changes in the conditions for workers from suppliers of companies engaged in those sector initiatives towards the better. We see this as a beneficial approach for further research, as it is currently not only unclear whether or not and how the efforts of these initiatives lead to measurable improvements which can be felt by the respective and affected workers, but also how to measure the potential impacts in a comparable manner, an issue previously analysed with non-comforting results by Beske-Janssen *et al* (2015). Although reporting frameworks like that of the Global Reporting Initiative (GRI, 2019) indicate a common base for the reporting of SSCM activities of corporations, and even if such a framework might be used by membership corporations, the comparability is still little – and sector initiatives usually do not provide stakeholders with a sustainability report. This is, however, not only true for the impact of sector initiatives, but also concerning the impact of SSCM activities of focal companies as well. The latter might even be harder to evaluate as they are strongly linked to company-internal documents.

In addition, no information currently exists on the view of suppliers in supplier networks in different value chains on whether or not and how they experience the activities of these sector initiatives. It is not known whether this leads to changes on the ground initiated by the efforts of these initiatives or whether it is a mere 'ticking the box' exercise, as discussed already by Crane (1999). Practitioners also mention that there is a lack of knowledge among some suppliers in some countries to fully address the information asked in the tools of the sector initiatives, or potentially even to understand which level of knowledge exists to benefit from capacity building activities. Therefore, there may also be a potential link between the current level of SSCM activities within an overall given value chain and the understanding thereof and the created impact. What if, after some maturation, the impact decreases because the overall level of SSCM had previously increased?

In conclusion, a broadned typology to further systematically analyse different sector initiatives is seen as beneficial because of the increasing relevance and engagement of focal companies via such initiatives, as well as to be able to analyse the impact such initiatives create, in combination with how they are legitimized in global supply chains.

References

AIAG (Automotive Industry Action Group) (2019) [accessed 23 September 2020] Southfield, MI: AIAG [Online] https://www.aiag.org/ (archived at https://perma.cc/64PX-HNRY)

Amnesty International (2017) [accessed 23 September 2020] Time to recharge: Corporate action and inaction to tackle abuses in the cobalt supply chain [Online] https://www.amnesty.org/download/Documents/AFR6273952017ENGLISH.PDF (archived at https://perma.cc/K9YZ-ZGJJ)

Ansari, ZN and Kant, R (2017) A state-of-art literature review reflecting 15 years of focus on sustainable supply chain management, *Journal of Cleaner Production*, **142** (4), pp 2524–43

Auswärtiges Amt (2016) [accessed 23 September 2020] *Nationaler Aktionsplan, Umsetzung der VN-Leitprinzipien für Wirtschaft und Menschenrechte, 2016–2020*, Auswärtiges Amt, Berlin [Online] https://www.auswaertiges-amt.de/blob/297434/8d6ab29982767d5a31d2e85464461565/nap-wirtschaft-menschenrechte-data.pdf (archived at https://perma.cc/4B45-PBT8)

Beske-Janssen, P, Johnson, MP and Schaltegger, S (2015) 20 years of performance measurement in sustainable supply chain management – what has been achieved? *Supply Chain Management: An international journal*, **20** (6), pp 664–80

Business for Social Responsibility (BSR) (2019) [accessed 23 September 2020] Business for Social Responsibility website [Online] http://www.bsr.org/en (archived at https://perma.cc/7QQH-W8E8)

Crane, A (1999) Are you ethical? Please tick yes or no: On researching ethics in business organisations, *Journal of Business Ethics*, **20** (3), pp 237–48

CSR Europe (2000–2019) [accessed 23 September 2020] CSR Europe [Online] http://www.csreurope.org (archived at https://perma.cc/5BT9-4MTX)

Drive Sustainability (2018) [accessed 23 September 2020] How we build our strategy, CSR Europe [Online] https://drivesustainability.org/how-we-build-our-strategy/ (archived at https://perma.cc/E2Y4-H7NV)

European Commission (2014) [accessed 23 September 2020] Directive 2014/95/EU of the European Parliament and of the Council of 22 October 2014 amending Directive 2013/34/EU as regards disclosure of non-financial and diversity information by certain large undertakings and groups Text with EEA relevance [Online] http://data.europa.eu/eli/dir/2014/95/oj (archived at https://perma.cc/4PNB-FHT9)

European Commission (2019) [accessed 23 September 2020] Conflict minerals: The regulation explained [Online] https://ec.europa.eu/trade/policy/in-focus/conflict-minerals-regulation/regulation-explained/index_en.htm (archived at https://perma.cc/DK29-282G)

Fischer, K (2020) Sustainability of global value creation and supply chains, in *Human Factors for Sustainability: Theoretical perspectives and global applications*, ed A Thatcher, KJ Zink and K Fischer, CRC Press, Boca Raton, FL, pp 237–57

Fischer, K, Hobelsberger, C and Zink, KJ (2009) Human factors and sustainable development in global value creation, in *Changes, Challenges and Opportunities: Proceedings of the 17th World Congress on Ergonomics, August 14–19, Beijing, China*, ed IEA, IEA Press, Santa Monica

Fischer, K, Jentsch, M and Zink, KJ (2018) Nachhaltigkeit in globalen Lieferketten – ausgewählte Forschungsarbeiten zu Einflussmechanismen und aktuellen Fragestellungen, in *Fortschritte in der Nachhaltigkeitsforschung*, ed M v Hauff and T Nguyen, Nomos, Wiesbaden, pp 55–86

Foerstl, K, Reuter, C, Hartmann, E and Blome, C (2010) Managing supplier sustainability risks in a dynamically changing environment: Sustainable supplier management in the chemical industry, *Journal of Purchasing and Supply Management*, **16**, pp 118–30

Frostenson, M and Prenkert, F (2015) Sustainable supply chain management when focal firms are complex: A network perspective, *Journal of Cleaner Production*, **107**, pp 85–94

Garcia-Torres, S, Albareda, L, Rey-Garcia, M and Seuring, S (2019) Traceability for sustainability: Literature review and conceptual framework, *Supply Chain Management: An international journal*, **24** (1), pp 85–106

Gereffi, G and Lee, J (2016) Economic and social upgrading in global value chains and industrial clusters: Why governance matters, *Journal of Business Ethics*, **133** (1), pp 25–38

Gimenez, C and Tachizawa, EM (2012) Extending sustainability to suppliers: A systematic literature review, *Supply Chain Management: An international journal*, **17** (5), pp 531–43

GRI (2019) [accessed 23 September 2020] The GRI Standards: The global standards for sustainability reporting [Online] https://www.globalreporting.org/standards (archived at https://perma.cc/N2PN-4UER)

Gunasekaran, A, Patel, C and McGaughey, R (2004) A framework for supply chain performance measurement, *International Journal of Production Economics*, **87** (33), pp 333–47

Humphrey, J and Schmitz, H (2001) Governance in global value chains, *IDS Bulletin*, **32** (3), pp 19–29

Joint Audit Cooperation (JAC) (2019) [accessed 23 September 2020] Cooperation beyond competition [Online] http://jac-initiative.com/ (archived at https://perma.cc/S4J9-SG36)

Klein, N (2010) *No Logo: No space, no choice, no jobs. 10th anniversary edition*, 3rd edn, Picador, New York

Know the Chain (eds) (2019) [accessed 23 September 2020] Three sectors, three years later: Progress and gaps in the fight against forced labor [Online] https://knowthechain.org/wp-content/uploads/KTC_Cross_sector_2019.pdf (archived at https://perma.cc/LTJ7-5JYJ)

Köksal, D, Strähle, J, Müller, M and Freise, M (2017) Social sustainable supply chain management in the textile and apparel industry: A literature review, *Sustainability*, **9** (11), p 100

Müller, M and Bessas, Y (2017) [accessed 23 September 2020] Potenziale von Brancheninitiativen zur nachhaltigen Gestaltung von Liefer- und Wertschöpfungsketten. Studie für das Bundesministerium für Arbeit und Soziales, Universität Ulm/ Bundesministerium für Arbeit und Soziales, Ulm/ Berlin [Online] https://www.bmas.de/SharedDocs/Downloads/DE/PDF-Publikationen/Forschungsberichte/fb483-potenziale-von-brancheninitiativen.pdf;jsessionid=E04A6E1C366FEEE33EF80F2C51A5E359.delivery1-replication?__blob=publicationFile&v=1 (archived at https://perma.cc/7RVW-76CK)

Newitt, K (2013) [accessed 23 September 2020] Private sector voluntary initiatives on labor standards: Background paper for the World Development Report, Ergon Associates Limited, London [Online] https://openknowledge.worldbank.org/bitstream/handle/10986/12142/WDR2013_bp_Private_Sector_Voluntary_Initiatives.pdf?sequence=1 (archived at https://perma.cc/CPZ4-PP25)

OECD (2013) [accessed 23 September 2020] *OECD Due Diligence Guidance for Responsible Supply Chains of Minerals from Conflict-Affected and High-Risk Areas*, 2nd edn, OECD Publishing, Paris [Online] http://dx.doi.org/10.1787/9789264185050-en (archived at https://perma.cc/9LNS-MFLS)

OECD (2018) [accessed 23 September 2020] Responsible business conduct: OECD guidelines for multinational enterprises [Online] https://mneguidelines.oecd.org (archived at https://perma.cc/T2WF-NM26)

Pagell, M and Wu, Z (2009) Building a more complete theory of sustainable supply chain management using case studies of 10 exemplars, *Journal of Supply Chain Management*, **45** (2) pp 37–56

Petersen, KJ, Prayer, DJ and Scannell, TV (2000) An empirical investigation of global sourcing strategy effectiveness, *Journal of Supply Chain Management*, **36** (2), pp 29–38

Railsponsible (2019) [accessed 23 September 2020] Railsponsible vision, mission and commitments of members [Online] http://railsponsible.org/how-it-works/mission/ (archived at https://perma.cc/A287-ETGG)

Reefke, H, Ahmed, MD and Sundaram, D (2014) Sustainable supply chain management – decision making and support: The SSCM Maturity Model and System, *Global Business Review*, **15** (4S), pp 1S–12S

Round Table on Sustainable Palm Oil (RSPO) (2019) [accessed 23 September 2020] RSPO [Online] https://www.rspo.org/ (archived at https://perma.cc/2X9B-EB3W)

Sancha Fernandez, C, Gimenez, C and Sierra, V (2016) Achieving a socially responsible supply chain through assessment and collaboration, *Journal of Cleaner Production*, **112** (3), pp 1934–47

Schöggl, J-P, Fritz, M and Baumgartner, R (2016) Sustainability assessment in automotive and electronics supply chains: A set of indicators defined in a multi-stakeholder approach, *Sustainability*, **8** (12), p 1185

Seuring, S (2011) Supply chain management for sustainable products: Insights from research applying mixed methodologies, *Business Strategy and the Environment*, **20** (7), pp 471–84

Seuring, S and Müller, M (2008a) Core issues in sustainable supply chain management: A Delphi study, *Business Strategy and the Environment*, **17**, pp 455–66

Seuring, S and Müller, M (2008b) From a literature review to a conceptual framework for sustainable supply chain management, *Journal of Cleaner Production*, **16**, pp 1699–710

Singh, A and Trivedi, A (2016) Sustainable green supply chain management: Trends and current practices, *Competitiveness Review*, **26** (3), pp 265–88

SOMO (Centre for Research on Multinational Corporations) (2016) [accessed 23 September 2020] Beauty and a beast: Child labour in India for sparkling cars and cosmetics', SOMO, Amsterdam [Online] https://www.somo.nl/beauty-and-a-beast/ (archived at https://perma.cc/7ZE2-KDN2)

Soundararajan, V, Brown, JA and Wicks, AC (2019) Can multi-stakeholder initiatives improve global supply chains? Improving Deliberative capacity with a stakeholder orientation, *Business Ethics Quarterly*, **29** (3), pp 385–412

State of California (2010) [accessed 23 September 2020] Senate Bill No. 657 CHAPTER 556 (California Transparency in Supply Chains Act) [Online] https://oag.ca.gov/sites/all/files/agweb/pdfs/cybersafety/sb_657_bill_ch556.pdf (archived at https://perma.cc/9TJ9-PD84)

UK Government (2015) [accessed 23 September 2020] Modern Slavery Act 2015 [Online] http://www.legislation.gov.uk/ukpga/2015/30/contents/enacted (archived at https://perma.cc/QA6M-AMM6)

von Geibler, J (2013) Market-based governance for sustainability in value chains: Conditions for successful standard setting in the palm oil sector, *Journal of Cleaner Production*, **56**, pp 39–53

Walker, H and Jones, N (2012) Sustainable supply chain management across the UK private sector, *Supply Chain Management: An international journal*, **17** (1), pp 15–28

Wang, C and Wood, LC (2016) The influence of supply chain sustainability practices on suppliers, *Handbook of Research on Global Supply Chain Management*, **2016**, pp 531–44

Wolf, J (2014) The relationship between sustainable supply chain management, stakeholder pressure and corporate sustainability performance, *Journal of Business Ethics*, **119** (3), pp 317–28

An institutional framework of urban logistics 13

Policy options and the role of the government

MARCUS SIDKI AND IGOR IVANOV

Urban logistics is a topic with growing relevance for economic, environmental and social issues, especially in cities and densely populated areas. While the demand for the commercial use of the public inner-city road networks increases constantly, strategic concepts that ensure its efficient and effective utilization and also take into account the possible mitigation of various negative externalities are lacking. We address the institutional setting introducing a framework of urban logistics from the focal point of a public good. Within this framework, we identify the relevant protagonists and discuss their individual or collective interests. Furthermore, we discuss how they are interconnected and, most importantly, what their negative and positive contributions are to a welfare-optimizing but also sustainable flow of goods within an urban setting. While companies have received a high amount of attention in the past, we will extend our focus to include the less-developed area of municipal governmental structures and the toolbox available to them. We identify areas that should be taken into account when designing or evaluating strategic solutions for urban logistics.

Urban logistics and policy

The demand for transportation and mobility in urban areas is on the rise: freight transport activity will rise by up to 40 per cent in the 2020s, with overall traffic also increasing by a comparable amount (Witkowski and Kiba-Janiak, 2014). This trend is compounded by high urbanization rates, which in Europe and Northern America exceeded 74–81 per cent in 2018 (Population Reference Bureau, 2018). While this indicates positive economic development, it also produces high and difficult to manage externalities (Piecyk, Cullinane and Edwards, 2015; Piecyk, McKinnon and Allen, 2015). Their successful management and mitigation will be instrumental in avoiding economic and long-term environmental impacts. Since profit margins are low for logistics companies, externalities and inefficiencies could even outweigh the potential benefits and the profitability of urban freight transport (Cardenas *et al*, 2017). A strong economy, a healthy environment and access to efficient transportation are also important factors in maintaining high levels of quality of life within urban areas (Steg and Gifford, 2005). While many individual stakeholders, ie freight transport and passenger transport companies, as well as citizens themselves, are involved, local governments play a key role (Witkowski and Kiba-Janiak, 2014). They have the necessary organization, centralization and authority to address these issues with the scope required for citywide problems, which – while arising from actions by individual agents – have collective consequences. It should be mentioned that the scope of this chapter lies on the municipal level. Hence, overland transport is excluded, because policy options pertaining to it are decided on a higher level (state, federal or even international, ie EU) and are less directly applicable to local urban environments. Although past research and actual policies have been documented for a wide variety of regions and urban areas (LEAN, 1999; Muñuzuri *et al*, 2005; Piecyk, McKinnon and Allen, 2015; Witkowski and Kiba-Janiak, 2014), these efforts mostly had a specific focus. Researchers and policy makers often do not take a strategic view that might uncover overarching patterns and solutions and can be applied in more diverse situations (Allen *et al*, 2015). In this regard, research and efforts under the umbrella term of 'urban logistics' have been instrumental in filling the gap.

But what does the term urban logistics entail? First, it should be noted that there are many (sometimes conflicting) definitions, synonyms and systematizations of the term in the literature (Cardenas *et al*, 2017). For example, a seminal definition by Taniguchi *et al* (2001; as cited in Taniguchi and Thompson, 2002: 45) uses the term 'city logistics' to describe the whole of the topic as 'the process for totally optimizing the logistics and transport activities by private companies with the support of advanced information systems in urban areas considering the traffic environment, its congestion, safety and energy savings within the framework of a market economy'.

Others (Cardenas *et al*, 2017) see 'city logistics' as a subset of urban logistics, alongside 'urban goods distribution' and 'last mile delivery'. Since the scope of this chapter is creating a framework to describe the stakeholders' motivations and interactions in order to shift the focus to a more holistic and strategic approach, we do not try to enter this discussion. Instead, we propose a functional definition: the movement of goods that are affected by particularities associated with urban traffic and morphology (Muñuzuri *et al*, 2005). Specifically, this definition includes the delivery and collection of goods, provision of services and goods storage (Allen *et al*, 2015). The focus lies on the different and divergent interests of those carrying the goods and other agents involved in urban traffic. The general goal of urban logistics initiatives is usually defined as reducing the impact of freight vehicles on living conditions in urban areas, while at the same time ensuring that economic and social factors are not unduly limited (Crainic *et al*, 2009). This is an ambitious goal, which has to deal with conflicting interests between and within very diverse groups (citizens, companies, environment, government, etc). Accordingly, initiatives taken should be derived from a solid framework and be strategic as well as holistic in nature.

While local authorities have a vast array of policy measures at their disposal, they have to be systematized in order to meet the aforementioned need for strategy-based actions. One way is to cluster around types of measures (Cardenas *et al*, 2017): they can be regulatory (eg emission restrictions, delivery time restrictions, vehicle characteristics restrictions), market-based (eg fees, tolls and all efforts of internalizing externalities in general), based on land-use planning (eg designated zones for parking, loading/unloading and logistical activities in general) and concern the building of additional infrastructure (eg consolidation centres, truck lanes, parking bays). All of these policies have been used in different urban centres and can alleviate the problems of urban freight transport. Such a typology is useful for the organization of a very diverse set of policies. But it does not address the need for a guideline on how to strategically optimize urban logistics services, while taking into account their combined influence on externalities, as well as possibly having a negative impact on the overall welfare of citizens and companies. First of all, local authorities need to consider which measures are implementable given their individual setting (eg geography, political landscape, etc). Then, the sum of all the possible measures builds an urban logistics system to efficiently and effectively manage externalities. Externalities have to be reduced in sum, ie the net effect has to be negative. Lastly, unwanted effects on citizens' quality of life and companies' ability to work profitably have to be avoided. For this a framework is needed that focuses on protagonists, their goals and possible goal conflicts.

Literature overview

Literature on urban logistics focuses on solving problems stemming from increases in transport vehicle traffic in urban areas, which is in turn caused by rising consumer demand. The aim of a sustainable transport strategy is 'to answer, as far as possible, how society intends to provide the means of opportunity to meet economic, environmental and social needs efficiently and equitably, while minimizing avoidable or unnecessary adverse impacts and their associated costs, over relevant space and time scales' (UK Round Table on Sustainable Development, 1996). The process of sustainable urban transport can be set in two ways (Goldman and Gorham, 2006): first, in a pathway logic that focuses on the improvement of predefined indicators, without providing a final aim and definition of what sustainable transport ought to be; and second, with an explicit end-state in mind, which also relies on indicators, but requires a clear definition of what sustainable transport is.

While oftentimes a distinction is being made between commercial and private logistical chains, the former as well as the latter produce unwanted externalities that affect all major stakeholders in different ways. These externalities include air pollution, noise, accidents, vibration, congestion, land-take, visual intrusion, etc, and cause economic, social and environmental issues. This happens directly and indirectly through first-order impacts, eg emissions or increased traffic, as well as second-order impacts, such as the need for additional infrastructure and its maintenance due to an increase in global logistical traffic (Piecyk, Cullinane and Edwards, 2015). Freight transport related externalities influence citizens' quality of life (Steg and Gifford, 2005), especially such important indicators (as judged by people themselves) as health and safety. On the other hand, a functioning logistical system can also influence quality of life in a positive way through indicators such as comfort and freedom of movement. One aspect that might diminish the effects of improved urban logistics is the rebound effect (Otto *et al*, 2014): improvements in efficiency can lead to more wasteful behaviour, which balances the gains from improved efficiency. For example, if congestion is reduced, people might use their car more often to travel within the city because it becomes more feasible (but for a critique see Gillingham *et al*, 2013; Gillingham *et al*, 2016).

In order to combat the aforementioned negative effects of freight transport, urban logistics is fundamentally concerned with consolidation and coordination (Crainic *et al*, 2009). It is noteworthy that consolidation efforts (which are often done through city distribution centres) mostly focus on inbound traffic and rarely look into outbound or inner-city traffic. Also, the question arises how much government intervention – through regulations and/or financial backing – is required to make consolidation efforts viable. Crainic *et al* (2009) report that most private city logistic projects were not financially viable. Once external funding ran out, such projects had to be abandoned. In contrast, examples where governments intervened more severely persevered, like in the Netherlands or, in the most extreme case, Monaco (Crainic *et al*, 2009). This suggests that the tight budgetary restrictions, especially of 'last mile logistics' are a hindrance that needs to be considered. One way in which the interests of freight companies and regulators might meet is in the discussion about the optimal size of transport vehicles. Larger vehicles have a higher impact per unit, but might have a lower impact overall, because fewer vehicles are used in total (Taniguchi *et al*, 2014). For businesses, this might raise efficiency and hence provide a workable solution to low margins. Municipalities can provide incentives through regulation. Then again, some policies aim to prevent vehicles of a certain weight or size from entering urban areas as a measure to lower congestions levels and road accidents that involve large trucks. Hence, goal conflicts exist between the different types of externalities caused by urban logistics services, which might lead to contradictory policy measures.

In sum, innovative solutions to urban logistics services have many things in common. A holistic perspective is adopted that considers transportation as part of the larger integrated system of urban life (Goldman and Gorham, 2006). Transport agencies have to undergo a shift in organizational culture in order to become modern 'mobility managers', that take more goals and indicators into account when evaluating their success. This means that not only the financial bottom line or passenger kilometres are taken as important, but also welfare aspects. Lastly, none of the solutions was a transportation megaproject, meaning that the steps taken, while bold, are more incremental in their nature and hence more affordable than long-term and big (construction) projects.

But some drawbacks and open questions have also been identified in past research: public authorities try to use regulations in order to optimize the flow of goods in urban environments. But these regulations have to be grounded in a systematic approach (Cardenas *et al*, 2017) and involve relevant stakeholders (Taniguchi *et al*, 2014). Otherwise, there are the risks of them either being short-sighted, producing unwanted secondary effects or simply not working when being applied in a new context. In order to minimize these negative effects of regulations, the interdependencies between relevant protagonists have to be taken into account.

This leads to another obstacle. When municipalities introduce policies, they have to rely on good data in order to tailor them to the needs and challenges their cities face. Although there are many sources available, reliable data collection remains a major concern (Cardenas *et al*, 2017). In this regard, feedback from and involvement of relevant stakeholders is important (Taniguchi *et al*, 2014). Otherwise policy makers face the risk of a lack in support and understanding of the measures taken. But information asymmetries have to be taken into account here: businesses won't share internal information and citizens self-select in such roundtables. So the municipality has to work with incomplete or even biased information when designing its actions. Also, there are vast differences in methodology and typology between data collection efforts, and research is often focused on specific regions and/or projects from which 'lessons learned' are derived in an attempt to give guidelines for future attempts at optimizing urban logistic systems. Although such a problem-oriented approach is sensible given the need for tangible solutions of real-world problems, there is the need for a more theoretical analysis, which specifically focuses on commonalities between urban freight systems and their associated challenges. Such an approach may find patterns and associated solutions that can lead to generalized insights and be broadly applied to new settings.

All of this can make the comparison of outcomes between different cities or urban areas problematic. An overarching framework that focuses on basic economic principles and interactions between relevant protagonists might alleviate this problem. Such a framework needs to be on a sufficiently abstract level to be applicable to new situations, but also specific enough as to not miss the needs and goals of important stakeholders involved in a local urban logistics system. The latter point is demonstrated by approaches that, for example, do not consider citizens (the main drivers of urban logistical activity) directly (Muñuzuri *et al*, 2005). As we will demonstrate, the interests and actions of citizens are not necessarily best understood by solely looking at the actions taken by local governments. Although local governments are beholden to the people and their main purpose may be seen as the improvement of the quality of life of their respective citizens (Witkowski and Kiba-Janiak, 2014), they still have distinct goals and preference structures, especially when it comes to the introduction of policies that tackle one problem by exacerbating another.

Institutional framework for urban logistics

The institutional framework serves to describe, categorize and analyse the main protagonists of urban logistics. It emphasizes their interconnectedness and possible goal conflicts or conflicts of interests that might arise between and within them. We attempt to achieve a holistic approach, which is why the framework does not only include citizens and logistics companies as parties directly involved in logistics transactions. Furthermore, it also includes different levels of the public sector as a regulator that has the capacity to set and define the rules under which a system of urban logistics takes place. The visualization of the framework can be found in Figure 13.1.

First, we discuss the individual behaviour and motivation of each protagonist based on economic theory. For the logistics companies we assume profit maximizing behaviour, that is, they are economic goal-oriented in maximizing the difference between turnover and the respective costs for offering urban logistics delivery services. Suppose company i offers the amount of urban logistics delivery services d_i for an average price per delivery p and that it faces the cost function $c_i(d_i)$. Its behaviour can then be modelled as:

$$\pi_i^* \overset{\text{def}}{=} \max_{d_i} \pi_i = p \cdot d_i - c_i(d_i). \tag{1.1}$$

Note that we assume market competition in a way that no single logistics company can influence the average price for delivery services. Solving this optimization results in an optimal level of d_i where the price for delivery services equals the company's marginal costs:

$$p = \frac{dc_i(d_i)}{dd_i}. \tag{1.2}$$

If price p would either be larger or smaller than the marginal costs, a company could further raise profits by offering additional or less output. The resulting optimal profit π_i^* holds for a given set of input and output prices and unchanged production technology. Of course, as is typical for markets with negative external effects, the individual profit of a company does not match its social value-added, ie, the profit taking the externalities' impact into account. Logistics companies suffer from urban logistics externalities in terms of traffic congestion resulting in higher fuel consumption and time losses due to heavy traffic. Hence, profitability declines and overall profits are lower than they would be without having to consider externalities.

Figure 13.1 Institutional framework of urban logistics

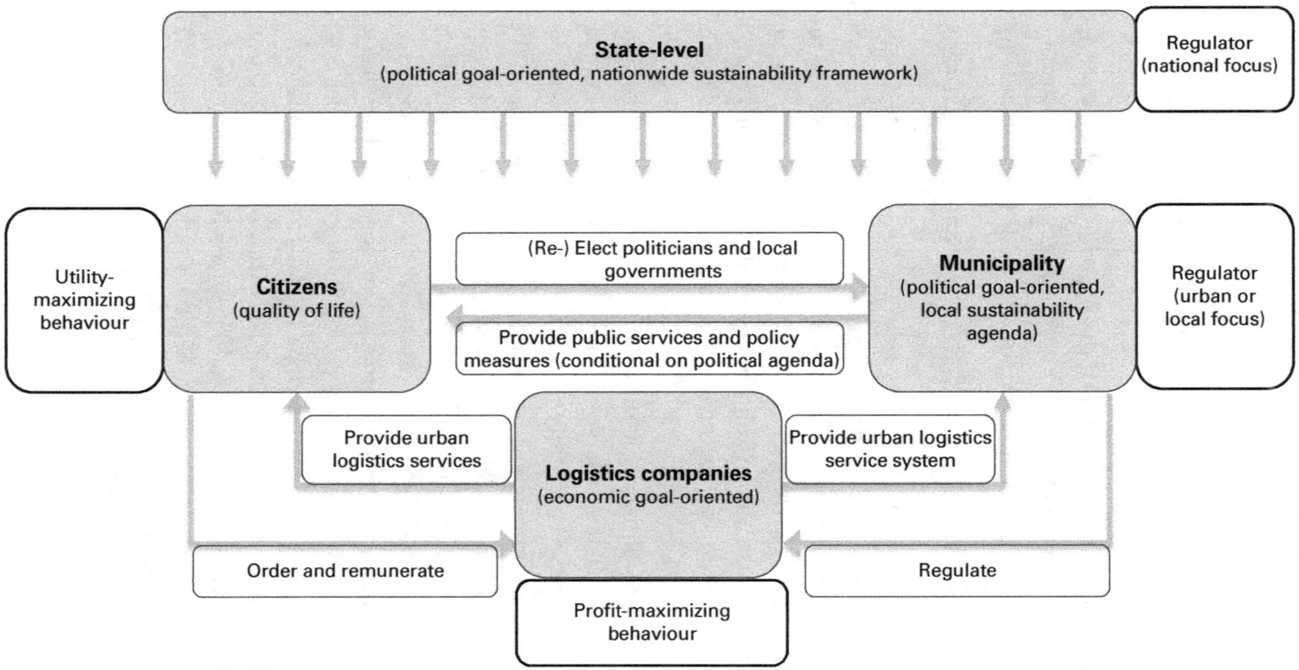

To include externalities in our considerations, we assume a firm-specific externalities cost function E^f that is mainly driven by the amount of total delivery services in an urban area d. A logistics company's value-added then calculates as:

$$Social\text{-}value_i = \pi_i^* - E_i^f(d), \ with \ d = \sum_{i=1}^{N} d_i. \tag{1.3}$$

Because d consists of the sum of the individual delivery services of all N logistics companies operating in an urban area, a single firm i can only influence d and thus $E_i^f(d)$ to a minor extent. It is reasonable to assume rising marginal costs of $E_i^f(d)$, ie, $\frac{dE_i^f(d)}{dd} > 0$ and $\frac{d^2E_i^f(d)}{dd^2} > 0$. This assumption states that a constant increase in the total amount of deliveries leads to rising additional costs due to congestion and reflects that costs are disproportionately high once traffic is close to or even above the limit that an installed road network can process. That is why it does not include the externalities costs into its idiosyncratic profit maximization. For reasons of simplicity we do not assume any other specific form or characteristic of function $E_i^f(d)$.

Citizens maximize their utility based on the consumption of goods and restricted by their available income. For reasons of simplicity, we do not distinguish between (utility-maximizing) private households and (profit-maximizing) commercial customers, eg local businesses, on the demand side. The scope of our model accounts for the receiving and sending demand of urban logistics simultaneously and no further differentiation to categorize the type of demander seems necessary. We assume that citizen j has an income of m_j and wants to consume a basket of goods and services consisting of a certain amount of delivery services by logistics companies d_j and many other goods. It is convenient to aggregate the latter into a composite good consisting of all other goods and services citizen j wants to consume except d_j. Hence, we denote x_j as the spending on such a composite good. Citizen j's individual preferences are described by a utility function u_j. Thus, she faces the following problem:

$$u_j^* \stackrel{\text{def}}{=} \max_{d_j, x_j} u_j(d_j, x_j) \ subject \ to \ m_j \geq p \cdot d_j + x_j. \tag{1.4}$$

Both goods are assumed to be subject to diminishing marginal utility, ie, $\frac{\partial u_j(d_j,x_j)}{\partial d_j} > 0$ and $\frac{\partial^2 u_j(d_j,x_j)}{\partial d_j^2} < 0$ as well as $\frac{\partial u_j(d_j,x_j)}{\partial x_j} > 0$ and $\frac{\partial^2 u_j(d_j,x_j)}{\partial x_j^2} < 0$ respectively. If we further assume that citizen j will consume at least some positive amount of both delivery services d and other goods x, we can rule out a boundary optimum and focus on the interior solution instead. Hence, maximum utility must satisfy the following condition:

$$\frac{\partial u_j\left(d_j,x_j\right)}{\partial d_j} \Big/ \frac{\partial u_j\left(d_j,x_j\right)}{\partial x_j} = p. \tag{1.5}$$

Equation 1.5 states that the marginal rate of substitution must equal the price for delivery services. Combining this equation with the budget constraint results in citizen j's optimal combination of delivery services and residual consumption. The equation gives the necessary condition for finding the consumer's optimal choice. There is no need to check the sufficient condition of whether the found solutions are indeed maximum values if we assume convexity of preferences. The resulting optimal utility level u_j^* holds for a given set of income and prices for goods and services and unchanged preferences to consume.

As before, citizens face negative externalities due to the intense usage of urban logistics services that occur in form of eg air and noise pollution, congestion of road networks, rising numbers of traffic accidents, land use and waste or visual intrusion. As before, a citizen's welfare, or quality of life, does not match their maximum utility based on the optimal choice of goods. We incorporate this in our model by defining a citizen-specific externalities cost function E^c that is, again, dependent on the amount of total delivery services in an urban area d. Comparable to equation 1.3, citizen j's quality of life then calculates as:

$$Quality\text{-}of\text{-}life_j = u_j^* - E_i^c\left(d\right), \, with \, d = \sum_{i=1}^{N} d_i. \tag{1.6}$$

Again, d consists of the sum of the individual delivery services of all N logistics companies operating in an urban area. The individual amount of delivery services has thus an ambiguous effect on citizens' quality of life. First, an increase in demand for delivery services goes along with a direct increase in citizens' utility as is specified by the assumption of a diminishing marginal utility which also results in a higher quality of life. Second, the total amount of delivery services as sum of the citizens' individual demand (and the logistics companies' supply) in an urban area increases negative external effects and reduces quality of life. Since an individual citizen's optimal delivery service demand is only a minor part of the total amount of d in a way that they can only influence d to an infinitesimal extent even if d_j is reduced to zero, the individual choice of making use of delivery services is nearly completely detached from the negative effects resulting from the service per se.

To summarize the total welfare, we aggregate the social-value functions and quality-of-life function of all protagonists to receive the following welfare function:

$$\Omega = \sum_i \sum_j \pi_i^* - E_i^f(d) + u_j^* - E_i^c(d). \tag{1.7}$$

We denote total profit of all logistics companies as $\pi^* = \sum_i \pi_i^*$ and total utility of all citizens as $u^* = \sum_j u_j^*$. Also, the total of individual firm-specific externalities costs are $E^f(d) = \sum_i E_i^f(d)$ and the total of citizen-specific externalities costs are $E^c(d) = \sum_j E_j^c(d)$. The sum of all externalities costs simply adds up to E(d) = Ef (d) + Ec (d). Equation 1.7 can then be rewritten as:

$$\Omega = \pi^* + u^* - E(d). \tag{1.8}$$

Thus, total welfare suffers under negative external effects in the form of addition costs E(d), which can only be influenced by each protagonist to a minor degree. Rational behaviour then suggest that each individual company or citizen maximizes their profit or utility while disregarding external costs E(d). In a case where $\pi^* + u^* < E(d)$ this could even lead to a situation of negative social welfare, ie market failure.

Preventing such market failure in reducing the negative effects of urban logistics-based externalities is the task of the public sector as regulator either on the state (or national) or on the municipal level. Following the subsidiarity principle, which states that decisions about public policy should always be made as close to the citizens as possible, we assume the state (or national) level to set the legal framework of urban logistics service provision based on societal needs and political goals. While this mainly addresses supra-regional issues in terms of a nationwide or even international sustainability framework, the municipality as local authority shapes the specific arrangement of logistics services within the framework set by the state level in the urban context for which it is responsible. In other words, municipalities follow a local sustainability agenda. Measures to influence this arrangement include the prohibition and permission of certain actions as well as the setting of (dis-)incentives.

It is important to notice that measures undertaken by the state or municipal level do not necessarily follow the goal of reaching a solution that is socially beneficial to all protagonists (eg in maximizing welfare Ω). Instead, political decision making that defines political goal-orientation can best be described by rent-seeking behaviour which can be further distinguished in vote-seeking, ie, receiving a maximum of votes during the election process, office-seeking, ie, receiving and retaining a maximum of political offices and policy-seeking behaviour, ie, implementing a maximum of the own (ideology-based) policy (Strom, 1990). Depending on the specific election mechanism, reaching these goals might to a certain extent be positively connected to overall social welfare, but not necessarily to the full extent. We include this in our framework by assuming that the state or municipal level aims at increasing (and not necessarily maximizing) welfare Ω based on a certain status quo. Policy measures that aim to reduce the total amount of logistics services d would only be effective if the sensitivity of externalities costs with respect to d is greater than the respective sensitivity of the sum of total individual (companies') profit and (citizens') utility, ie:

$$\left|\frac{dE(d)}{dd}\right| > \left|\frac{d\left(\pi^* + u^*\right)}{dd}\right|. \tag{1.9}$$

If this condition would be met, a reduction of d by eg applying quantity or price regulation measures leads to a stronger decline of externalities costs E(d) than the sum of individual profit and utility $\left(\pi^* + u^*\right)$ decrease, hence increasing overall welfare Ω – but supposing this condition to hold in every possible state is certainly a too restrictive assumption to become a recommended course of action for public (political) decision makers. It is also important to keep in mind that neither companies nor citizens would approve such measures because their behaviour is solely focused on maximizing π^* and u^*. Therefore, they disapprove of public policies that reduce their individual maximum outcome. Since a politician's behaviour is subject to lobbying efforts to consider industry interests and contingent on the interests of their respective voter group, applying such policy measures might not be a high priority. In summary, reducing the level of d remains an ambiguous measure based on a pure welfare-increasing point of view.

A second type of policy measure could address the externalities cost function E(d). Public policy can provide measures that (dis-)incentivize or impose companies' and citizens' behaviour in order to arrange logistics services more efficiently. In terms of our considerations, this would transform the externalities cost function E(d) to a new function E'(d), with E'(d) < E(d), hence increasing welfare Ω without directly decreasing the individual optimal profit or utility. Of course, this does not rule out the possibility that indirect costs might arise when implementing policy measures to move from E(d) to E'(d) which could subsequently be imposed on the companies and citizens. Such policy measures require the existence of a gap between current cost function E(d) and a hypothetical optimized cost function E*(d) in which the impact of an additional cost-reducing measure equals the marginal effort to implement this measure. If we assume a diminishing marginal impact of cost-reducing measures, the effect to increase cost efficiency is larger the greater the gap between the current and the hypothetical optimized cost function is. Transferring this type of policy to practical implementation requires effective measures in order to arrange urban logistics services more efficiently, especially when considering the social costs arising from externalities, as well as an understanding of how possible costs to implement such measures are distributed among the protagonists.

Next, we briefly highlight the interactions and possible resulting goal conflicts between the main protagonists. The companies not only provide logistics services to the citizens. All logistics companies in an urban setting form a local logistics service system. While services to citizens take place on an individual transaction basis, the logistics service system provided to municipalities can be interpreted as a service of general interest which would otherwise have to be supplied by the local authorities or other public bodies. In other words, one can think of a local logistics service system as a public good operated by profit-maximizing (often privately organized) companies that act in a competitive environment. Problems arise when the provided services are connected to negative externalities that stem from the usage of a municipal road network – especially when free of charge or of other limitations of utilization.

Citizens order and remunerate either receiving or sending logistics services (the former oftentimes happens indirectly in connection with mail-ordering goods). They also (re-)elect politicians that form the municipal governments. Since we focus on the interests and interactions on the local level, we omit any dependencies between the local protagonists and the state level other than the latter possibly implementing a nationwide sustainability framework that might hold consequences for citizens, logistics companies and municipalities as stated above. Conflicts of interest can arise from the citizens wanting more (or faster) delivery services from the companies while at the same time expecting the local governments to lower welfare-reducing externalities costs stemming from an increase of such services.

The public sector, ie the state level and the municipalities, is foremost responsible for providing public goods and services as well as policies to set the framework in which everyday life takes place (and, of course, to take measures, if citizens or companies overstep the framework). In the context of urban logistics, this translates into a possible regulation of the market to reach a market design that is in line with the national or local sustainability agenda. A source for possible conflicts arises when such agendas contradict the responsible politicians' inherent motivations to act, ie, the types of political rent-seeking as stated above.

Implications and research questions

We can derive multiple implications and research questions from the framework. Basic economic theory on externalities usually states that regulation measures ought not aim to completely avoid the production of goods and services that provoke negative external effects on uninvolved third parties but rather find ways to prevent such transactions that have a negative impact on total welfare while at the same time enabling transactions that even after including costs of external effects still add value. Our framework further specifies this insight considering the institutional setting of the involved protagonists. Effective regulation should not aim to reduce the total amount of delivery services which has an ambiguous impact on total welfare. Instead, measures considered by the regulator should rather undertake efforts to lower externalities that accompany deliveries as such. Technically speaking, preferred policy measures should aim to reduce the externalities cost function $E(d)$ to a new function $E'(d)$, with $E'(d) < E(d)$. This is the target level to evaluate policy measures that a (local) regulator considers implementing. Hence, the question should not be whether, for example, access time or vehicle weight restrictions reduce the overall amount of delivery services in an urban area. Instead, one should ask whether access time or vehicle weight restrictions are the most effective measures to lower the externalities caused by the delivery services in an urban area, and if not, what measures are more able to reach that goal on a cost-benefit basis. Based on this, a first recommendation for future research is the development of an evaluation framework for policy measures that specifically focuses on the ability the reduce externalities while keeping the total amount of delivery services constant.

Second, a more holistic perception on how a delivery service system should be structured can be derived as well. Are there more effective ways of organizing urban logistics? One consideration based on the aforementioned thought of local logistics service systems as a public good could be that the externalities provoke market failure to an extent that justifies more intense interventions by the regulator. One possible implication could be the creation of regulated local monopolies in accordance with how local gas and electricity distribution networks are organized in Germany. If we interpret an installed urban road network as a public good, its commercial use by logistics companies could be restricted to, eg, one temporarily accredited sole operator. This can be achieved since, usually, the networks are owned by the respective municipality. They could be temporarily sold – say, for a duration of 20 years – in a regulated and competitive bidding procedure to a public or private enterprise that runs the networks as local monopolist. To prevent socially negative monopoly pricing, the German Federal Network Agency (Bundesnetzagentur) as the nationwide regulator sets individual maximum revenues for each network on a yearly basis. The ways to organize such a system in order to effectively shape urban logistics to include the imposed negative external effects remains an interesting field for future research.

A third implication can be derived from the result that measures introduced by local governments can affect the utility functions of citizens and logistics companies alike. Hence, effective communication by the policy makers is required to convince relevant stakeholders about their necessity. In this regard, how the goals of urban logistic strategies are set becomes important: as pathways or as end-states (Goldman and Gorham, 2006). While both use indicators to measure success, the former is probably easier to implement because no specific definition of a well-working and sustainable transport system needs to be provided. On the other hand, end-states have the advantage of being more palatable. Also, they can be framed in different ways: either in what a sustainable logistics system should not do, or in what it should do. This sort of goal framing (Kahneman and Tversky, 1984; Levin *et al*, 1998) can have a significant influence on how the general public evaluates these propositions (Krishen *et al*, 2014). For example, Krishen *et al* (2014) used this communication technique in a transportation related context, specifically for a vehicle miles tax, and found that loss framing leads to higher acceptance by the public. These findings can be extended to effects on citizens that are not direct (like a tax) but rather indirect (for example, through limitations in delivery hours, etc). They can also be contrasted with Goldman and Gorham's (2006) framework with either goals as end-states or goals as pathways. In the end, another research question derived from the framework is what an effective communication strategy looks like when policies have direct influences on people (say, through lowering utility u*) but work through more obscure and indirect means (by trying to tackle the externalities cost function E(d)).This cumulates in the broader topic of 'public acceptance of policies', which has been looked at by different disciplines, ranging from political psychology, political science, sociology to economics. Many aspects are combined in the emerging field of behavioural political economy (Schnellenbach and Schubert, 2015), which allows for the analysis of the interplay between citizens, politicians and bureaucrats. Our institutional framework focuses on such interactions as well and can thus be used as a jumping-off point to approach follow-up questions like: What are common goals and especially goal conflicts among the protagonists of local urban logistics systems? How can common solutions be found? How should this information be presented in order to be most accessible and convincing to policy makers, citizens, logistics companies and bureaucrats? Do municipal policy makers even know about the numerous options they have in order to design urban logistics systems? Since the behavioural political economy approach uses economic analysis the scope of possible research questions is even broader and includes questions about optimal incentive structures and the optimal level of regulation or direct state intervention (for example through logistic centres; Goldman and Gorham, 2006) as well.

Conclusion

Urban logistics is not simply the sum of individual measures. It is a strategic approach, which takes into account all relevant stakeholders and employs a toolbox managing externalities in a way that is not detrimental to citizens' and businesses utility provided by urban freight transport systems. In order to help achieve these ambitious goals the proposed institutional framework in this chapter identifies key protagonists, their needs as well as their connections, and formalizes them through basic economic analysis. Through this goal, conflicts and contradictory demands are highlighted and venues for future research established:

- First, the development of an evaluation framework for policies that establishes whether a proposed solution addresses externalities directly or merely indirectly through the reduction in the amount of transportation activities.

- Second, the ways in which urban logistics systems can be fundamentally structured.
- Third, policy makers should strive for public acceptance of their solutions, which is especially relevant when there might be negative effects in the short term and improvements are felt only after longer time periods (Muñuzuri *et al*, 2005).

Urban logistics lies at the intersection of political, societal and scientific megatrends (urbanization, globalization, climate change, digitization, etc) so it won't lose its importance any time soon. However, through strategic and intelligent action it will be a resource rather than a hindrance for the developments to come.

References

Allen, J, Browne, M and Holguín-Veras, J (2015) Sustainability strategies for city logistics, in *Green Logistics: Improving the environmental sustainability of logistics*, 3rd edn, ed A Mckinnon, M Piecyk and M Browne, Kogan Page London, pp 293–319

Cardenas, I, Borbon, Y, Verlinden, T, Van de Voorde, E, Vanelslander, T and Dewulf, W (2017) City logistics, urban goods distribution and last mile delivery and collection, *Competition and Regulation in Network Industries*, **18** (1–2), pp 22–43

Crainic, TG, Ricciardi, N and Storchi, G (2009) Models for evaluating and planning city logistics systems, *Transportation Science*, **43** (4), pp 432–54

Gillingham, K, Kotchen, MJ, Rapson, DS and Wagner, G (2013) The rebound effect is overplayed, *Nature*, **493**, pp 475–76

Gillingham, K, Rapson, D and Wagner, G (2016) The rebound effect and energy efficiency policy, *Review of Environmental Economics and Policy*, **10** (1), pp 68–88

Goldman, T and Gorham, R (2006) Sustainable urban transport: Four innovative directions, *Technology in Society*, **28** (1–2), pp 261–73

Kahneman, D and Tversky, A (1984) Choices, values, and frames, *American Psychologist*, **39** (4), pp 341–50

Krishen, A, Raschke, R, Kachroo, P, LaTour, M and Verma, P (2014) Promote me or protect us? The framing of policy for collective good, *European Journal of Marketing*, **48** (3–4), pp 742–60

LEAN (1999) Integration of lean logistics into urban multimodal transport management in order to reduce space requirements and optimize the use of transport, PL97-2113, DGVII European Union

Levin, IP, Schneider, SL and Gaeth, GJ (1998) All frames are not created equal: A typology and critical analysis of framing effects, *Organizational Behavior and Human Decision Processes*, **76** (2), pp 149–88

Muñuzuri, J, Larrañeta, J, Onieva, L and Cortés, P (2005) Solutions applicable by local administrations for urban logistics improvement, *Cities*, **22** (1), pp 15–28

Otto, S, Kaiser, FG and Arnold, O (2014) The critical challenge of climate change for psychology, *European Psychologist*, **19** (2), pp 96–106

Piecyk, M, Cullinane, S and Edwards, J (2015) Assessing the external impacts of freight transport, in *Green Logistics: Improving the environmental sustainability of logistics*, 3rd edn, ed A Mckinnon, M Piecyk and M Browne, Kogan Page, London, pp 32–54

Piecyk, M, McKinnon, A and Allen, J (2015) Evaluating and internalizing the environmental costs of logistics, in *Green Logistics: Improving the environmental sustainability of logistics*, 3rd edn, ed A Mckinnon, M Piecyk and M Browne, Kogan Page, London, pp 80–104

Population Reference Bureau (2018) 2018 world population data sheet [Online] https://www.prb.org/wp-content/uploads/2018/08/2018_WPDS.pdf (archieved at https://perma.cc/7MPD-4U7H)

Schnellenbach, J and Schubert, C (2015) Behavioral political economy: A survey, *European Journal of Political Economy*, **40**, pp 395–417

Steg, L and Gifford, R (2005) Sustainable transportation and quality of life, *Journal of Transport Geography*, **13** (1), pp 59–69

Strom, K (1990) A behavioral theory of competitive political parties, *American Journal of Political Science*, **34** (2), pp 565–98

Taniguchi, E and Thompson, RG (2002) Modeling city logistics, *Transportation Research Record: Journal of the Transportation Research Board*, **1790** (1), pp 45–51

Taniguchi, E, Thompson, RG and Yamada, T (2001) Recent advances in modelling city logistics, *City Logistics II*, Institute of Systems Science Research, Kyoto

Taniguchi, E, Imanishi, Y, Barber, R, James, J and Debauche, W (2014) Public sector governance to implement freight vehicle transport management, *Procedia: Social and behavioral sciences*, **125**, pp 345–57UK Round Table on Sustainable Development (1996) *Defining a Sustainable Transport Sector*, UK Round Table on Sustainable Development, London

Witkowski, J and Kiba-Janiak, M (2014) The role of local governments in the development of city logistics, *Procedia: Social and behavioral sciences*, **125**, pp 373–85

INDEX

Note: Numbers within main headings (including roman numerals) are filed as spelt out, with the exception of VDI entries, which are filed in numerical order. Acronyms are filed as presented. Page locators in *italics* denote information contained within a figure or table.

From 4 December 2025 the EU Responsible Person (GPSR) is:
eucomply oÜ, Pärnu mnt. 139b – 14, 11317 Tallinn, Estonia
www.eucompliancepartner.com

www.ingramcontent.com/pod-product-compliance
Lightning Source LLC
LaVergne TN
LVHW050301210926
848481LV00014BA/367
* 9 7 8 1 7 8 9 6 6 2 6 2 7 *